TRADITIONS IN SOCIAL THEORY

Founding Editor: Ian Craib
Series Editor: Rob Stones

This series offers a selection of concise introduc
sociological thought. It aims to deepen the reader's knowledge of particular theoretical approaches and at the same time to enhance their wider understanding of sociological theorising. Each book will offer: a history of the chosen approach and the debates that have driven it forward; a discussion of the current state of the debates within the approach (or debates with other approaches); an argument for the distinctive contribution of the approach and its likely future value. The series is a companion to the *Themes in Social Theory* series, edited by Rob Stones.

Published

PHILOSOPHY OF SOCIAL SCIENCE (Second Edition)
Ted Benton and Ian Craib

CRITICAL THEORY
Alan How

MARXISM AND SOCIAL THEORY
Jonathon Joseph

THE SIMMELIAN LEGACY
Olli Pyyhtinen

MICRO SOCIAL THEORY
Brian Roberts

WEBER AND THE WEBERIANS
Lawrence A. Scaff

STRUCTURATION THEORY
Rob Stones

Forthcoming

POST-STRUCTURALISM AND AFTER
David Howarth

THEMES IN SOCIAL THEORY

Series Editor: Rob Stones

This series explores how cutting-edge research within the social sciences relies on combinations of social theory and empirical evidence. Different books examine how this relationship works in particular subject areas, from technology and health to politics and human rights. Giving the reader a brief overview of the major theoretical approaches used in an area, the books then describe their application in a range of empirical projects. Each text looks at contemporary and classical theories, provides a map of primary research carried out in the subject area and highlights advances in the field. The series is a companion to the *Traditions in Social Theory* series, founded by Ian Craib and edited by Rob Stones.

Published

CRIME AND SOCIAL THEORY
Eammon Carrabine

HEALTH AND SOCIAL THEORY
Fernando De Maio

POLITICS AND SOCIAL THEORY
Will Leggett

TECHNOLOGY AND SOCIAL THEORY
Steve Matthewman

HUMAN RIGHTS AND SOCIAL THEORY
Lydia Morris

INTERNATIONAL MIGRATION AND SOCIAL THEORY
Karen O'Reilly

ENVIRONMENTS, NATURES AND SOCIAL THEORY
Damian F. White, Alan P. Rudy and Brian J. Gareau

INSTITUTIONS, INTERACTION AND SOCIAL THEORY
Will Gibson and Dirk vom Lehn

Forthcoming

GENDER WORK AND SOCIAL THEORY
Kate Huppatz

IDENTITY AND SOCIAL THEORY
Stephanie Lawler

The Simmelian Legacy

A Science of Relations

Olli Pyyhtinen

© Olli Pyyhtinen 2018

All rights reserved. No reproduction, copy or transmission of this publication may be made without written permission.

No portion of this publication may be reproduced, copied or transmitted save with written permission or in accordance with the provisions of the Copyright, Designs and Patents Act 1988, or under the terms of any licence permitting limited copying issued by the Copyright Licensing Agency, Saffron House, 6–10 Kirby Street, London EC1N 8TS.

Any person who does any unauthorized act in relation to this publication may be liable to criminal prosecution and civil claims for damages.

The author has asserted his right to be identified as the author of this work in accordance with the Copyright, Designs and Patents Act 1988.

First published 2018 by
PALGRAVE

Palgrave in the UK is an imprint of Macmillan Publishers Limited, registered in England, company number 785998, of 4 Crinan Street, London, N1 9XW.

Palgrave® and Macmillan® are registered trademarks in the United States, the United Kingdom, Europe and other countries.

ISBN 978–1–137–00665–3 hardback
ISBN 978–1–137–00666–0 paperback

This book is printed on paper suitable for recycling and made from fully managed and sustained forest sources. Logging, pulping and manufacturing processes are expected to conform to the environmental regulations of the country of origin.

A catalogue record for this book is available from the British Library.

A catalog record for this book is available from the Library of Congress.

Contents

Chronology	viii
Preface and acknowledgements	xi
List of abbreviations	xiii

1	**Introduction**	1
	The legacy	3
	The structure of the book	7
	Notes	8

PART I: MAIN IDEAS

2	**Method and Key Principles**	11
	Dialectics without reconciliation	12
	Form and content	15
	Wechselwirkung	22
	Conclusion	26
	Notes	28
3	**Sociology of Association**	30
	A science of society	33
	Dissolving society into relations	37
	How is society possible?	39
	Beyond methodological individualism	43
	Conclusion: an alternative scalar imaginary	45
	Notes	47
4	**The Bustle of Modern Life: Fashion and the Modern Metropolis**	50
	Restless and feverish modern life	52
	The dualism of fashion	54
	Fashion as a metaphor for modernity	57
	The metropolis and the intensification of nervous life	60
	Shock experience and blasé attitude	63
	Conclusion	66
	Notes	67

5	**Money**	69
	Value, desire, and exchange	70
	Money as a means of exchange and measure of value	73
	Money and modern lifestyle	76
	Conclusion	80
	Notes	81
6	**Studying Social Forms**	83
	Time, space, and number	83
	Friendship, love, and the stranger	91
	Sociability	95
	Conclusion	98
	Notes	99
7	**Philosophy of Culture and Life**	102
	Philosophy	104
	The background of Simmel's life-philosophy: Goethe, Schopenhauer, Nietzsche, and Bergson	106
	Life as pre-individual flux and dynamic inter-subjectivity	111
	Life as more-life and more-than-life	113
	Life and boundary	116
	Culture as cultivation	117
	Tragedy of culture	119
	Conclusion	122
	Notes	123

PART II: INFLUENCE

8	**From Fame into Oblivion: Simmel's Early Reception and Influence**	127
	Evocative lecturer and bestselling author	127
	Ambivalent influence on contemporaries in Germany	130
	Influence on continental philosophy: the case of Simmel and Heidegger	138
	Early reception in France and the broken collaboration with Durkheim	143
	Early North American reception	147
	Oblivion	154
	Notes	157

9	**Renewed Interest: Post-War Reception**	161
	Canonizing the European classics with the exception of Simmel: the case of Talcott Parsons	162
	Diffusion of Simmel's ideas in North American sociology between the 1950s and 1970s	165
	German Simmel renaissance	174
	Conclusion	178
	Notes	179
10	**Resonance with Contemporary Discussions and Debates**	180
	Simmel's actuality	180
	Lines of flight	185
	Notes	187

References   189

Index   205

An e-appendix, 'Works by and on Simmel', is available at
www.palgravehighered.com/pyyhtinen

Chronology[1]

1858	1 March, Georg Simmel is born as the youngest child to a family of seven children. Both his parents are of Jewish origin, yet his father, Edward (b. 1810), had converted to Catholicism, and mother, Flora, had been baptized into Evangelism as a child.
1874	Edward, a well-off businessman and founding partner of a chocolate factory, dies.
1876	Graduates from Friedrich-Werdersches Gymnasium. Begins studies at the University of Berlin. First studies history but soon changes into philosophy. In addition to history and philosophy, also studies psychology and Italian. Teachers include the founders of *Völkerpsychologie* Moritz Lazarus and Heymann Steinthal; historians Theodor Mommsen, Heinrich von Treitschke, Heinrich von Sybel, and Johann Gustav Droysen; art historian Hermann Grimm; philosophers Friedrich Harms and Eduard Zeller, as well as psychologist Adolf Bastian.
1880	The first doctoral thesis, *Psychologisch-etnographische Studien über die Anfänge der Musik* ('Psychological and Ethnographic Studies on the Origins of Music'), is rejected for being too speculative, aphoristic, and stylistically careless.
1881	Obtains doctorate for the thesis *Das Wesen der Materie nach Kants Physischer Monadologie* ('The Nature of Matter According to Kant's Physical Monadology'), which had received an academic prize a year earlier.
1883	Submits a study on Kant's doctrine of space and time as Habilitation work. The permission for habilitation is given, but the trial lecture is rejected due to disregard for academic etiquette. Simmel ridicules Professor Zeller for claiming the soul to be located in a certain brain lobe.
1884	The second trial lecture is accepted. Publishes the work 'Dantes Psychologie' ('Dante's Psychology').
1885	Appointed as *Privatdozent*, an unpaid lecturer, at the philosophical faculty of the University of Berlin – a post which he held for an unusually long period of 15 years.

---

[1] The chronology partly overlaps with a 'timetable' (*'Zeittafel'*) of Simmel's life presented by Klaus Lichtblau (1997), pp. 178–80.

1889	Inherits from Julius Friedländer, the founder and owner of the Berliner music publisher C. F. Peters and a friend of the Simmel family, who became Simmel's patron after his father's decease. Though Friedländer lost some of his fortune to pay debts caused by failed speculations, Simmel's inheritance is large enough to allow the *Privatdozent* a fairly sheltered bourgeois life.
1890	*Über sociale Differenzierung* ('On Social Differentiation'). Marries Gertrud Kinel (b. 1864), who is a philosophical author herself, publishing, for instance, the books *Vom Sein und Haben der Seele* ('On the Being and Having of the Soul') in 1906 and *Realität und Gesetzlichkeit im Geschlechtsleben* ('Reality and Legality in Gender Life') in 1910 under the pseudonym Marie Luise Eckendorff. Gertrud outlives her husband by 20 years.
1891	Son Hans is born. Later he becomes *Ausserordentlichen Professor* in medicine at the University of Jena. Under National Socialist rule Hans is incarcerated in the Dachau concentration camp, but he manages to escape in 1939 and flees into exile to the United States, where he dies in 1943.
1892	*Die Probleme der Geschichtsphilosophie* ('The Problems of the Philosophy of History').
1892–3	*Einleitung in die Moralwissenschaft* ('Introduction to the Science of Morality').
1898	Application for *Extraordinarius Professor* at the philosophical faculty of the University of Berlin is rejected.
1900	First edition of *Philosophie des Geldes* ('The Philosophy of Money').
1901	Appointed as *Ausserordentlichen Professor* at the philosophical faculty of the University of Berlin.
1904	*Kant*. Has a child, Angela, with Gertrud Kantorowitz resulting from an extramarital affair. Later Angela moves to Palestine where she dies in an accident in 1944.
1905	*Philosophie der Mode* ('Philosophy of Fashion') and the second, completely revised edition of *Die Probleme der Geschichtsphilosophie*.
1906	*Kant und Goethe* ('Kant and Goethe') and *Die Religion* ('Religion').
1907	*Schopenhauer und Nietzsche* ('Schopenhauer and Nietzsche').
1908	*Soziologie. Untersuchungen über die Formen der Vergesellschaftung* ('Sociology. Enquiries into the Forms of Association'). Application for the chair in philosophy at the University of Heidelberg is unsuccessful, largely because of the harsh, anti-Semitic review by historian Dietrich Schäfer and despite the support of Eberhard Gothein and Max Weber, and Heinrich Rickert withdrawing his application. Participates actively in the founding of the German Sociology Association, *Deutsche Gesellschaft für Soziologie* (DGS), which is founded the next year, in 1909.

1910	*Hauptprobleme der Philosophie* ('Main Problems of Philosophy'). In October, has the honour of presenting the opening paper at the first meeting of the German Sociology Association held in Frankfurt, with the title 'Soziologie der Geselligkeit' ('Sociology of Sociability'). Participates in the founding of the journal *Logos* and joins the editorial board.
1911	*Philosophische Kultur. Gesammelte Essais* ('Philosophical Culture. Collected Essays'). Receives honorary doctorate at the University of Freiburg.
1913	*Goethe*.
1914	Receives full professorship in philosophy at the Kaiser Wilhelm University in Strasbourg.
1916	*Rembrandt* and *Das Problem der historischen Zeit* ('The Problem of Historical Time').
1917	*Grundfragen der Soziologie* ('Basic Problems of Sociology') and a collection of wartime writings under the title *Der Krieg und die geistigen Entscheidungen* ('The War and Spiritual Decisions').
1918	*Der Konflikt der modernen Kultur* ('The Conflict of Modern Culture'). Dies of liver cancer 26 September. Last book *Lebensanschauung: Vier metaphysischer Kapitel* ('The View of Life: Four Metaphysical Essays with Journal Aphorisms') comes out posthumously, a few weeks after his death.

Preface and acknowledgements

In many ways this book presents a sequel to my first book, *Simmel and 'the Social'*, which came out in 2010. There's certain continuity and congruence between them, and the book at hand returns to some of the same themes that I discussed in the first one. However, the present volume has a much broader scope: whereas *Simmel and 'the Social'* focused more narrowly on the notion and constitution of the social, this book displays a wider range of his ideas, while also attending to their latter-day reception, transmission, and appropriation. In the present volume I also explicitly take the role of a teacher. My attention to the importance of writing the book grew out of my experiences in teaching courses on both sociological theory and on Simmel's work to undergraduates. I have noticed that the general awareness of Simmel's work and influence among students (and scholars as well) does not match that of other classical sociologists, like Émile Durkheim and Max Weber, or that of more contemporary eminent authors. This goes as much for his key ideas and main works as for the background and influence of his thought.

Accordingly, the somewhat 'evangelical' aim of the book is to broaden the understanding of Simmel's work and stress his relevance to many contemporary debates. The entire book is crafted so as to read as an argument concerning Simmel's legacy and stressing why an assessment of his work is timely for sociology *today*. It presents a critical engagement with his work, though its critical ethos is not about passing judgements where Simmel has erred and made mistakes, but rather about bringing his work alive, about intensifying and multiplying signs of life. In one of his journal entries, Simmel remarks how he 'find[s] utterly regrettable that modern man [sic] adopts the *critical* standpoint – as self-evidently the first and only standpoint – towards his [sic] reading'. Instead, he suggests, 'One should gratefully accept from a book whatever appeals to us and simply pass over the rest' (a very similar standpoint has been embraced and emphasized more recently by Gilles Deleuze, though without a connection to Simmel). What is more, Simmel suggests that the tendency towards criticism tends to focus on particulars – and generalize them into a condemnation of the whole. To some extent, this has also been the case in the reception of Simmel's own work: it has largely focused on particular texts, ideas, and topics, and it is only recently that a more comprehensive appreciation of the full scope of his work has been emerging.

While the book makes an effort to cover a wide spectrum of Simmel's ideas and texts, it is in no way exhaustive. It has Simmel's relationalism as a leitmotif that runs throughout the text. The book suggests that Simmel's most substantial contribution lies especially in the relational mode of thought that he cultivates.

This book has been coming for a long time, as other books, projects, and professional responsibilities – or, simply: *life* – intervened and kept me at a distance from it. The fact that I was actually able to come back to the project, at a point when in my research I had already moved elsewhere, and complete it owes to several people. I would like to express my gratitude especially to the following colleagues: to Tom Kemple, with whom I edited a volume on Simmel for Anthem Press (not to mention our numerous nerdy conversations on Simmel!); to Jukka Gronow, with whom I authored a lengthy article discussing works by and on Simmel for Oxford Bibliographies (its extended version is the e-appendix of this book); to Carlos Frade with whom I got the opportunity to present an imagined dialogue between Weber and Simmel (with Carlos as Weber and myself as Simmel) at a conference in Edinburgh in December 2015, which we then worked into an article for *The Journal of Classical Sociology*; to Mikko Joronen for crafting with me a paper on Simmel and Heidegger for a German volume edited by Johannes Weiß and Gallina Tasheva; to Leopoldo Waizbort, who made me consider thoroughly some key Simmelian matters when he interviewed me in autumn 2014 for the Brazilian journal *Sociologia & antropologia*; and to Christian Abrahamsson for inviting me to Oslo to give a lecture in December 2015 as well as to Boris Traue for asking me to talk at the 'Re-thinking Relationality in the Socio-Technological Condition' symposium organized at the Digital Cultures Research Lab of the University of Lüneburg in May 2016. Both occasions gave me some entirely new ideas I had not come to think of before.

I am also grateful to Natàlia Cantó-Milà for sharing her knowledge, for instance about Simmel archives and about the reception of his work in Latin America (unfortunately only a small fraction of that insight ended up in this book). Further, Jarno Valkonen read the manuscript and gave very helpful feedback, as did the students who read early drafts of some of the chapters in a reading group organized in spring 2016 at the University of Tampere. Turo-Kimmo Lehtonen is to be thanked for a long and mutually respectful philosophical friendship.

The series editor Rob Stones and editorial assistant Tuur Driesser have been incredibly patient with this book. I really appreciate all the support, feedback, and encouragement I've received from both. Finally, I would also like to thank Cathy Tingle for the copyediting and Ville Savolainen for compiling the index.

List of abbreviations

GSG 1   *Das Wesen der Materie nach Kants Physischer Monadologie; Abhandlungen 1882–1884; Rezensionen 1883–1901.* Georg Simmel Gesamtausgabe Band 1. Ed. Klaus Christian Köhnke. (Frankfurt am Main: Suhrkamp), 1999.

GSG 2   *Aufsätze 1887–1890; Über sociale Differenzierung; Die Probleme der Geschichtsphilosophie.* Georg Simmel Gesamtausgabe Band 2. Ed. Heinz-Jürgen Dahme. (Frankfurt am Main: Suhrkamp), 1989.

GSG 3   *Einleitung in die Moralwissenschaft. Eine Kritik der Ethischen Grundbegriffe.* Erster Band. Georg Simmel Gesamtausgabe Band 3. Ed. Klaus Christian Köhnke. (Frankfurt am Main: Suhrkamp), 1989.

GSG 4   *Einleitung in die Moralwissenschaft. Eine Kritik der Ethischen Grundbegriffe.* Zweiter Band. Georg Simmel Gesamtausgabe Band 4. Ed. Klaus Christian Köhnke. (Frankfurt am Main: Suhrkamp), 1991.

GSG 5   *Aufsätze und Abhandlungen 1894–1900.* Georg Simmel Gesamtausgabe Band 5. Eds Heinz-Jürgen Dahme & David Frisby. (Frankfurt am Main: Suhrkamp), 1992.

GSG 6   *Philosophie des Geldes.* Georg Simmel Gesamtausgabe Band 6. Eds David Frisby & Klaus Christian Köhnke. (Frankfurt am Main: Suhrkamp), 1989.

GSG 7   *Aufsätze und Abhandlungen 1901–1908 Band I.* Georg Simmel Gesamtausgabe Band 7. Eds Rüdiger Kramme, Angela Rammstedt & Otthein Rammstedt. (Frankfurt am Main: Suhrkamp), 1995.

GSG 8   *Aufsätze und Abhandlungen 1901–1908 Band II.* Georg Simmel Gesamtausgabe Band 8. Eds Alessandro Cavalli & Volkhard Krech. (Frankfurt am Main: Suhrkamp), 1993.

GSG 9   *Kant; Die Probleme der Geschichtsphilosophie.* Georg Simmel Gesamtausgabe Band 9. Eds Guy Oakes & Kurt Röttgers. (Frankfurt am Main: Suhrkamp), 1997.

GSG 10 *Philosophie der Mode; Die Religion; Kant und Goethe; Schopenhauer und Nietzsche.* Eds Michael Behr, Volkhard Krech & Gert Schmidt. Georg Simmel Gesamtausgabe Band 10 (Frankfurt am Main: Suhrkamp), 1995.

GSG 11	*Soziologie: Untersuchungen über die Formen der Vergesellschaftung.* Georg Simmel Gesamtausgabe Band 11. Ed. Otthein Rammstedt. (Frankfurt am Main: Suhrkamp), 1992.
GSG 12	*Aufsätze und Abhandlungen 1909–1918 Band I.* Georg Simmel Gesamtausgabe Band 12. Eds Rüdiger Kramme & Angela Rammstedt. (Frankfurt am Main: Suhrkamp), 2001.
GSG 13	*Aufsätze und Abhandlungen 1909–1918 Band II.* Georg Simmel Gesamtausgabe Band 13. Ed. Klaus Latzel. (Frankfurt am Main: Suhrkamp), 2000.
GSG 14	*Hauptprobleme der Philosophie; Philosophische Kultur.* Georg Simmel Gesamtausgabe Band 14. Eds Rüdiger Kramme & Otthein Rammstedt. (Frankfurt am Main: Suhrkamp), 1996.
GSG 15	*Goethe; Deutschlands innere Wandlung; Das Problem der historischen Zeit; Rembrandt.* Georg Simmel Gesamtausgabe Band 15. Eds Uta Kösser, Hans-Martin Kruckis & Otthein Rammstedt. (Frankfurt am Main: Suhrkamp), 2003.
GSG 16	*Der Krieg und die geistigen Entscheidungen; Grundfragen der Soziologie; Vom Wesen des historischen Verstehens; Der Konflikt der modernen Kultur; Lebensanschauung.* Georg Simmel Gesamtausgabe Band 16. Eds Gregor Fitzi & Otthein Rammstedt. (Frankfurt am Main: Suhrkamp), 1999.
GSG 20	*Postume Veröffentlichungen; Ungedrucktes; Schuldpädagogik.* Georg Simmel Gesamtausgabe Band 20. Eds Torge Karlsruhen & Otthein Rammstedt. (Frankfurt am Main: Suhrkamp), 2004.
GSG 22	*Briefe 1880–1911.* Georg Simmel Gesamtausgabe Band 22. Ed. Klaus Christian Köhnke. (Frankfurt am Main: Suhrkamp), 2005.
GSG 23	*Briefe 1912–1918; Jugendbriefe.* Georg Simmel Gesamtausgabe Band 23. Eds Otthein Rammstedt & Angela Rammstedt. (Frankfurt am Main: Suhrkamp), 2008.
GSG 24	*Nachträge; Dokumente; Gesamtbibliographie; Übersichten; Indices.* Georg Simmel Gesamtausgabe Band 24. Ed. Otthein Rammstedt in collaboration with Angela Rammstedt & Erwin Schullerus. (Frankfurt am Main: Suhrkamp), 2016.

1

Introduction

The German sociologist, philosopher, essayist, and cultural theorist Georg Simmel (1858–1918) remained for a long time one of the great unknowns of sociology. Akin to the figure of the 'stranger', which he analysed in one of his best-known texts, entitled 'The Stranger' (orig. 'Exkurs über den Fremden'), Simmel has been standing both near to and far from us, at the borderline between the inside and outside of the discipline: he has been in but not necessarily considered to be essentially *of* sociology. This is not to say that Simmel remained largely without recognition. On the contrary, he was one of the foremost thinkers of his day, depicted by contemporaries for example as 'the most versatile, wittiest, and the most fruitful of all living philosophers' (cited by Landmann, [1958] 1993, p. 31). He also had active relations with several other eminent and influential German figures of his day, such as political theorist, sociologist, and philosopher Max Weber, philosophers Edmund Husserl and Heinrich Rickert, and poets Rainer Maria Rilke and Stephan George, and he was well-connected internationally. His French contacts included, for instance, political economist René Worms, who established the journal *Revue Internationale de Sociologie* and founded the *Institut International de Sociologie*, sociologist Célestin Bouglé, sociologist, philosopher, and criminologist Gabriel Tarde, sociologist Émile Durkheim and philosopher Henri Bergson, as well as sculptor Auguste Rodin, and he also had connections to the United States, corresponding, for example, with Albion W. Small, the founder and first editor of *The American Journal of Sociology*, and Lester F. Ward, who served as the first president of the American Sociological Association.

So, in certain respects Simmel was anything but the academic outsider he is usually described as (and which is also implied by the epithet 'stranger'). His ideas significantly inspired and informed both students and colleagues. Already at a time when he had not yet succeeded in securing himself a permanent position he was considered to exercise 'a more powerful influence on the spiritual development of the younger generation than the majority of his colleagues in the philosophical chairs of Germany' (Fechter, [1918] 1993, p. 157; trans. Goodstein, 2017). Simmel was an immensely popular lecturer, 'a virtuoso on the platform' (Coser, 1977, p. 196), whose lecture courses built even something of a 'Berlin tradition' over the years (Ludwig, [1914] 1993, p. 154), and Simmel himself, too, realized what a 'great attraction' he was in academia (Simmel, 2005, p. 615, in *Georg Simmel Gesamtausgabe* 22, hereafter GSG). His individual lectures were 'leading intellectual events' which were covered in newspapers (Coser, 1965, p. 3) and they drew students as far as from North America, among them sociologist Robert E. Park and philosopher Frank Thilly. Simmel was also one of the first academics in Germany who welcomed women to his lectures.

Simmel's reputation was not confined within Germany; he enjoyed a wide international fame. For example, by the 1910s no other European sociologist had more pieces translated into English than Simmel. His first programmatic text on sociology, 'Das Problem der Sociologie' ('The Problem of Sociology'), which he published in 1894 as an early career scholar (in GSG 5), came out as a French translation the next year, followed soon by the Italian, Russian, and Polish translations.

Nevertheless, despite his influence and wide reputation, in Germany Simmel remained in a somewhat marginal institutional position in academia – indeed, akin to a 'stranger'. Simmel's career was anything but a success story. He suffered from constant refutations: his first doctoral dissertation as well as his habilitation lecture were rejected; he remained in the unpaid *Privatdozent* post for an unusually long period of 15 years and 13 years as *Ausserordentlich Professor* ('extraordinary professor', an honorary title to which Simmel was promoted in 1901); and he had no success in securing himself a senior position at German universities until 1914, when he received a full professorship in Strasbourg at the age of 56, four years before his death. Commentators have explained the failures of making steady progress in his career by referring to his Jewish background and unorthodox mode of thought, as well as his ambiguous position between the roles of an academic scholar and a public intellectual, but none of these can be considered as being a sufficient explanation in itself.[1]

What is more, Simmel had no true disciples. There is no tradition of thought that would go by his name, and intellectual history knows of no 'Simmelians'. Simmel remained a 'stimulator', not 'a great educator' nor 'one who brought matters to a close' by establishing a unified system, as one of his former students, Georg (György) Lukács ([1918] 1993, p. 171; trans. 1991, p. 145), once characterized him. In 1957, Simmel's friend, journalist, essayist, and poet Margarete Susman ([1957] 1993, p. 278) complained that 'time and again a question poses itself to me: why did he, one of the most renowned philosophers of his time, remain without followers; why is he forgotten, at least by name'? Strangely enough, it is as if Simmel had foreseen the oblivion his legacy was to suffer though he himself did not seem to regard the lack of heirs as a great misfortune. Perhaps already aware of his approaching death, Simmel wrote an entry in his large brown leather-bound journal, comparing the legacy he was about to leave to money, one of his best-known topics:

> I know that I shall die without spiritual heirs (and that is as it should be). Mine is like a cash divided by many heirs, and each converts his share into whatever business suits *his* nature, in which the provenance from that legacy cannot be seen. (GSG 20, p. 261; 2010, p. 160)[2]

The prediction turned out to be very accurate. As I will show later in this book, while Simmel's ideas have been widely distributed and appropriated, their use has not always revealed its indebtedness to him, but in many cases the origin of those ideas has remained unacknowledged, unrecognized, and hidden.

The legacy

If Simmel remained something of a stranger in the academia of his day, to some extent his posthumous reception, too, has been characterized by marginality. For example, compared to the mounting masses of works on other canonized sociological giants like Émile Durkheim, Max Weber, or Karl Marx, until recent years especially the Anglophone secondary literature on Simmel has remained somewhat scarce. And, in a sense, it is not at all very surprising that Simmel's work has not quite fitted in the grand sociological tradition – it is too nonconformist and unorthodox for that. While it does cover such canonical sociological themes as the problem of sociology, social differentiation, power, group structures, and the relation of the individual and society, Simmel's oeuvre also contains an incredibly rich variety of unusual and peculiar topics ranging from the sociology of senses to flirtation, the bridge and the door, fashion, style, gratitude, the letter, the picture frame, the handle, the ruin, and the landscape, for example. In addition, not even those of his writings that have the most explicit focus on sociological matters are only sociological, but they, too, may cut across several perspectives and disciplines, including philosophy, psychology, aesthetics, and ethics. In his time Simmel was also criticized in a highly controversial manner. He was scorned both for being too one-sided and too versatile, as only a sociologist and yet too philosophical and essayistic. Simmel also published a large amount of his writings in non-scholarly publications, such as newspapers, art magazines, and literary monthlies, thus blurring the line between serious scholarship and more popular writings.

In relation to the nonconformist nature of Simmel's work, in this book I contend that Simmel's legacy consists not so much in formulating answers to well-established sociological questions as in transforming the whole landscape of sociological problems by offering altogether different abstractions.[3] Hugh Dalziel Duncan (1965, p. 108) captures something of the scope and depth of this originality when he writes:

> As many of us have discovered in our excursions into sociological theory, the figure of Simmel often appears toward the end of the journey. We greet him with dismay as well as respect, for he is coming back from a point we are still struggling to reach. (Duncan, 1959, p. 108)

I argue that Simmel restructures the landscape of sociological thought basically in three ways:

First, instead of explaining concrete phenomena by categories and abstract principles, his work is *explanatory of abstraction*.[4] It is not uncommon for sociologists to treat 'society', 'power', 'class', 'structure', 'norms', 'capitalism', and 'social context' as entities external to individuals, acting behind the scenes, as it were, and pulling the strings.[5] Simmel's approach, however, is somewhat different. What sociologists usually take for granted as a cause Simmel tries to explain as an effect. His conception of society is a most revealing case in point. In his sociological theory, he does not start from an abstract and all-encompassing notion of society, but looks at the ways in which society is built up out of concrete and particular relations. For Simmel, society does not pre-exist the relations of interaction and interdependence between people, but it is produced and actualized in and by those relations. Another aspect of the steering away from abstract explanations is the way Simmel introduces such concrete and mundane objects into the sociological and philosophical analysis as money, jug handles, bridges, doors, and picture frames. Especially within the field of philosophy, the shift was dramatic. Until then, philosophy had concerned itself mostly with what is universal, eternal, and deeply significant. By theorizing concrete objects, Simmel, by contrast, attends to what is mundane, ephemeral, and seemingly insignificant. Even Theodor Adorno, who lashed Simmel in many other aspects, acknowledged him for having accomplished this shift in philosophy's focus to concrete objects. According to Adorno, the shift 'remained canonical for anyone dissatisfied with the chattering of epistemology or intellectual history' (Adorno, 1984, p. 558; trans. Frisby, 1997, p. 24).

The second manner in which Simmel transforms sociological enquiry has to do with *how* his work comes to explain the emergence of the more abstract things from the concrete ones. Simmel cultivates a *relational mode of thought* by examining phenomena in and through relations. Simmel develops a sociology suggesting the priority of relations against the overly substantialist perspectives that still populate many strands of sociology today. Centring on the interdependencies, togetherness, and associations between people, his work places relations into the heart of sociology. Each and every unit(y) is for him comprised of relations. All in all, whatever topics Simmel chooses to consider, he always seems to work them out in a similar manner: instead of starting from an abstract concept or problem, he begins with a concrete object. Then he reveals the complexity of its seemingly simple make-up and a deeper meaning beneath its assumed superficiality, and proceeds by uncovering surprising connections between the object under investigation and objects (seemingly) most distant from it in order to ultimately get a better view not only of the essence of the object but also of the extensive network of relations it is woven into. Thereby his thought connects the most heterogeneous phenomena and builds the most unexpected assemblages out of them.

Third, while Simmel typically explores the objects that he treats in his writings, to borrow Spinoza's formulation, as if *sub specie aeternitatis*, 'under the aspect of eternity', as he pays attention to what is universally and ahistorically valid about them, he also makes sociology and philosophy responsive to the situation and crisis of modernity. Of course, he is by far not the only classical sociologist to pay attention to modernity; after all, as a discipline sociology was born to explain and understand what is novel in the emerging modern society. However, what is unique about Simmel is that unlike Weber, Durkheim, and Marx, for instance, Simmel is interested not so much in the social structure or system of modern society resulting from the modernization process as in the modern *experience*. He aspires to analyse in detail what it is like to *live* in the modern world. Whereas with the other sociological classics this mundane, everyday aspect of the bustle of modern life remained largely disregarded and undertheorized (Frisby, 1992), Simmel dissects it to the minutest detail: he attends to urban life; to the dissolution of fixities and secure footholds; to the increasing pace of life; to the mature money economy; to the predominance of means over ends; and to the overwhelmingly external culture and technique of life within the modern socio-technological mechanism.

What we have inherited from Simmel is above all a certain *mode of thought*, a method of approach, or a form of questioning. Simmel regarded his relational mode of thought as being perfectly compatible with the conceptual framework of modern science. In *Einleitung in die Moralwissenschaft* ('Introduction to the Science of Morality'), Simmel suggests that modern thought is characterized by a tendency towards the 'dissolution of substance into functions, of the solid and the lasting into the flux of restless development' ([1893] GSG 4, p. 330). Indeed, instead of positing self-identical and self-contained substances or some 'primordial elements' as the ultimate reality, from quantum physics to cognitivism and systems theory modern science takes as its starting point 'desubstantialized processes', such as 'string vibrations', 'emerging properties' and 'self-organization' (Prigogine & Stengers, 1984; Žižek, 2004, p. 664). Given the central place that processes and relations inhabit in his thought, Simmel's sociology can itself be regarded as embodying such a shift from substance to event. In his work, he rejects substances and static things, be they individuals or structures, as valid starting points for sociological study and dissolves them into processes and unfolding, dynamic relations. Yet his relational thought does not simply one-sidedly embrace constant process and change, but it also tackles the problem of how to think – both sociologically and philosophically – in the modern world of flux, where no secure philosophical foundation is available any more, and where one thus easily falls into nihilism or bottomless subjectivism and scepticism (see e.g. Simmel, GSG 20, p. 304; Goodstein, 2017).

It is his mode of thought that is Simmel's legacy for us, and I claim that it still has great potential to enrich our thinking. The present book sets out to make this legacy more explicit. In Part I, it does this first and foremost by exploring the characteristics of this mode of thought within Simmel's own writings, bringing it firmly into the foreground. Part II of the book follows some of the traces of its distribution to latter-day uses. In the book, Simmel's 'legacy' is thus intended in two senses, referring not only to the posthumous reception of his work but also to its not yet fully actualized creative potential, the actualization of which could make a difference and provide sociology with novel lines of becoming.

By returning to Simmel and by rediscovering his legacy, the book gives voice to a neglected force in the history of sociology, to an intellectual and creative corpus of vast significance that has lived too much in the shadows. The story that emerges in *The Simmelian Legacy* is based on a gathering together of neglected lines of flight, modes of thought, and framed insights. The result, which subverts conventional conceptions of sociology's history, is narrated, first, as the rediscovery of key dimensions of Simmel's thought from within Simmel's own writings. Second, it is also laid out as the gradual and uneven re-emergence of this thought within the subsequent history of sociology. The story the book tells can be seen as an alternative history for at least two reasons. First, because Simmel's influence has remained largely invisible, unrecognized, and anonymous. While his thought has certainly had an international following, it has not formed any tradition nor fitted the grand tradition of the discipline with ease. The second reason has to do with relationality itself having remained a secret, subterranean undercurrent, as it were, in the discipline of sociology and even in the whole of Western thought. Our ways of speaking and thinking are reifying in the sense that we tend to perceive the world as consisting of relatively static things, not of dynamic relations and processes. As German sociologist Norbert Elias (1978, pp. 111–12) notes, our languages are constructed in such a way that that even movement and change seem to imply an isolated object at rest, to which is added a verb that expresses the fact that the thing changes: we say 'the river flows' and 'the wind is blowing', as if the river was somehow separate from its flowing and the wind from its blowing. According to philosopher Alfred North Whitehead, the entire history of philosophy attests to the fact that the mind 'tends to ignore the fluency, and to analyse the world in terms of static categories' ([1929] 1978, p. 209).

Here the reason behind the return to Simmel is the ambition to bring Simmel and his legacy back to prominence in sociological theory. The point of going back to Simmel is not, however, just to promote or reverence his work and restore its past glory to it. Rather, the return is motivated above all by an aspiration to reconsider the tradition of sociology on the basis of the *relational turn* Simmel's work provides for sociological theory and to make his sociology bear on our present. This is also to say that this book is not attempting to cover the whole of Simmel's work, but it focuses on issues, themes, and concepts that matter most for readers today. The book aims to show how Simmel's work is still highly relevant for contemporary discussions and debates within the social sciences.

The structure of the book

The book is divided into two parts. Part I delineates the key ideas of Simmel's sociology by emphasizing its relational point of departure and introduces the reader to the general context, organizing principles, and key areas of his work. The reader will be taken on a journey through Simmel's thought, proceeding from a discussion of its main principles, his major works, and areas of interest (Chapter 2) to the relational basis of his sociology (Chapter 3) all the way to more specific themes (Chapters 4–6). Chapter 4 focuses on Simmel's sociological diagnoses of modernity by looking at his writings on fashion and the modern metropolis, Chapter 5 examines Simmel's analysis of money and the modern money economy, and Chapter 6 discusses his analyses of specific social formations, such as friendship and love, his treatment of the temporal and spatial aspects of social relations, and the social type of the stranger. Not only are the phenomena discussed of utmost importance for the understanding of modern life, but Simmel also shows how each has undergone a major change in the transformation into modernity. Chapter 7, for its part, deals with Simmel's philosophy of culture and life, in relation to the debates and problems it draws its inspiration from. For Simmel, the notion of 'life' stands as the key category of modern worldview. It also enables him to conceptualize the modern world of flux and flows.

Part II will aim to uncover the distribution and circulation of the legacy of Simmel's sociology. Chapter 8 discusses Simmel's influence on his contemporaries in Germany and elsewhere and also tackles the question of how it is possible that such a 'first-rate stimulator of academic youth and academic colleagues', as Weber (1972, p. 158) described Simmel around 1908, fell into oblivion so soon after his decease. Chapter 9 looks into how Simmel's legacy was revived and interest in his work renewed after World War II in North America and Germany. As already implied above, tracing and detecting Simmel's impact is unusually difficult, as on several occasions it remains anonymous. Like money, its origin is not necessarily always apparent to the ones using it. The value of examining Simmel's reception in American sociology not only allows us to better understand the background of the Chicago School, for example, but it is also important for understanding the European reception of Simmel's work. This is because, after World War II, the rediscovery of Simmel in Europe is partly an effect of the re-import of his sociology from North America. Chapter 10, finally, teases out Simmel's resonance with contemporary discussions and debates. Neither Simmel's significance nor actuality are any longer denied, but contemporary scholars draw from his work in various ways, and a more comprehensive appreciation of Simmel's oeuvre has also been gradually emerging.

Notes

1 See e.g. Wolff (1950, pp. xviii–xix); Dahme & Rammstedt (1986, p. 11); Köhnke (1996, pp. 20–1); Noro (2005, pp. 8–12).
2 Exact original date unknown.
3 The present book focuses in particular on Simmel's intellectual legacy, but in his study *Georg Simmel and Avant-Garde Sociology* (2000) Ralph M. Leck provides a fascinating picture of Simmel's cultural legacy by examining his influence on politics and aesthetics during his lifetime.
4 I borrow the expression 'explanatory of abstraction' from Alfred North Whitehead ([1929] 1978, p. 20).
5 For more on this, see Latour (2005, p. 137).

PART I

MAIN IDEAS

2

Method and Key Principles

Simmel's work lends itself to no easy summary. Although he is remembered today primarily as a founding father of sociology, his writings cover a variety of other fields as well, including epistemology, psychology, aesthetics, ethics, and metaphysics. It is easy to agree with Michael Landmann's (1968, p. 8) apt remark that 'Simmel's thinking is kindled by the variety of phenomena'. After all, in his writings he treats topics as diverse as sociability, the Alpine journey, the adventurer, money, religion, flirtation, the ruin, female culture, the landscape, death, the senses, the handle, the bridge and the door...Like a Harlequin's cape, his work is just too rich, versatile, and diverse to be subsumed under some overarching unity. Instead of presenting a closed system, it is rather susceptible to constant variation and modulation. Indeed, rather than a system builder, Simmel is 'an adventurer in ideas' (Salomon, 1993, p. 363). He is constantly on the move, uncovering connections between ideas and swinging between standpoints, without being fixed in one place or the other. Ultimately, it is by connecting seemingly separate and alien objects that Simmel also tries to make his way to a synthesis and get a glimpse of the whole of things. For him, the totality of the world does not amount to an absolute, substantial unity, but to a multiplicity of heterogeneous entities connected to one another by relations of reciprocal interdependence.

In this chapter, I discuss the general design of Simmel's work and the key principles of his thought. I will begin by examining his dialectical mode of thinking that presents something of his overall 'method'. Simmel's dialectics is of a particular kind, since while he seeks to establish continuity or common ground between the two opposing poles of the dualities into which he conceptually orders the phenomena he deals with, the mediating 'third' hardly ever brings a final, totalizing synthesis. Thus it amounts to dialectics without a reconciling synthesis. After outlining Simmel's dialectical approach, I will focus on one specific duality, the form–content distinction. It is not just one contrast among many, but it holds a special place in Simmel's thought, figuring as one of its two key principles. I will look at how the distinction between form and content appears in various fields of his work, focusing especially on his epistemology, sociology, and metaphysics. The other key principle discussed in the chapter is that of *Wechselwirkung* ('reciprocal effect'), which presents the basis of Simmel's relational approach. I will examine how it, too, just like the distinction between form and content, manifests in his theory of knowledge, sociology, and, finally, metaphysics. The concluding section will sum up the discussion and bring the two principles together.

Dialectics without reconciliation

It is characteristic of Simmel's style to think via paradoxes, contrasts, dualities, and polarities. For him, the world is constituted by contradictoriness: he perceives phenomena in the form of struggle and combination of antagonistic forces, tendencies, or principles. Overall, Simmel thinks that thought cannot grasp the immediately lived reality as a unity, but he remarks in various of his writings that the basic motifs and determinations of our being and thought are typically organized into dualities. For example, in the essay 'Fashion' ([1904] 1957, p. 541) Simmel writes:

> We are constantly seeking ultimate forces, fundamental aspirations, some of which controls our entire conduct. But in no case do we find any single force attaining a perfectly independent expression, and we are thus obliged to separate a majority of the factors and determine the relative extent to which each shall have representation. To do this we must establish the degree of limitation exercised by the counteraction of some other force, as well as the influence exerted by the latter upon the primitive force.

Given this dialectical conviction, it should not come as a surprise, then, that Simmel's texts abound with dualities and polarities. Henry Schermer and David Jary (2013) divide these neatly into 'fundamental dualisms' and 'general polarities'. The former are much more limited in number and underpin the latter ones. Simmelian fundamental dualisms include, for example, the pairs subject–object, absolute–relative, and life–form (or becoming–being/flux–fixity/potential–actual).[1] The number of general polarities is significantly greater, and they include such dualities as (with some but not all of them also mentioned by Schermer and Jary) abstract–concrete, freedom–necessity, general–particular, passivity–activity, part–whole, individual–society, feminine–masculine, subjective culture–objective culture, means–ends, qualitative–quantitative, inclusion–exclusion, conformity–distinction, resistance–submission, distant–close, and openness–secrecy. Obviously, not all of them share the same level of generality, but some are more abstract or general than others, with the contrast individual–society, for instance, being subsumable under the part–whole polarity.

When thinking through dualities and contradictions, it is also characteristic of Simmel that he does not merely lay out the antagonism or tension of mutually exclusive principles, tendencies, or forces, but he repeatedly finds unity in the conflicting sides through a 'third' (*Dritte*) that mediates their relation and allows both of the poles to appear in a new light, as dialectically intertwined and occasionally even as co-constituted. This interplay of the juxtaposed opposites and the 'third' even constitutes something of the 'method' of Simmel's work, though the term is to be used only with some reservations, because method usually implies repetition and predictability. While Simmel repeats – and varies – his dialectical approach from text to text by analysing in a fairly similar, recognizable manner all the objects that he treats, his dialectical approach does not really amount to a proper method that would be applicable for anyone.[2] Hence it might be more appropriate to call it the basic 'schema' (Noro, 1991) or *diagram* of Simmel's thought.

In any case, Simmel is constantly in search for '"third" categories' which, as Anna Wessely (1990, p. 376) suggests, 'might comprehend opposites and make us comprehend how mutually exclusive forces and principles do not annihilate each other but create, in their interaction, new forms by finding, as it were, a third way out of a dilemma'. Sometimes the thirds may appear as the 'excluded third' of logic, sometimes as the mutual source of the opposites being examined, and at some other times as a mediating midpoint, or an expression of an encompassing unity between surface level polarizations (cf. Levine, 1971, p. xxxv). The third may culminate the tension in the contradiction, dissolve apparently monolithic unities into inner contradictions, and also establish a common ground or continuity between conflicting tendencies or forces. However, importantly, unlike famously in the thought of the German idealist philosopher Georg Wilhelm Friedrich Hegel (1770–1831), hardly ever does the contrast of thesis and antithesis result in Simmel's writings in a final, totalizing synthesis. Rather, following Landmann (1968, p. 16), Simmel's thought can be described as 'dialectics without reconciliation'. The third provides an underlying unity that preserves the tension between the contrasting poles in all its vigour.

One of the most famous thirds explored by Simmel is the 'stranger' (*Fremde*).[3] For Simmel, the stranger highlights the borderline between the inside and the outside of the group; the stranger is included only insofar as s/he is excluded. Simmel stresses that the stranger does not just stand outside a group but is rather 'an element of the group itself'; 'to be a stranger is naturally a very positive relation, a specific form of interaction'. Yet the stranger's position in the group is 'determined, essentially, by the fact that he [sic] does not belong to it from the beginning'. Rather, the stranger has arrived only recently. S/he is a 'potential wanderer', a 'person who comes today and stays tomorrow'. This endows her/him with a greater freedom of movement when compared to the insiders of the collective: although the stranger has not moved on, s/he has not abandoned 'the freedom of coming and going'. By being a newcomer, the stranger imports qualities into the group 'which do not and cannot stem from the group itself' ([1908] GSG 11, p. 765). Thereby s/he is able to transform the whole social milieu. Before her/his emergence, the stranger had occupied no space at all; s/he was literally nothing (to us). By her/his arrival, however, the stranger takes up space and becomes something. S/he is there, among us, and does not go away.

The figure of the third plays a significant role also in Simmel's view of the dynamics of social relations, as we will see in more detail in Chapter 6. Simmel suggests that the typical differences between all social constellations can be analysed by looking at the differences between the formations of two elements and those involving three, that is, between 'dyad' and the 'triad' or the 'two' (*die Zwei*) and the 'third' (*der Dritte*). While the relationship of two elements presents according to him the first embodiment of not only synthesis and unification but also of separation and antithesis, Simmel contends that the 'third' brings a 'crossing, reconciliation, rejection of the absolute contrast' to this antithesis ([1908] GSG 11, p. 124). The third provides the twosome a wider, solidifying 'social frame' (p. 115), producing hence 'a completely new formation' (p. 121): a supra-individual social whole irreducible to its individual members ([1908] GSG 8, p. 349; [1908] GSG 11, p. 101).

Ultimately, Simmel presents his own thought, too, as a 'third', mediating or reconciling the opposing poles of the dualities explored by him. Simmel belonged to no school, but his work rather presents a combination of a large variety of influences, from German idealism to materialism, from socialism to romanticism, and from evolutionism to vitalism, for instance. Although his thinking bears affinities with all of these movements, it cannot justifiably be placed within any one of them. Rather, he grounds his thought in the infinite interaction between them. The way he writes of other philosophers is telling in this respect. It is not rare that philosophers appear in his texts as pitted against one another; sometimes we can see this already in the titles of his writings, the books *Kant and Goethe* and *Schopenhauer and Nietzsche* being good examples. In exploring the polarities between the philosopher Immanuel Kant (1724–1804) and writer Johann Wolfgang von Goethe (1749–1832) or philosophers Arthur Schopenhauer (1788–1860) and Friedrich Nietzsche (1844–1900), Simmel does not simply prefer the thoughts of one to the other or use the one against the other. Instead of making a choice between them or reaching for a final reconciling synthesis, he discloses their contrast and retains it in force. In the closing remarks of the small book *Kant and Goethe* (published in English in 2007 in article format), Simmel suggests that while the worldview of the epoch that was then approaching its end could be characterized by the slogan 'Kant or Goethe!', the 'coming epoch may be under the sign Kant *and* Goethe, rejecting any half-hearted mediation between them' ([1906] GSG 10, p. 166; 2007, pp. 189–90). And here Simmel presents his own thinking as a kind of 'third', bridging the opposing poles of Kant and Goethe to one another, much like those of Schopenhauer and Nietzsche as well. His own stand is never a final synthesis between whichever two thinkers he pits against one another, but it rather presents a shifting balance between them, developing their standpoints in infinite reciprocity, on shifting sands, as it were. Simmel uses the authors as means to develop his own ideas and illuminate the problems he is engaged with himself, rather than pursuing a faithful reading of them.

Form and content

A key duality that runs throughout Simmel's work is that between *form* and *content*. The concept of form is perhaps the most fundamental organizing principle of his thought. However, as Guy Oakes (1977, p. 19) suggests, in its vagueness and elusiveness it may also be 'the most perplexing and inaccessible concept in Simmel's thought'. In this regard it is telling that Simmel manages to elaborate the distinction between form and content only by way of illustration and analogies.

Oakes (1977) has made a valuable contribution by clarifying the properties of Simmelian forms. He identifies seven features characteristic of them:

(1) A form is 'a *category* or a *collection of categories*' (p. 19; italics added). According to Simmel, the real can become an object of knowledge and experience only insofar as it is organized by some form. Form designates thus a certain perspective on reality and its phenomena. For example, social forms, as we shall see, uncover a specific layer of reality, its social dimension.
(2) From this it follows that forms have an *epistemological status*, pertaining to our access to the world and how and whether we can know things. A given form 'constitute[s] the conditions under which the world can be experienced and conceived in a certain way' (p. 19). The way in which the world appears to us is dependent upon the categories or concepts with the help of which we view it.
(3) However, forms also have an *ontological status*, as they condition and structure the existence of phenomena. For example, exchange is a particular kind of form organized in a different manner than free giving, paratism, or robbery.
(4) The characteristic features of forms are immanent to forms themselves and cannot be deduced from contents.
(5) Forms are also '*incommensurable*' (p. 24; italics added). For example, science and religion both amount to forms. Each is not correctable let alone refutable by the other. While scientific criticism can cast doubt on some specific contents of religious faith, such as faith cure, resurrection, or the existence of divinities, it is incapable of annulling religion as such, as a form (Simmel, 1997b, p. 5). This is because religion is organized according to different principles than science.

(6) Forms are also *incomplete* (Oakes, 1977, pp. 20–1). No form is ever exhaustive. There exists, for example, no art as such, but only historically specific forms of art and artworks characterized by particular techniques, certain possibilities of expression, and stylistic features (Simmel, [1918] GSG 16, p. 240).
(7) Finally, there are *hierarchical* relations between forms (Oakes, 1977, p. 24). An item can be classified as a poem, for example, only provided that it falls under the conceptual category of writing. Likewise, economic exchange, exchange of words in a conversation, mutual gaze, and gift exchange can all be subsumed under the more generic form of 'exchange'.

In a rare short autobiographical text later named 'Anfang einer unvollendeten Selbstdarstellung' ('Beginning of an Incomplete Self-portrait')[4] of which it is not known when exactly it was written,[5] Simmel states that in his work the distinction between form and content appears originally in the context of his theory of knowledge, where it grounds his philosophy of history. In the text he also mentions how the epistemological principle is transformed in his sociology into a 'methodical principle' (*methodisches Prinzip*) that allows him to define sociology as an independent discipline (Simmel, GSG 20, p. 304). Finally, as Antonius M. Bevers (1985, p. 23) suggests, in Simmel's life-philosophy and philosophy of culture the distinction develops into one between form and life, and is used as a *metaphysical principle*. I will look into these epistemological, sociological, and metaphysical renderings of the form–content distinction in more detail in what follows.

In epistemology

Simmel's use of the conceptual pair form and content owes much to Kant. In the philosophy of Kant, the notion of form plays a crucial role in how he sees the relation of knowledge and reality. Kant insists that we have no access to 'things in themselves' (*Dinge an sich*), that is, to things as they really are, but we can know things only in their manner of appearing to us. Accordingly, as he thought that it is not possible for us to transcend our consciousness, in other words to step outside it, Kant focused on questions of epistemology, and thereby he transformed the question of the world into one of how it is that we can know it. What we call nature, for instance, is according Kant something ordered by our reason. As Simmel ([1908] GSG 11, p. 42) puts it, for Kant nature is a 'certain manner in which our intellect assembles, orders, and forms sense impressions'. Solving the preconditions of nature necessitates in Kant's view that one identifies the forms that give our intellect its structure. Kant thus understood consciousness as a mirror, as it were, in which various phenomena are reflected. What kind of images the mirror reflects is dependent on how the mirror is structured.

Method and Key Principles

In Simmel's early work, his epistemology is centred especially on the philosophy of history, and it is in this context that the distinction between form and content initially appears, too. At the time, many scholars concerned themselves with the question of history's status as a science, among them historian and philosopher Wilhelm Dilthey (1833–1911), who was Simmel's more senior colleague in Berlin and one of the originators of the philosophy of history, as well as the neo-Kantian Wilhelm Windelband (1848–1915). In 1892, Simmel published the book *The Problems of the Philosophy of History* (1977; orig. *Die Probleme der Geschichtsphilosophie*), of his early works the only one which he republished later as a revised edition (in 1905/7). In the book Simmel asks – analogous to the question of the preconditions of nature that Kant posed in the *Critique of Pure Reason* – how history is possible. The book reads as a critique of historical realism. Simmel argues that the value of Kant's question 'How is nature possible?' was, first, that it endowed the human subject with a sense of freedom over against nature: the soul is not subjected to the same blind forces of nature as the falling stone, for example. Second, for Simmel Kant's importance lies equally in the fact that he did not reduce subjective freedom to the 'arbitrariness and idiosyncratic vicissitudes' of the assumedly sovereign ego. On the contrary, for Kant the freedom of human subjects is conditioned by 'categories which inhere in the knower alone' (Simmel, 1971, p. 4).

Simmel extends Kant's idea of form as an a priori precondition of knowledge to the study of history. Instead of providing a sheer copy or representation of the past 'as it really was' (p. 3), historical knowledge is based on 'form-giving creativity' (p. 5), which is to say that history is constructed; it is a product of the formative powers of the human mind (p. 3). For Simmel, the knowing subject has thereby a constitutive role in the production of historical knowledge. Unlike Dilthey, who thought that human experience as such was distinctive about history, and unlike Windelband, for whom history consists of concrete and unique events in themselves (Levine, 1971, p. xxii), Simmel insists that history is a form into which the knowing subject orders singular events. Accordingly, in *The Problems of the Philosophy of History* (1977), Simmel advances a thesis of history as a constitutive form and asks: how does the mere event of a phenomenon become a historical fact? For Simmel, history is formed out of immediately experienced events in accordance with 'a priori preconditions of the mind that constructs science' (*Apriofitäten des wissenschaftsbildenden Geistes*) (GSG 20, p. 304). To become history, events need to be ordered into a sequential order by the creative and active knowing subject. With regard to knowledge, this makes the human being ultimately a double, both an object and a subject: 'Man [sic], as something known, is made by nature and history; but man [sic], as knower, makes nature and history' (1971, p. 4).

In sociology

In the excursus 'How is Society Possible?' to his work *Sociology* (Simmel [1908], GSG 11; trans. 2009), Simmel takes up the idea of the a priori preconditions of knowledge, which he used in *The Problems of the Philosophy of History* to conceptualize history, and applies it now to the constitution of society. But unlike in Simmel's epistemology, in his sociology the distinction between form and content appears primarily as a *principle of method*, which plays a highly significant role in his endeavour to found and justify sociology as an independent discipline in the family of sciences. Namely, Simmel defines the subject matter of sociology by making a distinction into the form and content of society.

Whereas in Simmel's epistemology 'contents' refer to the events experienced by human subjects, in his sociology he calls 'contents' the various sorts of interests, motivations, inclinations, and reasons that individuals may have to engage in interaction. Contents make up the 'materials', so to speak, of social relations. While it is on the basis of their interests and motivations that individuals form associations with each other, according to Simmel those interests and motivations are nevertheless not yet social in themselves. As he writes in *Sociology*: 'Neither hunger nor love, neither labour nor the religious sentiment, neither technique nor the contents of intelligence, are in and of themselves alone social in character' ([1908] GSG 11, pp. 18–19). Social life cannot in Simmel's view be grasped in a satisfactory manner by reference to the subjective meanings, aims, intentions, or interests of individuals, as contents merely take place in society without constituting it. Therefore an abstraction of form is called for.

While contents without doubt fill the life of individuals and propel it, they become actual and effectual only in the relations of reciprocal influence (*Wechselwirkung*) of individuals. In other words, the interests, inclinations, and motivations of individuals are actualized only due to the relations spun between the individuals. In Simmel's sociology, the other term of the conceptual pair, namely that of *form*, refers precisely to these relations, connections, bonds, or associations. Forms designate for Simmel what is purely social, the social as such. Forms are 'what in society is really "society"' ([1908] GSG 11, p. 25), and therefore sociology, as a science of society, should according to him focus on studying them. While 'everything which takes place in society' (p. 23) may pass for a subject matter in various other social sciences, this cannot be the case in sociology, Simmel insists, but sociology must investigate the constitutive processes of society and the principles on which its unity rests. Society is for him 'the form (realized in innumerably different ways) in which individuals grow together into a unity and within which their interests are realized' (p. 19).

With regard to the perplexity of the concepts of form and content it is telling that Simmel is able to explain what he means by making the form–content distinction in sociology only through an analogy. He compares the sociology of forms to geometry, which pays attention solely to form, examining 'the form through which matter becomes empirical objects in the first place'. So, just as only geometry defines what is spatial in spatial objects, only sociology – insofar as it focuses on forms – discloses what is society as such in historical-social life.

Simmel's conception of sociology has been criticized by several scholars for being too narrow, classificatory, and formalistic (e.g. Small, 1909; Sorokin, 1928; Abel, 1929; Mills, [1959] 2000). It has been felt that as he excludes subjective motivations, aims, intentions, and meanings from what for him amounts to society or the social, Simmel's programme leads to an all-too-restricted understanding of sociology. However, this criticism is more or less based on a misconception of the nature of the Simmelian abstraction of form. Simmel explicitly states that in reality form and content belong together: there is no form devoid of any content, but the social form always only appears as the form of some specific content, and any content necessarily makes appearance always in some form. In the context of his sociology, form is for him a methodological concept with the help of which he tries to uncover a specific layer of the real, its social dimension. It is a viewpoint that organizes events and conditions in a different manner than the perspective of content does. Simmel thereby intends the abstraction of form, as Friedrich Tenbruck (1959, p. 75) has argued, not as an 'abstraction from content-*phenomena*', but as an 'abstraction from a content-*perspective*'. This is to say that Simmel's programme of sociology does not disregard contents, but it insists that sociology should view reality with regard to forms of relations between humans instead of subjective contents.

There are two facts on the basis of which Simmel justifies the isolation of the social form from its content by way of abstraction. The first is that one and the same form may manifest in diverse contents. Exchange, for instance, is a social form that may occur in monetary exchange, in the exchange of gifts such as Christmas presents or reciprocal dinner invitations, just as it may occur whenever people engage in conversation or look at each other, for example. Likewise, competition may take place in various spheres of life from sports to politics, economy, science, and erotic life, and one may compete for various kinds of things such as medals, glory, reputation, votes, wealth, truth, academic positions, and conquests. All in all, Simmel suggests that people may actualize a similar form of reciprocity in several spheres of life and despite acting on varying interest and reasons. In his own words: 'as diverse may be the reasons why people overall [...] are associated, the forms of association may nevertheless be the same' ([1908] GSG 11, p. 21). Simmel's second justification for the abstraction of form from content is that what was noted above applies also vice versa: one and the same content may appear in various forms. Economic strivings, for example, may manifest in capitalism as much as in socialism, in market economy as much as in planned economy or in gift economy, in free competition as much as in monopoly (p. 21). It is important to acknowledge that the distinction into form and content is not absolute but relative. '[F]orm and content' Simmel stresses, are merely relative concepts'. They are 'categories of knowledge' for grasping and organizing phenomena, and thereby, as Simmel puts it, 'the very same thing that in one relation, as if seen from above, appears as form, must be described as content in another' (p. 492).

In metaphysics

It is quite common in the secondary literature to view the last ten years of Simmel's life as a dramatic and sudden 'turn' away from sociology towards philosophy, especially towards metaphysics of life and philosophy of culture marked by the influence of Johann Wolfgang von Goethe, Friedrich Nietzsche, and Henri Bergson (see, for example, Landmann, 1968, p. 8; 1976, pp. 4–5). For instance, Tenbruck states that Simmel published his magnum opus *Sociology* at a time, in 1908, when 'sociological study was already left far behind him and he had definitely turned his attention to philosophical and aesthetic questions' (Tenbruck, 1958; cited by Frisby, 1981, p. 24). However, it may very well be that the turn is not quite as radical as Tenbruck assumes. To me David Frisby seems to hit the mark better, as he suggests that while the publication of *Sociology* signified, perhaps, 'the end of Simmel's *major* occupation with sociology' (Frisby, 1981, p. 4; italics added), Simmel did not abandon sociology completely. In his life-philosophy, Simmel only digs deeper into the presuppositions of his thinking, as it were. We can see this also in the distinction between form and content, which is present in Simmel's life-philosophy as well, though by being supplemented by a new, more fundamental layer.

This deep storey is that of *life* (*Leben*). In Simmel's life-philosophy (which will be discussed in more detail in Chapter 7), life constitutes the ultimate horizon of thought: it is something that both must be thought and yet constantly escapes thought. Ultimately, the notion of life is for Simmel a way of conceptualizing the pervasive processuality of things and the world, including the social one. Simmel perceives movement, process, and flows in terms of life, and life as movement and becoming. For Simmel, life amounts to an emblem of movement, a radical becoming. In *Rembrandt*, Simmel notes of life: 'It never *is*; it is always *becoming*.' ([1916] GSG 15, p. 321; 2005, p. 11)

In Simmel's life-philosophy, the tension between life and form is given a privileged position in cultural change. According to Simmel, their contrast is 'the innermost motive for cultural transformation' ([1918] GSG 16, p. 226) and 'the ultimate grounds for the fact that culture has a history' (p. 183). Life constantly tries to overcome forms. While forms encompass life and provide it with shape, stability, and actuality, they 'do not share the restless rhythm of life, its ascent and descent, its constant renewal, its incessant divisions and reunifications' ([1918] GSG 16, p. 183; 1971, p. 375). In his life-philosophy, Simmel describes form as actuality, surface, timeless, and powerless in contrast to life, which he gives such attributes as potentiality, inner current, temporality and force ([1916] GSG 15, pp. 377–80; 2005, pp. 51–3). Life cannot be fully accommodated in form, since forms funnel and dam its ever-flowing stream. This is why life ceaselessly reaches out beyond old forms and creates new ones. In the essay 'Der Konflikt der modernen Kultur', Simmel illustrates this process by taking the transformation of the forms of production as his example:

> The economic forces of every epoch generate forms of production appropriate to their nature. Slave economy, guild constitution, peasant obligation, free wage labour, and other kind of work organizations – all these expressed, when they were formed, adequately the capacities and wishes of their times. Within their own norms and limitations, however, there grew economic forces whose volume and manner could not fulfil themselves in these forms. Either through gradual or more acute revolutions the forces burst the oppressive bonds of their respective forms and replaced them with modes of production more appropriate. A new mode of production, however, as a form has no energy of its own that could supersede another form. It is life itself, here in its economic dimension – with its drive and its desire for advancement, its internal changes and differentiation – that provides the dynamics for this whole movement; yet life as such is formless, it can only become a phenomenon as formed. ([1918], GSG 16, pp. 184–5)

At first glance, Simmel seems to be echoing here Marx, who sees the conflict between the forces of production and the forms of social relations as the root of social and economic change. However, for Simmel, the conflict is only one manifestation of the more pervasive antagonism between life and form to which it is subordinate.

The emphasis on life as process is what Simmel shares, for example, with Bergson (1859–1941), whose 'vitalism' – with its key concepts of duration, memory, and élan vital – was remarkably influential and fashionable in Europe, especially in Weimar Germany, in the early decades of the 20th century. However, unlike Bergson (see, e.g., 1999, p. 30), Simmel does not think that we should renounce rigorously defined concepts in favour of 'intuition'. This separates Simmel significantly not only from Bergson but from most other life-philosophers as well. He is well aware of the logical difficulty present in the attempt to come to grips with life with the help of concepts, since fixed and static concepts inevitably obliterate life's characteristics of flux and processuality (Simmel, [1918] GSG 16, p. 235). Nevertheless, rather than insisting on the necessity of grasping life via intuition, like Bergson did, Simmel rejects the very possibility of viewing 'life proper'. Owing to his Kantian background, Simmel thinks that we are denied access to life as such. Life can never be grasped in itself, but only in some form, through the relative contrast of life and form.

Wechselwirkung

Several commentators have asserted the essential role of the notion of *Wechselwirkung* ('reciprocal effect') not only in Simmel's sociology but also in his thought in general.[6] Moreover, Petra Christian (1978, pp. 115–20) and later Andreas Ziemann (2000, pp. 117–31) have traced the pre-Simmelian history of the concept; Christian as a path leading from Kant to Hegel, Friedrich Schleiermacher (1768–1834), Dilthey and finally to Simmel; and Ziemann, following otherwise the same route, except for the fact that he substitutes Hermann von Helmholtz (1821–94) for Hegel. The word *Wechselwirkung* does not translate into English without difficulties. For example, the term 'interaction', which is an often seen translation, problematically implies that *Wechselwirkung* would be based on (social) *action*. However, relations of *Wechselwirkung* cannot be explained by reference to the action of individual actors and their motivations, ambitions, or ends, but *Wechselwirkung* presents a 'third', as it were, in relation to the actions of each party. What is more, for Simmel, *Wechselwirkung* consists not only of what the individuals involved actively 'do' (*tun*), but also of how they are influenced. It refers to the dynamics and interplay of affecting and being affected. Further, Simmel also insists that individuals affect each other not only actively, but passively, too: for example, the way one receives a gift – whether by being grateful or ungrateful, by having expected it or by having become surprised by it, by loving it or feeling humiliated by it 'has a crucial effect [...] on the donor', as Simmel remarks in *Sociology* ([1908] GSG 11, p. 663, n. 1).

Like the distinction between form and content, the notion of *Wechselwirkung*, too, holds a significant position in Simmel's epistemology just as much as in his sociology and metaphysics. Thereby, we can also make an analytical distinction between three types of relationalism in Simmel: epistemological, sociological, and metaphysical.

Epistemological relationalism

In Simmel's epistemology, the principle of *Wechselwirkung* is connected to the notion of truth. Simmel insists on the relativity of truth. Whereas Simmel himself calls his view 'relativism' (*Relativismus*), I feel that it is more accurate to call it *epistemological relationalism*, for while relativism in its conventional form sees that truth is weakened by its relativity, Simmel, on the contrary, aspires to disclose how truth is *founded upon* relations. In a letter to Heinrich Rickert, Simmel notes that his version of 'relativism' should not be identified with the subjectivism and scepticism commonly associated with the term: 'What I understand by relativism is an entirely positive metaphysical worldview, and [it has] so little scepticism [in it] as does Einstein's or [Max von] Laue's physical relativism' ([1916] GSG 23, p. 638). A few lines later, he elaborates on this a bit further, explaining that for him the relativity of truth 'does not mean at all that truth [*Wahrheit*] and falsehood [*Unwahrheit*] are relative to one another; but truth means *a relation between contents* of which none possesses truth in and by themselves' (p. 638; italics added). Simmel explains also in *The Philosophy of Money* how relativity needs to be understood:

> Relativity does not mean – as in common usage – a diminution of truth [...]; on the contrary, it is the positive fulfilment and validation of the concept of truth. Truth is valid, not in spite of its relativity but precisely on account of it. ([1900/7] GSG 6, p. 116; 2004, p. 116)

This means that every claim is relative; either in 'a rising or falling series', as in logical derivation, 'where every link depends upon another, and a third one is dependent upon it', or in a circular fashion, so that 'each part of the circle determines the position of other parts' ([1900/7] GSG 6, pp. 120–1; 2004, p. 119).

Interestingly, Simmel connects his discussion of the relativity of truth to the sociocultural changes of his time as well as to transformations in the scientific worldview. He asks how it is possible to think in the modern world of flux without falling into subjectivism and scepticism. He provides an answer in the 'incomplete self-portrait', the short biographical text mentioned above:

> The recent dissolution of everything substantial, absolute, eternal into the flux of things, into historical mutability, into merely psychological reality is, as it appears to me, secured against an unstable subjectivism and scepticism only if one sets in the place of the substantial fixed values the living reciprocity of elements, which themselves are subject to the same dissolution ad infinitum. The central concepts of truth, value, objectivity, etc. expressed themselves to me as reciprocities, as contents of a relativism that now no longer signified the sceptical dissipation of all that is solid but precisely protection against it via a new concept of solidity. (GSG 20, pp. 304–5)

So, Simmel thinks that 'relativism' or relationalism provides a new notion of solidity: the dissolution of absolute objectivity can be carried in such a way that no 'absolute is [...] required as a conceptual counterpart to the relativity of things' ([1900/7] GSG 6, p. 97; 2004, p. 104). It is according to Simmel precisely here where lies the strength of 'relativism'/relationalism compared to other epistemological principles. While other principles suffer from the difficulty of subjecting their own content to the judgement they pronounce upon knowledge in general, this does not apply to 'relativism'/relationalism ([1900/7] GSG 6, p. 116; 2004, p. 116). Therefore, Simmel claims, 'the relativity of things is the only absolute' ([1900/7] GSG 6, p. 307; 2004, p. 238). To elaborate:

> Only a relativistic epistemology does not claim exemption from its own principle; it is not destroyed by the fact that its validity is only relative. For even if it is valid – historically, factually, psychologically – only in relation and in harmony with other absolute, or substantial principles, its relation to its own opposite is itself only relative. ([1900/7] GSG 6, p. 117; 2004, p. 117)

Simmel also regards 'relativism'/relationalism as 'the most appropriate expression of the contemporary contents of science and emotional currents', and it 'decisively exclude[s] the opposing world picture' ([1900/7] GSG 6, p. 13; 2004, p. 56). In practice, it does not make a difference whether one thinks 'that there is an absolute but it can be grasped only by an infinite process, or that there are only relations but that they can only replace the absolute in an infinite process' ([1900/7] GSG 6, pp. 117–8; 2004, p. 117). Either way, we end up with relationality. Interestingly, the quotation also suggests a link between epistemological relationalism and process: the dissolution of absolutes into relations is necessarily 'an infinite process' or 'a never-ending process' ([1900/7] GSG 6, p. 118; 2004, p. 117). It is established on a fleeting basis: for relativism, truth, value, and objectivity appear as reciprocities.

Sociological relationalism

As Simmel's sociological relationalism will be discussed in more detail in Chapter 3, here the issue will be touched on only briefly. Its core is the notion of *Wechselwirkung*. In *The Philosophy of Money*, Simmel insists that '[t]he starting point of all social formations can only be the reciprocity of effects [*Wechselwirkung*] between person to person' ([1900/7] GSG 6, p. 208; 2004, p. 173; translation altered). As a science of society, sociology should according to Simmel take interpersonal forms of *Wechselwirkung* as its object of enquiry. While 'everything which takes place in society' (Simmel [1908] GSG 11, p. 23) may pass for a subject matter in various other social sciences, this cannot be the case in sociology, Simmel insists, but sociology must investigate 'what in society is really "society"' (p. 25). That is, it needs to study the constitutive processes of society and the principles on which its unity rests. And, according to Simmel, the production and reassembling of society can be grasped only by examining the *Wechselwirkungen* of its elements ([1896] GSG 1, p. 370). As he puts it in *Sociology*: 'Should there be a science, whose object of study is society and nothing else, it can examine only […] reciprocal effects [*Wechselwirkungen*], […] ways and forms of association.' ([1908] GSG 11, p. 19)

Simmel regards the independent and autonomous forms (social classes, family, politics, the economy, the church, etc.) that make up the traditional objects of sociology as merely secondary phenomena compared to the *Wechselwirkungen* between individuals ([1890] GSG 2, p. 130; see also [1900/7] GSG 6, pp. 208–9; Frisby, 1992, p. 10). Accordingly, society, too, is nothing autonomous or absolute for him. He does not regard society as the defining feature of the social, as a general framework for social phenomena that the notion of the social would always already presuppose. On the contrary, society is for Simmel only a result of the relations among individuals and groups, something that has to be produced and connected rather than being always there. The relational turn that Simmel's work initiates in sociology resonates, for example, with the work of Gabriel Tarde and Norbert Elias. In addition, his relationalism also figures with varying degrees in much more recent calls for a relational programme for sociology (see, e.g., Emirbayer, 1997; Crossley, 2011; Donati, 2011; Dépelteau & Powell, 2013; Powell & Dépelteau, 2013).

Metaphysical relationalism

In the aforementioned rare autobiographical note, Simmel mentions that while *Wechselwirkung* originally appears in his work as a sociological concept, it later broadens up in his metaphysics into a general 'metaphysical principle' that ultimately concerns the whole of reality (GSG 20, p. 304). To put it simply, Simmel's metaphysical relationalism is characterized by the idea of *the real as relational*. In *Über sociale Differenzierung*, he suggests that it should be held as a 'regulative world principle' that 'everything interacts in some way with everything else' ([1890] GSG 2, p. 130). He maintains that it is only because of the interconnectedness of all things that there can appear something like a world in the first place. As he puts it in *Sociology*, 'We could not say that the world is one, unless its every element somehow affected every one else.' ([1908] GSG 11, p. 18)

Thereby, as Simmel notes in a letter, he does not regard the world as 'a substantial, absolute oneness' (GSG 22, p. 872), but as a multitude of individual, separate elements woven together by reciprocal relations. Both Simmel's metaphysical and sociological relationalism dissolve things into reciprocal effects and processes. They establish the 'interdependence of things' as 'their essence', to quote Simmel's own words in *The Philosophy of Money* ([1900/7] GSG 6, p. 120; 2004, p. 114). This interdependence suggests that entities are only what they are through the relations that they come to have with others. Any entity involves others as its components; the influences and effects of others do not distort the being of an entity but participate in making it what it is. Simmel's goal is thus to strip things off their false isolation, self-sufficiency, and absoluteness. For Simmel, as Siegfried Kracauer (1995, p. 250) has proposed, 'there is nothing absolute that exists unconnected to other phenomena and that possesses validity in and for itself'. Nothing exists solely in and by itself, but each and every entity is made up of relations. Relatedness has primacy over quality.

Indeed, whatever objects Simmel treats in his work he never conceives them as monolithic or isolated substances, but he dissolves them into relations. And he tackles their interconnectedness by way of operating with two different kinds of relations (Kracauer, 1995). On the one hand, Simmel attends to how entities are actually bounded, connected, and linked to each other in reality. To pick one example, in *The Philosophy of Money* Simmel shows how money establishes wide-ranging relationships of mutual dependence. For instance, due to the mediating role played by money, 'it is possible for a German capitalist but also for a German worker to take part in the swap of a minister in Spain, in the profits of African gold mines, and in the outcome of a South American revolution' ([1900/7] GSG 6, pp. 663–4; 2004, p. 476).

On the other hand, the interconnectedness of phenomena reveals itself to Simmel also through relations of analogy. Simmel's writings are full of analogies: for example, he compares money to God in that in modernity the first has become the common denominator of most opposed and distant things; he makes an analogy between sociability and art as well as play; and he suggests that boundaries are to social relations what the picture frame is to a work of art. What is more, as we saw earlier, Simmel even predicted the fate of his work by comparing his legacy to money.

Simmel's extensive use of argument by analogy has been criticized by several commentators, including Max Weber (1972). However, what Simmel undeniably loses in systematic argument he wins in the ability to suggest surprising links between seemingly unconnected and distinct things. Analogies are a way of grasping the unfamiliar in terms of the familiar. They allow us to comprehend what we do not know by relating it to what we already know. To propose an analogy between sociability and art, for example, is to highlight their similarity and shared properties. Rather than say that there is a perfect equivalence, a homology, between them, the comparison draws attention to similarity between the related terms while at the same time acknowledging their difference. In a sense, then, one could argue that for Simmel analogies are a way of seeing similarity *through difference*. And, by using analogies, Simmel not only succeeds in making graspable something new or less familiar by comparing it to the more familiar, but also in discovering new and unfamiliar aspects in the familiar. So, by comparing sociability with art and play, for example, he sheds new light on art and play, too. Thanks to the relations of analogy established, we are able to see both of the related terms from a different perspective and in a new light.[7]

Conclusion

In this chapter, I have discussed Simmel's dialectical method and explored two key principles of his work, the form–content distinction and the principle of *Wechselwirkung* ('reciprocal effect'), and presented how they manifest in Simmel's epistemology, sociology of forms, and metaphysics. For the sake of clarity, above the two principles have been examined separately, but it is also possible to sum them up in one table (Table 2.1).[8]

The form–content distinction row displays, first, the manifestation of the principle of form and content in Simmel's epistemology, sociology of forms, and life-philosophy. Second, it also indicates the object of Simmel's thought in each perspective: whereas in his epistemology Simmel takes the a priori forms of knowledge as his subject matter, in his sociology he focuses on the social

Table 2.1 Key principles of Simmel's thought (adaptation from Bevers, 1985, p. 25)

	Epistemology	Sociology of forms	Metaphysics
Form–content distinction	epistemological principle: a priori forms of knowledge	methodical principle: social forms	metaphysical principle: contrast of form and life
Principle of Wechselwirkung	epistemological relationalism: relativity of truth	sociological relationalism: society and the social as relational	metaphysical relationalism: the real as relational

forms of *Wechselwirkung*, and, finally, his life-philosophy is organized around the contrast of form and life. As for the bottom row, it presents how the principle of *Wechselwirkung* figures in the aforementioned fields or disciplines: in Simmel's epistemology, it appears as the basis of his epistemological relationalism, arguing truth to be founded on relations; in his sociology, it forms the key concept of his sociological relationalism, which looks at society and social phenomena by starting from relations; and in his metaphysical worldview the principle of *Wechselwirkung* is related to a metaphysical relationalism, which regards the real as relational.[9]

None of Simmel's contemporaries or any one of the scholars that he has influenced has assumed Simmel's method as such, as employed by him. Scholars have rather embraced one particular dimension of it or used selected concepts and ideas. As we shall see more closely in Chapter 8, Leopold von Wiese, for example, based his sociology largely on Simmel's principle of form, but in his hands the Simmelian sociology of forms turned into a much more classificatory undertaking. Another example is presented by Robert E. Park (also discussed in Chapter 8), who received his key concept, 'interaction', from Simmel, and also insisted that sociology should investigate the ideal types of forms of interaction. However, what Park meant by interaction differs significantly from the Simmelian notion of *Wechselwirkung*, and he also understood social facts in a manner different from Simmel.

Even though the principle of the form–content distinction and that of *Wechselwirkung* were discussed separately above, it is important to think of them in connection with each other, since that gives us a more comprehensive sense of Simmel's ways of knowing. On its own, the sociological principle of form–content distinction is a classificatory practice. It provides a means to discover the typical features from varied phenomena. When studying competition, for example, Simmel is interested not so much in specific kinds of competition – such as that in the economy, science, arts, weapons, or sports – as in delineating the typical characteristics of all types of competition, so as to see what kinds of conflicts and alliances it involves, and what kind of consequences it may have (Bouglé, 1965, p. 59). Accordingly, as was already noted, some scholars have criticized Simmel's sociology for being overly classificatory. However, when the abstraction by form is coupled with relationalism we get a more versatile image of how Simmel operates in his thought. While the form–content distinction splits things apart, relationalism draws things together. Connecting heterogeneous, seemingly most distant phenomena, Simmel's relational mode of thinking in a sense even amounts to a kind of topological or geographical notion of knowledge, which fathoms knowing as travelling, as a journey along a web or mesh of relations. This is to say that one knows not only based on classifications, but also '*alongly*', to borrow a brilliant notion by Tim Ingold (2011, p. 154). Knowledge necessitates movement, and moving is itself a way of knowing. Together the principles of form–content distinction and *Wechselwirkung* present something of a system of Simmel's work, though it is one based on constant variation, modulation, and change instead of invariance and stability. Simmel's thought is not static, merely classificatory, or particularly formal, but fluid and flexible. When studying social forms, Simmel's analysis does not attempt their taxonomy, but he stresses the dynamics of social life by attending to the emergence, becoming, and cessation of the forms. What is more, language and thought themselves are for Simmel above all something 'living' (Christian, 1978, p. 50; see, e.g., Simmel, [1914] GSG 13, p. 54; [1918] GSG 16, p. 258), not systems of meanings and propositions. To understand him it is therefore important to attend to the movement of thought. In the remaining chapters of Part I, I will trace that movement by mapping both the beaten tracks and some less familiar if not altogether undiscovered paths in his thinking. Part II then follows how Simmel's ideas have spread out and emanated within academia along varied routes.

Notes

1 Schermer and Jary (2013) identify the two first ones as fundamental dualisms, but instead of life–form they mention nature–culture, which I would merge with object–subject.
2 For instance Weber, too, suggests that Simmel's manner of thought is unrepeatable and inimitable. According to Weber (1972, p. 158), Simmel's 'mode of exposition is simply brilliant and, what is more important, attains results that are intrinsic to it and not to be attained by any imitator'. In his assessment of Simmel, Leopold von Wiese notes pretty much the same thing: 'From a certain aspect I would even call his sociology the sociology of an aesthete, a sociology for the literary salon. [...] But in its mosaic form and its aestheticism, this sociology has a distinctly personal, Simmelean character. The same method in the hands of – (no, I had better name no names!) would be unbearable.' (von Wiese, 1965, pp. 56–7)

3   The figure of the stranger will be discussed in more detail in Chapter 6.
4   In GSG 20, the text is titled 'Fragment einer Einleitung' ('Fragment of an Introduction').
5   Torge Karlsruhen and Otthein Rammstedt (2004, p. 549) suggest in their editorial to GSG volume 20, however, that the text cannot have been written before year 1910, when Simmel's first texts on metaphysics were published.
6   See, e.g., Becher (1971); Christian (1978, pp. 125–33); Dahme (1981, pp. 253, 368–75); Nedelmann (1984, pp. 93–6); Ziemann (2000, pp. 113–6); Gross (2001, pp. 397–8).
7   See also Swedberg (2014) for Simmel's use of analogies.
8   The table is adapted from Bevers (1985, p. 25) with slight alterations. The most important ones are, first, that Bevers has *Kultur-/Lebensphilosophie* ('Culture-/Life-philosophy') as the title of the column on the far right; and, second, that he specifies metaphysical relationalism as being about the 'dialectical nature of life and cultural process' (*dialektischer Charakter von Leben und Kulturprozeß*).
9   It must be noted that what is meant by 'metaphysics' in the table in relation to the distinction between form and content differs to some extent from what is referred to with it in relation to the principle of *Wechselwirkung*. Whereas in the first case it refers to Simmel's life-philosophy, what is meant by it in the latter is Simmel's overall relational approach to the world and the real.

3
Sociology of Association

Although Simmel saw himself primarily as a philosopher, from very early on his career was entangled with sociology and its development. Simmel also cared a great deal about the discipline. As he wrote in a letter to Célestin Bouglé in 1894, 'the tasks of sociology' were for him 'so close to the heart'.[1] In the same letter, Simmel also replies to Bouglé's enquiries about the future direction of his work by stating: 'In the near future I dedicate myself completely to sociological studies and will not step into any other field' (GSG 22, p. 112). The same year, he published his first major programmatic statement 'Das Problem der Soziologie' ('The Problem of Sociology'), which seeks to delimit the scope of sociology and thereby define and justify it as an independent discipline. Later, Simmel also played an active part in the institutionalization of German sociology (see e.g. Härpfer, 2014, pp. 14–15). With Rudolf Goldscheid (1870–1931) he initiated the founding of the *Deutsche Gesellschaft für Soziologie* (DGS), the German Sociological Association. In November 1908, Simmel wrote a letter to colleagues suggesting that a committee be organized with the founding of the Association as its purpose (see Simmel, [1908] GSG 22, pp. 669–70). As a result, the following month an invitation, signed by Simmel, Georg Jellinek, Werner Sombart, Ferdinand Tönnies, Max Weber and others, was sent out (pp. 672–7). The Association was founded the next year, in 1909.

Simmel was the first to use the word *Soziologie* ('Sociology') as a book title in the German language (Tönnies, 1965, p. 50). This major work came out in 1908, and it is highly significant with regard to sociological analysis for at least three reasons. First, it sets out to lay the foundations of sociology as a discipline. While doing so it also comes to give a precise meaning to the term 'sociology'. Up until then the notion had remained fairly vague. For example, in his letters to René Worms from 18 December 1893 and 28 January 1894, Simmel laments that, as a discipline, sociology is so varied that 'no two people have the same conception of it' (GSG 24, p. 99), and thus the ones practising it share merely the name 'sociologists', which is 'a name under which everyone thinks something different' (GSG 24, p. 105). Second, the book also presents Simmel's programme of sociology in its most advanced and extensive form.

And, third, it includes a remarkably wide array of concrete analyses of social forms as examples of how to put the programme into practice. The topics discussed include themes such as conflict, the stranger, space, the significance of the number of participants for social formations, sub- and superordination, secrecy, the senses, gratitude, and faithfulness. The choice of themes, which at first glance seems more or less arbitrary, was deliberate on Simmel's part. He intended the topics as fragments of the ground that the sociology of forms could cover when matured. As he writes in a footnote to the first chapter:

> The further the here presented remains from a unified system, and the further apart its parts lie from one another, the more extensive will the circle be to which the future completion of sociology will tie its already determinable individual points. ([1908] GSG 11, p. 31 n. 1)

However, the book *Sociology* only presents a culmination of Simmel's work on sociology that he had begun almost 20 years earlier, and most of the book's materials had also already been published as individual essays. His first major sociological work, *Über sociale Differenzierung* ('On Social Differentiation'), appeared in 1890. The book already contains many of the themes, such as individuality, the concept of society, and the epistemological foundation of the social sciences, on which Simmel was to work throughout nearly his whole career. Its first chapter deals with the epistemology of the social sciences or, more exactly, of sociology (which he at that point wrote with c, 'Sociologie', and not z). In the chapter, Simmel seeks to overcome the individualistic approach to social life by identifying 'the forms of being-with of people' (*die Formen des Zusammenseins von Menschen*) as the specific object of sociological investigation (Simmel, [1890] GSG 2, p. 118). He argues that even though in the last instance there exist only individual human beings in their situations and movements, sociology reveals a specific layer of reality by focusing on its social dimension. In the chapter Simmel also highlights the importance of the notion of *Wechselwirkung*, which I identified in Chapter 2 as one of the two key principles of his work. Simmel suggests that each and every unity is ultimately based on the interaction of its parts, and that this is also how we must understand society (Simmel, [1890] GSG 2, pp. 129–30).

In *Über sociale Differenzierung*, Simmel identifies the relationship of the individual and the social group or society as the foundational problem of the social sciences. Simmel was to retain this view throughout the years up until the book *Grundfragen der Soziologie*, which was published in 1917, one year before his death. In his description of the book, Simmel writes that the 'basic question of all sociology' is 'what kind of relations there exist between society and its elements, the individuals?' (GSG 16, p. 444). In *Grundfragen der Soziologie*, Simmel names three different sociological approaches to this question: general sociology, pure sociology, and philosophical sociology. Whereas general sociology amounts for him to the study of the societally formed historical life, with its focus especially on the problem of the relation between individuals and the collective behaviour of a group or a mass (what Simmel calls the *Niveauproblem*), pure sociology, which is *the* sociology Simmel seeks to define in *Sociology* ([1908] GSG 11), takes as its object the forms of *Wechselwirkung* between individuals. Philosophical sociology, lastly, examines the epistemological and metaphysical aspects of the relation between individuality and society or, more broadly, humanity.

While Simmel regards the individual and society as irreconcilable *as principles*, his sociological work importantly insists that the two are not separate entities but mutually constitutive. They are bound by relations of *Wechselwirkung*. With the notion of *Wechselwirkung* as its basis, Simmel's sociology places 'relation' as the final unit of sociological analysis. In *Über sociale Differenzierung*, Simmel insists that the unity of any entity is based on *Wechselwirkungen* of parts (Simmel, [1890] GSG 2, p. 129). In *Sociology*, Simmel foregrounds relations even more explicitly by proposing that the purely sociological concepts concern relations, more exactly the 'form of relation' (*Beziehungsform*), not their substance. And, following from this, he suggests that the purest sociological concept is that of 'relationship' (*Verhältnis*), for while the term can also be used to refer to a certain kind of relationship, namely 'love affair', it is not limited to any one single type of relation but can stand for all kinds (GSG 11, p. 710 n. 1).

In this chapter, I examine how Simmel's insistence on the primacy of relations of *Wechselwirkung* initiates a relational approach in sociology against reifying substantialist assumptions, which conceive the world in terms of categories and more or less discrete and static entities. Mustafa Emirbayer (2013, p. 210) observes that 'substantialist assumptions are incorporated [so] deeply in our everyday and scholarly discourse alike' that 'it is difficult to imagine their being supplanted anytime soon'. Nevertheless, I argue that Simmel's work provides an important example of how the underlying substantialist presuppositions could possibly be ousted. It not only acknowledges the fundamental entanglement and interconnectedness of beings but also helps us escape the long tradition of conceiving the world in terms of the micro–macro distinction, where the term 'micro' refers to individuals and their (inter)actions, and 'macro' to larger social formations, institutions, and processes. In what follows, I will first discuss Simmel's effort to lay a theoretical and philosophical foundation for sociology as an independent discipline. Then I will examine how Simmel dissolves society as an assumedly autonomous and static entity into relations. After that I will discuss Simmel's effort to lay the epistemological preconditions for society. The final two sections of the chapter focus on fleshing out Simmel's relational approach. The concluding section will also sum up the key implications of Simmel's relationalism for social theory.

A science of society

Simmel was among the first who made a serious attempt to lay a theoretical basis for sociology as an independent discipline. In his work, he refutes the then dominating view of sociology as an all-inclusive science, famously held for instance by Auguste Comte (1798–1857), who is commonly regarded as the 'father of sociology' and credited with inventing the term 'sociology'. Instead of seeing sociology as a synthesis of all existing scientific fields of enquiry, Simmel tries to define sociology as a specific science in its own right. In *Sociology*, he argues that no new discipline is gained by simply lumping all historical, psychological, and normative sciences together as if in a large jar and adding the label 'Sociology' (Simmel, [1908] GSG 11, pp. 14–15). In order to stand as an independent discipline, sociology needs a distinctive view, providing it with a subject matter of its own, an object not yet studied by any other existing field of enquiry.

Early sociology rested on an all-embracing notion of society. Besides Comte, among others Herbert Spencer and Émile Durkheim, too, considered society in totalizing terms, as a kind of pre-existing and comprehensive container within which the lives and actions of individuals are contained. Simmel states that for such a view society 'builds the individual existences like the sea builds the waves' ([1908] GSG 11, p. 14). In contrast to this, Simmel argues that the fact that the contents of life are actualized in human sociality, that is, in relations of interdependence between humans, easily misleads us to assuming that sociality and society are 'the only, and universally applicable, categories in terms of which we may contemplate the contents of human experience' ([1908] GSG 11, p. 858; 1971, p. 36). For Simmel, far from exhausting the whole of human experience, society is merely one possible *category* under which contents of life can be organized. It is equally possible to subject them to the categories of *objective contents*, *the individual*, and *humanity*. As regards the first, Simmel suggests that sciences, technologies, and arts, for example, have an 'inner validity, coherence, and objective significance' irrespective of the fact that they are actualized only within relations between individuals and in society ([1908] GSG 11, p. 859; 1971, p. 36). The individual presents another category of human experience. Simmel maintains that all 'contents of life are directly borne by individuals' in that someone must conceive them and they fill the consciousness of a person ([1908] GSG 11, p. 859; 1971, p. 37). While it is true that individuals always live in a society, in reciprocal relations with other individuals, the category of the individual nevertheless presents a point of view that is different from that of society. Finally, the contents of life could also be examined from the perspective of humanity, enquiring into the 'value and meaning which they possess as elements of the life of humanity, as stages of its development' ([1908] GSG 11, p. 861; 1971, p. 38). While humanity may occasionally overlap with the category of society,[2] Simmel stresses that the two viewpoints are in principle different ([1908] GSG 11, p. 861; 1971, p. 39).

For Simmel, society is thus a *methodological concept* that does not exhaust all of the real, but presents it from a specific viewpoint. It is based on the perspective of form independent of that of contents. Although the emotions, feelings, beliefs, strivings and motivations of individuals may modify social forms, forms uncover a specific layer of reality irreducible to individual actors and to the meaning they give to their action. The forms of *Wechselwirkung* cannot therefore be explained with reference to social action and subjective meaning. For example, just as in relations of power the one in the position of the superordinate is bound by the ones who obey without explicitly intending or striving for this, obedience is hardly an aim or motivation of the subordinate (Tenbruck, 1959, pp. 72–3). One cannot grasp super- and subordination unless one pays attention to the dynamics of relations between the subjects involved.

Dissatisfied with the 'peculiar fuzziness and uncertainty' (Simmel, [1908] GSG 11, p. 24) of the broad notion of society envisaged by Comte and other early sociologists, in his programme of sociology Simmel seeks to redefine society by giving it a more precise meaning. Hence, while 'everything which takes place in society' (p. 23) may pass for a subject matter in various other social sciences, in Simmel's view this cannot be the case for sociology. In order to qualify as a legitimate science of *society*, sociology must for him discover 'what in society is really "society"' (p. 25; see also [1894] GSG 5, p. 57), that is, investigate the principles on which the unity of society rests. It is for this purpose that Simmel makes the distinction between the form and the content of society, with contents referring, as was already mentioned in Chapter 2, to the impulses, urges, needs, desires, and motives of individuals, and forms designating the modes in which individuals affect others and are affected by them. It is only when married with the concept of form that the insight that people are mutually defined in their relations of being with, for, and against one another attains for Simmel genuine sociological relevance (Simmel, [1908] GSG 11; Dahme, 1981, p. 24; Ziemann, 2000, pp. 113–14).

For Simmel, society is constituted by *Wechselwirkung*. He acknowledges that the basic insight on which early – such as Comtean – sociology rests, namely that 'the human being is in one's whole essence determined by the fact that one lives in reciprocal interaction with other people must lead to a new manner of examination in the human sciences [*Geisteswissenschaften*]' ([1908] GSG 11, p. 15). In Simmel's view, this insight, however, does not yet provide sociology with a distinctive object and principle (p. 15). Such ground is gained only on the basis of the analytical abstraction of the perspective of form from that of content that was discussed in Chapter 2.

Simmel maintains that, apart from form, 'everything else found within "society" and realized through it within its framework is not itself society. It is merely a content that develops or is developed by this form of coexistence' ([1908] GSG 11, pp. 19–20; 1971, p. 25). A given number of human beings become a society only when the vitality of the contents that fill their life 'attains the form of reciprocal influence' ([1908] GSG 11, p. 19; 1971, p. 24). For Simmel, the only and entire basis of a special science of society lies therefore in the possibility of detaching the form of reciprocity from its content. While in reality the two are inseparable, it is only by separating them by analytical abstraction that we are able to examine what is 'society and nothing else' ([1908] GSG 11, p. 19; 1971, p. 25) and reach 'the plane of the purely social' (*die Ebene bloß Gesellschaftlich*) ([1908] GSG 11, p. 20; 1971, p. 25).

Because of Simmel's insistence that sociology should focus on the forms that remain invariable in a diversity of contents, several scholars have misunderstood his sociology as being particularly static. For example, in *The Sociological Imagination* ([1959] 2000, p. 30) C. Wright Mills asserts:

> [I]n the work of the formalists, notably Simmel and Von [sic] Wiese,[3] sociology comes to deal in conceptions intended to be of use in classifying all social relations and providing insight into their supposedly invariant features. It is, in short, concerned with a rather static and abstract view of the components of social structure on a quite high level of generality.

However, unlike Mills suggests, Simmel is not primarily interested in some classification of social forms, nor does he understand forms as particularly static, but his work rather stresses the dynamics and processuality of social life. In the final chapter of *The Philosophy of Money*, 'The Style of Life', Simmel remarks that while our categories for comprehending the world tend to stress the invariable and permanent aspects of phenomena, 'reality itself is in a restless flux' ([1900/7] GSG 6, p. 712; 2004, p. 509). He elaborates on this a page later:

> In reality itself things do not last for any length of time; through the restlessness with which they offer themselves at any moment to the application of a law, every form becomes immediately dissolved in the very moment it emerges; it lives, as it were, only in being destroyed; every consolidation of form to lasting objects – no matter how short they last – is an incomplete interpretation unable to follow the motion of reality at its own tempo. ([1900/7] GSG 6, p. 714; 2004, p. 510; translation altered)

Not surprisingly, then, modern thought, too, is characterized according to Simmel by a tendency towards the 'dissolution of substance into functions, of the solid and the lasting into the flux of restless development' ([1892/3] GSG 4, p. 330). Simmel's own thought makes no exception here. It can itself be regarded as an expression of the shift from substance to relation and process that he depicts. This has also been observed in the secondary literature on Simmel. With regard to Simmel's mode of thinking, Kracauer writes that, with Simmel, 'Everything shimmers, everything flows, everything is ambiguous, everything converges in a shifting form' (cit. and trans. Frisby, 1981, p. 98). But the emphasis on process also characterizes Simmel's sociological perspective. Heinz-Jürgen Dahme (1988, p. 416), for example, suggests that the 'emergence, development, and dissolution of social forms are central objects of investigation' in Simmel's work. Gregor Fitzi (2002, pp. 75, 263–4), in turn, emphasizes that Simmel aspires to grasp forms in their making, unfolding, and cessation. Much like Dahme and Fitzi, I, too, am of the view that in his sociology Simmel is interested above all in the emergence and movement of relations and their forms. According to Simmel, 'On every day, at every hour', relations from person to person that bind us together 'are spun, dropped, picked up again, replaced by others or woven together with them' ([1907] GSG 8, p. 277; 1997a, p. 110). Social forms are constituted by the interplay of forces flowing back and forth. When abstracted from their contents and viewed from a distance they may appear as invariable moulds,[4] but in reality they vary. Accordingly, Simmel gives primacy to the *becoming* of forms over their states of being. Social forms are not given in advance, but contents have formative power and play an active part in the process. Contents are not passive and form-receiving matter upon which a form is imposed, but forms are themselves generated in the confluence of various materials or contents and the effects from one individual to another, as people engage in relations with others on the basis of certain interests and motivations.

However, for all his emphasis on process and dynamic relations, it is important to note that not all that is solid melts into air for Simmel. In contrast to authors like Bergson or more recently Zygmunt Bauman, who lay emphasis on 'becoming' and 'liquidity' and thereby tend to disregard being and solidity (Fitzi, 2016), Simmel does not simply stress becoming, fluency, and variation. While giving precedence to process, he nevertheless explicitly sets out to bridge the gap between becoming and being that ever since the days of Heraclitus and Parmenides has continued to run throughout Western thought. Simmel stresses that the 'unity of the whole of being is completely comprehended in the unity of what simply persists and what simply does not persist' ([1900/7] GSG 6, p. 714; 2004, p. 510). That is, while the being of any entity is constituted in and by its becoming, there are also matters or aspects in phenomena that persist through time. Accordingly, the primary preoccupation of Simmel's sociology is the dynamics of stability and fluidity, of social life and social forms (Pyyhtinen, 2010; Fitzi, 2016).[5] A statement by Simmel in *Sociology* captures this well. He notes that society is always originally a 'fluctuating, constantly developing life-process', which 'nevertheless receives a relatively stable external form' ([1908] GSG 11, p. 659; 1971, p. 351). According to Simmel, we can experience and come to know life only in some form, never as an absolute flow. As he puts it in the essay 'The Crisis of Culture' (1997a, p. 107): 'Life is the opposite of form, but obviously an entity can be conceptually described only if it has a form of some sort.'

Dissolving society into relations

The problem with the overly broad notion of society, mentioned earlier, that Simmel rejected is not only the fact that it is awfully vague, as it pictures society as an all-encompassing and pre-existing frame or context of all human lives and (inter)actions, but it is also reifying: to assume the 'container' model is to start with the finished product instead of examining the processes that produce it. With regard to this assumption, Simmel insists that it is only when society is dissolved into complex constitutive relations that sociology may hope to be able to grasp society adequately. Analogous to biology, which did not gain solid ground until it abjured the approach on life as an 'undivided phenomenon' and focused instead on the microscopic processes and interactions between organs and cells, sociology according to Simmel needs to analyse society as a manifold of *Wechselwirkungen* without assuming a prior or more basic unity encompassing them (Simmel, [1908] GSG 11, pp. 24–5).

For Simmel, every entity emerges from the *Wechselwirkungen* of its components. In *Sociology*, he asserts that 'in empirical sense, [any] unity is nothing but interaction of elements [*Wechselwirkung von Elementen*]'. An organic body, for example, is held together by the fact that its organs exchange energies more regularly and intensively with each other than with any other entities (Simmel, [1908] GSG 11, p. 18). In an analogous manner, society is for Simmel nothing but 'reciprocal effects of its elements' (Simmel, [1890] GSG 2, p. 130). It is 'present' wherever and whenever several of these elements 'enter interaction [*Wechselwirkung*]' (Simmel, [1894] GSG 5, p. 54). This means that interpersonal interactions do not presuppose a prior, overarching society in which they would be contained, but society is rather produced in and by them. In an important passage in *The Philosophy of Money*, Simmel writes:

> Society is not an absolute entity which must first exist so that all the individual relations of its members [...] can develop within its framework or be represented by it: it is only the synthesis or the general term for the totality of these specific interactions. Any one of the interactions may, of course, be eliminated and 'society' still exist, but only if a sufficiently large number of others remain intact. If all interaction ceases there is no longer any society. ([1900/7] GSG 6, pp. 209–10; 2004, p. 175)[6]

Simmel's relational approach to society reminds us that society is no natural unity, but its unity is a product of processes and dynamic relations. To quote a formulation from *Grundfragen der Soziologie*: 'The reciprocal effects between the elements [...] carry the whole persistence and elasticity, the whole diversity and unity of the so palpable and so puzzling life of society' ([1917] GSG 16, p. 69). Thereby, Simmel radically reverses the conventional view: instead of examining how social relations take place in society, he proposes that sociology should study *the society in social relations*, that is, examine how society is actualized and produced in and by concrete relations between people.

To consider society as a process instead of seeing it as a being in a state of rest is to pay attention to it *in statu nascendi*, in its nascent state. This means to study not so much the historical origin of society, but its *logical* origin, that is, the underlying dynamics, the relations that account for its coming into being at 'every day and on every hour' (Simmel, [1907] GSG 8, p. 277). As Simmel writes in *Grundfragen der Soziologie*: 'The association between people folds, unfolds, and refolds itself without rest; it is an eternal flux and pulsation that links individuals to one another also where it does not give rise to actual organizations' ([1917] GSG 16, p. 69). Thus also Simmel's preference for the verbalization 'association' (*Vergesellschaftung*) over the noun 'society' (*Gesellschaft*), as the former expresses much better the processual and dynamic nature of society. We are not dealing with a 'substance', but with a process or an 'event' (*Geschehen*) through which society comes to existence and occurs (p. 70).[7]

Interestingly, Simmel conceived matter much along these lines in his doctoral thesis *Das Wesen der Materie nach Kants Physischer Monadologie* ('The Nature of Matter According to Kant's Physical Monadology'). In it, Simmel criticizes Kant for hypostasizing matter and maintains that matter and the forces that produce it are not separate but fold into each other. They may only separate momentarily: 'Process and result, event and the thing occurred, [are] kept apart only to flow into one another again' (Simmel, [1881] GSG 1, p. 35). Related to this notion, some pages earlier he notes that matter is not a finished product, but a 'molecular process'. It is not a mode of being but of becoming:

> If matter emerges out of forces, then one should no longer treat it as purely passive stuff upon which other forces can exercise their undisturbed interplay; for the product of these energies is no finished product, but a continuous process, not being [...], but becoming [...]'. (p. 26)

It is easy to see the remarkable resemblance between Simmel's later sociological conception of society and his early philosophical understanding of matter. Just as Simmel does not consider matter in molar terms, he understands society not as a whole that is, but as a molecular process that becomes.[8] In the essay 'The Sociology of Sociability', which is a written version of Simmel's talk at the first conference of the German Sociological Association held in October 1910 in Frankfurt, Simmel draws the analogy himself in most explicit terms:

> The energy effects of atoms upon each other bring matter into the innumerable forms which we see as 'things.' Just so the impulses and interests which a man [sic] experiences in himself [sic] and which push him [sic] out toward other men [sic] bring about all the forms of association by which the mere sum of separate individuals are made into a 'society'. ([1911] GSG 12, p. 177; 1971, pp. 127–8)

So, instead of starting from the finished product, Simmel tries to explain society by the processes that have produced it. Accordingly, I see the term 'realistic-dynamic' (*realistischdynamisch*) which Simmel uses to describe his position in his doctoral thesis as an apt label for how he sees society, too. For Simmel, the ancient controversy between realism and nominalism is a badly stated problem. He regards society neither as a self-subsistent entity with properties of its own, nor as merely a name for an aggregate of individuals. There is without doubt a reality to which the term 'society' refers, but it is not that of an independent entity. Instead, it is the relations of interaction that are the reality intended by the term (Simmel, [1908] GSG 11, pp. 17–19): society comes into being through the synthetic realities of mutual influences between individuals (Levine, 1971, pp. xxxiii–iv). It is produced and sustained in and by the mutual relations between its components. The becoming of society is never finished. It never stops becoming, and in its becoming it constantly involves new connections and drops others.

On the face of it, the difficulty of pursuing a relational approach such as Simmel's lies, of course, in the fact that interactions do not make the world each time anew, as if by beginning from scratch; they take place in at least partly pre-given settings. Nevertheless, despite his emphasis on relations and processes, Simmel does not simply dissolve society into constantly changing relations. When suggesting that society owes its existence to relations of interaction he does not dismiss the stability of society. On the contrary, what is wonderful about Simmel's relational take on society is that it helps us simultaneously meet two opposite aims: to both attend to how society is produced in and by relations, and account for its endurance and stability. What is more, this view is not restricted to society alone, but it can be generalized to apply to all entities. It allows us to consider entities as bundles of relations without disregarding their possible endurance. And, importantly, it gives us means to consider their endurance without resorting to substance or to an essence that sustains. While some of the features of an entity may endure even despite many of its relations being eliminated, this is so only because and insofar as there are a sufficiently large number of others that remain intact. So, in a sense, Simmel takes substance out of substantialism: there is indeed something in things that cannot be subtracted from them without them ceasing to exist, but this something is not essence or substance, but their relations. Another way to put this would be to say that there is no substance to things other than their relations or, more exactly, their event, actualization in relations. For Simmel, relations are one with the essence or the substance of a thing.

How is society possible?

In *Sociology*, Simmel examines society also from an epistemological perspective, by posing the question of the possibility of society. His discussion of it appears in 'How is Society Possible?', the excursus to the opening chapter of the book. The question is not only of philosophical interest; it is highly relevant for sociology as well. Simmel remarks that it permeates the whole book: 'In a certain sense, the entire content of this book [...] is the beginning of the answer to this question' ([1908] GSG 11, p. 45; 1971, p. 8).

Like the problem of the possibility of history that Simmel studies in *The Problems of the Philosophy of History* (1977), the question of the preconditions of society is analogous to Kant's question as to how nature is possible. Nevertheless, the question 'How is society possible?' has a quite different methodical sense: whereas a meadow, a stream, a tree, and a mountain, for example, make up a 'landscape' only in the mind of an observer, societal unification needs no observing third party outside the component elements, but it is 'directly realized by its own elements' (Simmel, [1908] GSG 11, pp. 43–4; 1971, p. 7). So, the preconditions reside a priori in the elements themselves, and not in the forms of cognition of an observing outsider synthesizing the given elements, as in the case of 'nature' (Simmel, [1908] GSG 11, p. 45; 1971, p. 8).

Accordingly, as the elements of society produce the unity by themselves without the effort of any intervening third parties, in 'How is Society Possible?' Simmel investigates the possibility of society as being built upon the interplay of two human subjects, myself and the other. Michael Theunissen (1984) has identified the existence of two philosophies of the Other: transcendental philosophy, which conceives the Other as the 'alien I', and the philosophy of dialogue, or 'dialogicalism', which understands by the Other the 'you' or the 'Thou' (Theunissen, 1984). Simmel's theorizing of the other is placed above all within the tradition of dialogicalism. He considers the relation between the component elements of association in terms of the dialogical relation between myself and other, I (*Ich*) and you (*Du*). The being of the I and the you is constituted by an essential, originary 'with' based on reciprocal determination. As Petra Christian (1978, p. 129) points out, the I and the you mutually ground themselves in a dialectical or dialogical fashion: as a primary category, you are a constituent component of my own existence, just as I myself am a you to the other person who perceives him/herself as a me to him/herself. The you thus has 'for me the same reality as I myself' (Simmel, [1908] GSG 11, p. 44); I do not perceive the other as an object, but as a subject inasmuch as I am a subject myself.

In the excursus, Simmel presents three preconditions for society. It is important to note that while he calls them, in a Kantian manner, 'aprioric' (*apriorisch*) (Simmel, [1908] GSG 11, p. 43), they are not really transcendental-logical but rather phenomenological preconditions, as they are grounded in the subject's experience in encounters with others.

The *first* precondition of association is that I perceive the other person as generalized to some extent (Simmel, [1908] GSG 11, pp. 47–8; 1971, p. 9), since it is impossible for us to fully know a subject different from ourselves; nor does the other person amount to an object endowed with fixed properties.

While our fellow humans are subjectively closer to us than any other beings, in his or her singularity the you is bound to remain a secret to us, in some measure. As Simmel writes in the essay 'Eros, Platonic and Modern', 'there is something unattainable in the other: [...] the absoluteness of the individual self erects a wall between two human beings' (Simmel, [1923] GSG 20, p. 188; 1971, p. 246). The I/you relation is thus marked by a paradoxical simultaneous proximity and distance. As Simmel describes it in the piece '*Vom Wesen des historischen Verstehens*' ('On the Nature of Historical Understanding'):

> On the one hand, the animated you is our only pair in cosmos, the only being with which we understand ourselves mutually and which can be felt as 'one' like nothing else, so that we place the other nature, whenever we mean to feel united with it, in the category of the you [...] On the other hand, the you has an individuality and sovereignty alongside us like no other [...]. ([1918] GSG 16, p. 162)

All relations of interpersonal knowledge between individuals are thus characterized by various degrees of inevitable incompleteness. As we are never able to know others entirely and without residue, in order to know them we cannot but resort to general categories. Nevertheless, those categories do not fully cover the other individuals, nor do the individuals fully cover the categories:

> The civilian who meets an officer cannot free himself [sic] from his [sic] knowledge of the fact that this individual is an officer. And although his [sic] officership may be a part of this particular individuality, it is certainly not so stereotypical as the civilian's prejudicial image would have it. And the same goes for the Protestant in regard to the Catholic, the businessman in regard to the bureaucrat, the layman in regard to the priest, and so on. (Simmel, [1908] GSG 11, p. 50; 1971, pp. 11–12)

No general category ever encompasses the person entirely. Any category, type or role is always at once more and less than the individual ([1908] GSG 11, p. 50; 1971, p. 12): more insofar as it holds for several individuals, less insofar as the individual is not exhausted by it, but has a personality beyond or apart from the classification. However, the general category does not simply hide or suppress who the other 'really' is as a person. On the contrary, it gives the individuality of the you 'a new form' ([1908] GSG 11, p. 50; 1971, p. 11). It is through the roles or general categories under which we classify other persons that their being and personality assume the quality and form required by sociality and those persons appear as members of a larger group. Classification constitutes a condition of social order: instead of just perceiving a disorderly flux of ever new incomparable and unique individuals, we are able to identify similarity and general characteristics in the people we encounter. This also allows us to generalize what we know of a person to a larger group of individuals and see the other as my like, as someone who inhabits the same world as I do ([1908] GSG 11, pp. 49–50).

For Simmel, the irreducibility of the individual to the type is suggestive of the fact that the you is not thoroughly social, a sheer social product. Instead of being mere carriers of social roles and general attributes, individuals also possess qualitative uniqueness that is not socially determined: 'It seems as if every human being had a deepest point of individuality in oneself which cannot be reproduced inwardly by anyone else with whom this point is qualitatively divergent.' ([1908] GSG 11, p. 48; 1971, p. 9; translation altered) Accordingly, Simmel formulates the *second* precondition of the social as follows: 'the a priori of the empirical social life is that life is not completely social' ([1908] GSG 11, p. 53; 1971, p. 14; translation altered). That is, 'every element of a group is not only a part of society, but is still something besides it'; the social being of an individual is crucially determined and co-determined by the way in which the individual is not social in other respects ([1908] GSG 11, p. 51). Importantly, for Simmel, the fact that we are not fully absorbed by and integrated into the social formations we participate in is not a sheer negative condition of society, but its positive moment. That we preserve part of us outside the relations we engage in affects the nature of the relationships, as is perceptible, for instance, in the phenomenon of secrecy. It also has an effect on the nature of individuality. It is only because one is not completely socially determined that the individual is able to self-determine and to identify one's action with one's person (Schrader-Klebert, 1968, p. 114) and have an underlying sense of continuity amidst the roles that one assumes (Jaworski, 1997, p. 40).

The second 'a priori' refers to a highly significant sociological phenomenon, namely that individuals simultaneously stand inside and outside of social formations. As Simmel puts it: 'the individual can never stay within a unit which he [sic] does not at the same time stay outside of, that he [sic] is not incorporated into any order without also confronting it' ([1908], GSG 11 p. 53; 1971, p. 15). Human subjects thus occupy a 'dual position' ([1908] GSG 11, p. 56; 1971, p. 17): they are at once associated and dissociated, connected and separate, beings who exist both for society as parts of a greater whole and for themselves as autonomous wholes. Importantly, Simmel stresses that the 'within' and the 'without' are not two unrelated properties of the human subject, but together they define the 'position of man [sic] as a social animal' ([1908] GSG 11, p. 56; 1971, p. 17). Our being forms a unity which we cannot conceptualize in any other way than 'as the synthesis or simultaneity of two logically contradictory characteristics' ([1908] GSG 11, p. 56; 1971, p. 18). So, here we once again perceive the juxtaposition of opposites that is characteristic of Simmel's mode of thinking.

The third condition, finally, concerns bringing the antagonism of the social and the individual to a 'principal harmony' (Simmel, GSG 11, p. 59; 1971, p. 20; translation altered). Here, Simmel is dealing not so much with the bond between I and you but with the relation of the individual to society as a self-sustaining social whole. He holds that, were one to perceive society from a purely objective perspective, it would appear as a system in which the individual has no weight whatsoever. Society would equal an order consisting of functions linked together systematically in terms of space, time, concepts, and values, completely devoid of the 'self' (*Ichform*) that, in the last resort, nevertheless carries its dynamics. On the other hand, were one to consider each function and quality as purely individual, society would become 'a cosmos whose diversity is [...] unfathomable in terms of being and movement' (Simmel, [1908] GSG 11, p. 57; 1971, p. 19; translation altered). In it, each element could be and act as it pleased without changing the overall structure the least bit. Thus, Simmel concludes, in order for society to be possible as a constellation of interrelated individuals, there has to be a pervasive correlation between the life of the individual and the social whole. According to him, when considered from the viewpoint of the individual, the causal nexus that produces the external network of society is transformed into a commitment, conviction, and a feeling of purpose (as expressed in 'vocation', for example). By way of this, 'every individual receives a specific position in the social milieu by oneself and in accordance with one's own nature', becoming thus associated or societalized ([1908] GSG 11, p. 59; 1971, p. 20). This produces the 'general value' of individuality, which means 'that the individuality of the individual finds a place in the structure of generality' ([1908] GSG 11, p. 61; 1971, p. 22). Then one exists as an individual in a social sense, by appearing as an individual to others, too, and not only in and by oneself.

To sum up, when sketching the preconditions for society Simmel focuses on individuals, enquiring into what is presupposed of the individual consiousness to make relations between subjects possible. For the sake of simplicity, the three preconditions could perhaps be termed *classification*, *singularity*, and *harmony*.[9] While classification deals with social roles and is a precondition for order (in terms of identifying likeness), singularity refers to the irreducibility of the individual to the social and is a precondition for individual self-awareness and action, and, finally, harmony relates to the congruence between the individual and social structure and is a precondition for social integration and membership in society.

Beyond methodological individualism

Based on what is noted above, Simmel's sociology of association would easily seem to suggest itself as a micro-reductionist solution to the individual–society problem mentioned in the beginning of the chapter. After all, Simmel does suggest that society amounts to nothing but microscopic relations of reciprocal action and effect between individuals. This impression is even stronger if we consider Simmel's epistemological justification of sociology that was just discussed. He starts from the view that the possibility of society is ultimately based on the individual subject becoming conscious of oneself as part of society. In the excursus 'How is Society Possible?' Simmel notes that 'the consciousness of constituting with others a unity is actually all there is to this unity' ([1908] GSG 11, p. 43; 1971, p. 7). This statement would seem to imply not only micro-reductionism, but also methodological individualism, which explains social wholes by the action of their parts, individual actors.

However, on closer examination Simmel's sociology of association does not reduce society to some assumed micro level of individuals, nor does it commit to methodological individualism.

First, Simmel stresses that cultural forms – society being one of them – are not reducible to the process of their emergence, but tend to gain a life of their own and affect their constituent elements retroactively.[10] The products of our own making, social forms among them, increasingly follow their own inner logic and, as a result, we become dominated by them. As William Outhwaite (2006, p. 63) puts it: 'We set up an organization and make ourselves its puppets; we adopt an innovative artistic convention and find ourselves unacceptably constrained by it.'

Second, Simmel avoids micro-reductionism and methodological individualism also because for him individuals are not the final or bottom-most layer of reality to which other, supposedly more derivative, phenomena could be reduced. As he phrases it in his own words, 'individuals are in no way final elements, atoms of the human realm' ([1917] GSG 16, p. 65). The unit(y) to which the notion of the individual refers is no absolute unity, a final, foundational base of (human) reality nor a self-sufficient, permanent substance, but it is socio-historically produced, a coming together of various forces, relations, and forms. As Simmel remarks in 'How is Society Possible?', 'as social beings we do not live around any autonomous core. Rather, at any given moment, we consist of reciprocal relations with others' ([1908] GSG 11, p. 55; 1971, p. 16; translation altered). Because of this, Simmel insists that the human individual is a 'multiplicity' (*Vielheit*), and he argues that this insight presents one of the most important preconditions for laying a 'rational basis' for the science of society ([1890] GSG 2, p. 127). Simmel's position is thus anti-essentialist. Even if he does have a concept of essence (as for example the statement: 'the human being is in one's whole essence determined by the fact that …' quoted above attests), he is not crudely 'essentialist'. Instead of having an inner essence, each individual is for him, literally, an 'assembled being' (*zusammengesetzte Wesen*) (Simmel, [1905/7] GSG 9, p. 323), an intersection of social circles (Simmel, [1890] GSG 2, p. 244), a 'point where the social threads woven throughout history interlace' (Simmel, [1905/7] GSG 9, p. 230; trans. Jalbert 2003, p. 264). Human beings admittedly appear to us as relatively lasting and stable bounded beings, but this is so only insofar as a sufficiently large amount of relations that constitute and define them remain in place.

While in Simmel's sociology the individual often is the smallest unit of analysis, Simmel nevertheless does not regard the individual as the elementary basis of (social) reality. On the contrary, the analytical process of dissolving beings into relations is in principle endless. Therefore, 'the individual', too, as Simmel himself remarks, is a 'completely arbitrary' place to end the process of dissolving substances into relations, because for an analysis that reaches further, the individual appears as a 'combination of qualities and fates, forces, and historical consequences'. In this picture, the qualities, fates, forces, and consequences are the 'elementary reality' vis-à-vis the individual, just as the individual may appear as the elementary reality in relation to society (Simmel, [1917] GSG 16, p. 66).

Conclusion: an alternative scalar imaginary

In this chapter I have discussed how Simmel's work places relations into the heart of sociology. Instead of beginning from static, self-enclosed entities of various kinds – such as individuals, groups, communities, social systems, or society – Simmel invites us to consider the very processes of their formation and coming into being. For him, social forms are not beings in a state of rest. On the contrary, they have to be considered in their becoming. Empirically, any unity is based on the reciprocity of effects between its elements. However, Simmel's approach does not simply dissolve bounded things into constantly changing or momentary relations, but, importantly, his relationalism also provides an account of how things endure. Entities endure as long as a sufficiently large amount of their relations remain intact. While an entity may break with some of the relations that have constituted it and made it emerge, it cannot lose all of them and remain (the same). If we removed all its relations we would not be left with its essence, but the entity would decompose into nothingness.[11]

Simmel's idea that the unity of any given entity is ultimately based on *Wechselwirkungen* among its components has the most significant implications for social theory.

First, it undoes the classical distinction (in philosophy) between natural substances and artificial aggregates. It suggests that not only society but also individuals (and in fact any entity) are made up of an infinity of parts. Individuals are not natural unities over and against the mere aggregate of society, but both the individual and society are manifolds composed of interactions of parts, since any given unity is an achievement, produced by the interactions of its parts. Because of this, there is also not much sense in arguing that individuals would be more real than society or vice versa. Both are as real as the other.[12]

Second, we cannot give individuals, any more than society, a privileged existence over the other, which also leads to the refutation of both micro-reductionism and macro-reductionism. The assumedly macro-scale phenomena such as society are not entirely reducible to the interactions of individuals, and individuals are never completely dissolved into the larger wholes they are part of. I think this is the important insight of the opposition Simmel makes between the individual and society on a principal level, which in many other respects appears as highly problematic (and with good reason: Bourdieu (1990, p. 31), for example, regards the opposition as 'absurd'). The irreducibility of individuals to society is suggested, for example, by one of the a preconditions of society that Simmel discusses in the excursus 'How is Society Possible?'. For Simmel, as was noted, society is conditioned by the fact that 'every element of a group is not only a part of society, but is still something besides it' ([1908] GSG 11, p. 51). Individuals both belong to society as parts of a greater whole, and every individual is also a whole in oneself, consisting in interactions of parts. And, as for society, the irreducible, stabilized, and durable existence of society vis-à-vis the fleeting, fluctuating lives of individuals is proposed by the contrast of life and form, which Simmel (2010) considers in terms of the tension between 'more-life' (*Mehr-Leben*) and 'more-than-life' (*Mehr-als-Leben*). The irreducibility of the individual and society to one another would thus seem to require that the examination of their relation is established on shifting sands, perhaps in a manner analogous to how Simmel treats the relation of historical materialism and idealism in *The Philosophy of Money*, that is, by basing his analysis upon the 'infinite reciprocity' of the two levels.[13]

However, on closer inspection – and this leads me to my third point – Simmel's sociological relationalism is not suggestive of there being only two levels to reality. While he occasionally insists on the dialectical nature of the individual and society, it is possible to tease out of his writings an idea that there is in fact *an infinite number of layers*. By emphasizing the constitutive role of *Wechselwirkung*, Simmel's sociology dissolves not only the individual and society into the interaction of their parts, but the idea also holds in principle for any entity at any given scale: every entity is composed of interactions of pre- and sub-entity materials, and every unity is a product of relations of interactions. This view helps us escape the long tradition in sociology of conceiving the world in terms of just two levels, with the individual or the micro level on the bottom and the larger-scale macro phenomena like society on top (or in those of three, if we place the 'meso-level' phenomena in between).[14] The problem with the micro-macro model is not only that it is reductionist, but also that more often than not it is assumed in advance, as something like a transcendent model. And, once set in place, it offers itself so naturally to us that it is difficult not to conceive the world along its contours (Marston, Jones & Woodward 2005, p. 422). George Ritzer (2011, p. 545), for instance, notes that '[w]e can clearly think of the micro-macro linkage in terms of some sort of vertical hierarchy, with micro-level phenomena on the bottom, macro-level phenomena at the top, and meso-level entities in between'. However, by presupposing that phenomena are placed on two (or three) levels only – or even privileging one of the scales, as is the case with micro- and macro-reductionism –

this paradigm remains blind to how processes crisscross various scales and how scales are produced in (inter)action.

In short, Simmel's sociological relationalism implies an entirely different scalar imaginary compared to the bi-(or tri-)focal micro-(meso-)macro model. Instead of modelling the world in accordance with two or three discrete levels forming a nested vertical hierarchy, it pictures it in terms of infinite chains of manifolds. The manifolds are wholes composed of interactions between their parts. The relation of whole and part of course implies a more or less vertical mode of ordering, with each whole being composed of interactions of elements at a sub-level, which, in turn, are manifolds in themselves consisting in interactions of their own sub-elements, and so on infinitely. However, the succession of manifolds is not ordered only vertically, in a bottom-up manner, with interconnected entities and materials at a sub-level giving rise to a greater whole. On the contrary, interconnectedness can be also conceived without assuming a vertical hierarchy. Notably, in *The Philosophy of Money*, Simmel examines how the circulation of money weaves the web of modern society (see also Frisby 1984, p. 51). It links individuals and their divergent interests, needs, valuations, and desires, but also different spaces, cultural contexts, and actions. Importantly, the refutation of verticality should not, however, be automatically taken as implying reliance on a pre-determined horizontal scale. The point cannot simply be to replace the vertical imaginary of the micro and the macro with a horizontal one – that of networks, for instance. This is because such a move would just implant things within another transcendent model that risks yet another form of reductionism. If we are to develop a genuinely non-reductionist social ontology we should start from relations, in the middle of things. The analysis should remain immanent to relations and avoid reliance on '*any* transcendent predetermination' (Marston et al., 2005, p. 422). We must integrate into social theory entities and materials of various sizes and on various scales, ranging all the way from, say, viruses and the tiny minerals of the smartphones we carry in our pockets to global markets and climate change (see Pyyhtinen, 2015). Society is not reducible to the level of individuals and their interactions, but rather designates a fabric of interdependent relationships, a *relation of relations*. Those relations may cross several scales and involve a plenitude of layers.

Notes

1 In the early 1890s, Simmel was also planning to found an international sociological journal, *Zeitschrift für Soziologie*; see his letters to Friedrich Jodl on 19 and 20 January and 3 July 1893 (GSG 22, pp. 83–6, 88–92), Lester F. Ward on 24 February 1893 (GSG 22, pp. 86–7), and René Worms on 19 February 1893 (GSG 24, p. 93). However, the plan was never actualized. Today there exists a journal of the same name, but it was not founded until 1971.

2 To quote Simmel on their overlap at length: 'It may be that what affects the entire history of humanity for better or for worse usually has the same significance for the narrower, socially bound circle; what is socially essential may without further consideration even be something essential for the development or for the system of humanity' ([1908] GSG 11, p. 861; 1971, p. 39).

3 Leopold von Wiese's appropriation of Simmel will be discussed in more detail in Chapter 8.

4 Durkheim (1964, pp. 355, 357), for instance, speaks of Simmel's concepts of 'form' and 'content' in terms of 'container' (*contenant*) and 'content' (*contenu*). Simmel's own phrasings, too, may occasionally give the impression of forms being invariable containers, for example when he suggests that social forms are valid irrespective of whether they are realized a thousand times or not even once (see Simmel, [1908] GSG 11, p. 26).

5 I will return to the issue of change and endurance in the last section of the chapter.

6 The very same idea can also be found in *Sociology* in almost identical form, see Simmel [1908] GSG 11, pp. 23–4.

7 I discuss Simmel's thinking of the event in more detail in Pyyhtinen, 2010.

8 For more on the distinction between the molar and the molecular, see Deleuze & Guattari (1987).

9 Thomas Kemple (2007, pp. 4–5) has introduced his own terms for the three apriorities by adding a dimensional aspect to each. Kemple calls the first a priori 'the *horizontal dimension of typification*', the second one 'the *diagonal dimension of membership*', and the third 'the *vertical dimension of commitment*'. I think both my conceptual trichotomy and his can only be employed with some reservations, as Simmel himself insists that the three preconditions 'cannot be designated by [...] simple slogan[s] like those which it is possible to use for the Kantian categories' (Simmel, [1908] GSG 11, p. 60; 1971, p. 22).

10 We will look at this dialectics of form and life more closely in Chapter 7.

11 Chris Fowler and Oliver Harris (2015, p. 132) make a similar point in their article on the paradoxes of the so-called new materialism.

12 To be sure, to some extent such an approach to social ontology entails reading Simmel against himself. After all, in some places he clearly privileges the individual level. In the essay 'Sociology of Senses' ('Soziologie der Sinne'), for example, Simmel suggests that it is only the 'delicate, invisible threads that are spun from one person to another', not the 'final finished pattern' of society's 'uppermost phenomenal stratum' that constitute 'the real life of society provided in our experience' ([1907] GSG 8, pp. 292, 277). However, as I have tried to show, there are also tendencies, formulations, and seeds of ideas in Simmel's work that problematize the micro-reductionist standpoint. First, the idea that cultural forms of our making gain a life of their own, independent of their creators and of the process of their creation, speaks against micro-reductionism. Second, while indeed occasionally insisting that individuals and their interactions are the basis of society, elsewhere Simmel contends that individuals are nevertheless not the bottom-most or final layer of reality, but just a layer among many others. And, just like any other entities at any given scale, individuals, too, can be dissolved into the interactions of their components.

13 As Simmel puts it in more detail: 'Every interpretation of an ideal structure by means of economic structure must lead to the demand that the latter in turn be understood from more ideal depths, while for these depths themselves the general economic base has to be sought, and so on indefinitely' ([1900/7] GSG 6, p. 13; 2004, p. 56).
14 For a more detailed and extensive critique of the fixed vertical scale of the micro–macro paradigm, see Pyyhtinen (2015).

4

The Bustle of Modern Life: Fashion and the Modern Metropolis

What is specific to our own time? What separates the present from the past? These are questions that already preoccupied the classical founders of sociology. All of them were baffled by the dramatic changes that were taking place before their very eyes, and they made painstaking efforts to conceptually come to grips with the new, modern world. While Durkheim, for instance, drew attention to the transition from mechanic to organic solidarity triggered by the division of labour, for Weber the modern epoch was characterized by an 'iron cage' (*Stahlhartes Gehäuse*)[1] of rationality resulting from a process of immense rationalization, and Marx emphasized the underlying laws of motion of history and the extensive and destructive crises that he saw as being intrinsic to capitalism, leading, via class struggle, ultimately to communism. Simmel, for his part, conceived modernization as a process of increasing social differentiation, by paying attention in particular to the correlation between the quantitative enlargement of the group and the development of individuality. He contends that larger groups allow more individual differentiation. The more distinctive and the smaller the group, the less individuated are its members; and, the other way around, the looser and the larger the social circles in which the individual lives, the more room there is for the development of individuality. Modern society is, for Simmel, a world of undifferentiated large groups or collectivities, on the one hand, and differentiated individuals, on the other. ([1890] GSG 2)

However, what distinguishes Simmel's writings on modernity from those of Durkheim, Weber, and Marx is the fact that in his analyses of modern life Simmel is concerned less with the structural aspects of modern society per se than with the modern *experience*. While modern experience is to be understood against the background of the forms of modernization, it nevertheless presents a very different conception of modernity than the diachronic approach, which focuses on the changes that society has undergone over time in the process of modernization. Simmel's theorizing on modernity has its background above all in the new artistic movements of the fin-de-siécle; he receives his concept of modernity in particular from aesthetic modernism, initiated by the French poet Charles Baudelaire (1821–67). In his famous essay *The Painter of Modern Life*, Baudelaire defines modernity (*modernité*) as 'the transient, the fleeting, the contingent' (Baudelaire, [1863] 1964, p. 13; translation altered). If Simmel is to be regarded as the 'first sociologist of modernity', as Frisby (1983, p. 17; 1985) suggests, it is in this Baudelairean sense that his modernity must be understood. In his work, Simmel translates the Baudelairean notion of modernity into sociological parlance.

What intrigues Simmel in the modern experience is not so much the inner life of individuals as such and in itself but, in line with his relational mode of thought, the *connection* between the social milieu or 'external culture' (*äußerlichen Kultur*) and the individual psyche. Simmel is of the view that the subjects' mental life is intimately connected to and conditioned by the social relations they participate in and the environment in which they live, and he pays attention to how the external signs and stimuli of modernity manifest in experience (see Frisby, 1992; Lichtblau, 1995, p. 33). Accordingly, he treats modernity as the movement of the external world that is manifest in the inner world of individuals. As he puts it in the essay 'Rodin':

> [T]he essence of modernity as such is psychologism, the experiencing and interpretation of the world in terms of the reactions of our inner life, and indeed as an inner world, as the dissolution of fixed contents in the fluid element of the soul, from which all that is substantive is filtered and whose forms are merely forms of motion. ([1911] GSG 14, p. 346)

In this chapter, I discuss Simmel's vision of modernity by using his analyses of fashion and the modern metropolis as my examples. They are not just any topics, as both are quintessential for understanding how Simmel conceives modernity. For Simmel, the modern experience is essentially intertwined both with the cycles of fashion and with the wealth of stimuli and the fleeting contacts of the modern metropolis (while also being entangled with the development of the modern money economy, as will be discussed in Chapter 5). Each also manifests a crucial aspect of the modern experience. With its perpetual flux, fashion embodies for Simmel the fleeting nature of modernity. Whereas fashion – which Simmel does not identify solely with clothing, but understands it much more widely, as functioning in a whole variety of domains of life – thereby relates above all to the *temporal* dimension of the modern experience, the modern metropolis embodies especially the *spatial* aspect of modernity. For Simmel, the metropolis is the breeding ground and main site of modernity. The modern experience is not only embedded in the urban space, but it is essentially also an experience of that space and of the social relations that take place in it and participate in producing it. I will examine Simmel's studies of fashion first, and then explicate his approach to the modern metropolis. I will conclude the chapter by summarizing Simmel's phenomenological approach on modernity and by discussing the sociology of the mundane of which his analyses of fashion and the modern metropolis are suggestive.

Restless and feverish modern life

The term 'modern', originating from the Latin *modernus*, dates all the way from the 5th century. Its contemporary meaning, however, can be traced to the writings of Baudelaire in the 1860s. In the critical text *The Painter of Modern Life* (Fr. *Le Peintre de la vie moderne*), originally published in three parts in the magazine *Le Figaro* in 1863, Baudelaire attacks classicism and sets as his aim to create a new theory of beauty to counter the theory of unique and absolute beauty. Baudelaire was not interested in the platonic, eternal, and classical beauty, but precisely in what he regarded as its opposite: modernity.

Baudelaire found his modernity in the crowds flowing through the cityscapes of Paris. The apex of a modern person in Baudelaire's eyes was the *flâneur*, a loafer idly strolling the streets of the urban landscape. The flâneur is entirely at home in the crowd. Baudelaire writes: 'The crowd is his element, as the air is that of birds and water of fishes' (Baudelaire, [1863] 1964, p. 9). The flâneur seeks something for which Baudelaire thought there is no better term than 'modernity' (*modernité*). Often, the flâneur is also something of a dandy, who 'makes it his business to extract from fashion whatever element it may contain of poetry within history, to distil the eternal from the transitory' (p. 12). From this, Baudelaire proceeds to his famous definition: 'Modernity is the transient, the fleeting, the contingent, the half of art whose other half is the eternal and the immutable' (p. 13; translation altered).

The transient or the fleeting is the most recent meaning that the term 'modern' has received over the course of its history. Historian Hans Ulrich Gumbrecht (1978) has discovered that the word has been used in three senses. According to Gumbrecht, modernity designated first *the present*, in distinction to the past. In this sense, the term was already used in the Middle Ages to express the opposition between *antiqui* and *moderni* (Gumbrecht, 1978, pp. 97–9). In the 17th century, the term began to take on a new meaning in the struggle between ancient and modern authorities. Now the word 'modern' referred also to the present as something *new* in contrast to the traditional and the old (pp. 109–10). It is important to note that this new time-consciousness manifested not only as a historical experience of the modern epoch that was felt to be different from the pre-modern, but it was also a mundane experience of the passing of time. The relationship to time became increasingly future-oriented. Reinhart Koselleck (1988) suggests that this narrowed down the experience of the present. Thereby, the present was experienced as *transient*, which is the third historical meaning of the term modern. It is important to note, however, that the third meaning did not replace the preceding two, but within the modernist tradition modernity is widely understood simultaneously through all three: the present, the new, and the transient. The three meanings co-exist in modernism, which tends to aestheticize the modern that appears as something present, new, and transient to our experience.

Simmel emphasizes similar features of modernity to Baudelaire. As already suggested above, it could be said that, in a sense, he conceptualizes sociologically what Baudelaire defined in aesthetic terms. Simmel understands the modern experience as a shift from the stable and the permanent to restless flux and the temporary. The dissolution of substance and fixed forms into flux and movement is for him observable above all in the increasing tempo of modern life. Simmel sees modern life as extremely restless:

> I believe that this secret restlessness, this helpless urgency that lies before the threshold of conscience, that drives modern man from socialism to Nietzsche, from Böcklin to impressionism, from Hegel to Schopenhauer and back again, not only originates in the bustle and excitement of modern life, but that, conversely, this phenomenon is frequently the expression, symptom and eruption of this innermost condition. The lack of something definite at the centre of our souls impels us to search for momentary satisfaction in ever-new stimulations, sensations and external activities. Thus it is that we become entangled in the instability and helplessness that manifests itself as the tumult of metropolis, as the mania for travelling, as the wild pursuit of competition and as the typically modern disloyalty with regard to taste, style, opinions and personal relationships. ([1900/7] GSG 6, p. 675; 2004, p. 484)

So, instead of arguing there to be a simple causal relation between the bustle of modern life and the restlessness that he sees as being characteristic of the modern psyche, Simmel sees the relation as much more complex by nature. The whirlpool of metropolitan modern life is both the cause and effect of the lack of foundation at the core of our psyche.

Interestingly, in the excerpt Simmel also implicitly refers to fashion. First, when he writes about how modern individuals are driven 'from socialism to Nietzsche, from Böcklin to impressionism, from Hegel to Schopenhauer and back again', he can be interpreted as alluding to intellectual fashions. On a second occasion, he refers to the 'disloyalty' that is typical of modern individuals when it comes to matters of taste and style. However, in his work Simmel also wrote on fashion explicitly and more extensively. In fact, the five essays that Simmel published on fashion make it one of the most frequent topics in his oeuvre. The first of them, 'Zur Psychologie der Mode' ('Towards Psychology of Fashion'), came out in 1895. In 1904, Simmel published the piece 'Fashion' in the journal *International Quarterly* in 1904 (republished in *The American Journal of Sociology* in 1957). The small German book *Philosophie der Mode* ('Philosophy of Fashion') published a year later, in 1905 (in GSG 10), is almost identical to it. Later the text reappeared in a slightly altered and enlarged form in the collection

Philosophische Kultur in 1911 under the title 'Die Mode' ('Fashion') (in GSG 14). In addition to these four texts, Simmel also published a piece 'Die Frau und die Mode' ('The Woman and Fashion') in 1908 (in GSG 8).

In his writings, Simmel analyses fashion as something not confined solely within clothing, but as a social form that is operative in a much wider range of domains; 'it has overstepped the bounds of its original domain'. According to Simmel, fashion 'has acquired an increasing authority over taste, over theoretical convictions, and even over the moral foundations of life', and this testifies to the broad influence that it exerts in modern culture on the consciousness of modern individuals. In consequence of its power, 'the great, permanent, unquestionable convictions are continually losing strength', while 'the transitory and vacillating elements of life acquire more room' ([1904] 1957, p. 548). Accordingly, Simmel suggests that with its ever-accelerating cycles fashion embodies the restlessness of modernity. In the essay 'Die Mode', he writes:

> The specifically 'impatient' tempo of modern life denotes not only the longing for the swift variation of the qualitative contents of life, but also the strength of the formal attraction of the boundary between beginning and end, coming and going. Through its play between the tendency towards broad diffusion and the destruction of its very purpose to which this diffusion leads fashion has the peculiar attraction of a boundary, the attraction of simultaneous beginning and end, novelty and transitoriness. ([1911] GSG 14, p. 197)

Fashion is essentially transitory; what is 'in' today may be 'out' tomorrow. As Simmel writes: 'Fashion [...] is concerned only with change' ([1904] 1957, p. 557). It never *is*, it only *becomes*. Finitude belongs to the mode of being of each fashion trend; no singular fashion lasts forever but every one is destined to fade away. According to Simmel, this perishableness presents a downright conceptual prerequisite for something to qualify as fashion. We do not call fashion anything that is 'new' and 'suddenly disseminated', if we believe in its 'continuance' and 'material justification'. On the contrary, we call something fashion only if we feel that the phenomenon 'will vanish as rapidly as it came' (p. 548). Once the model or example provided by fashion becomes widely accepted, it loses its attraction and capability to produce distinction, and subsequently dies as a fashion. It is deserted and substituted by a new one, one that is not worn out yet. Each new fashion tries to distinguish itself from the fashion of yesterday; novelty is produced here through negative distinction.

The dualism of fashion

Before exploring the connections between fashion and modernity further, let me first elaborate the idea of fashion as a social form that was mentioned briefly above. At the time they were published, Simmel's writings provided a novel approach to fashion. Until then fashion had been studied mostly by focusing on its contents, that is, on whatever has been in fashion over time. In accordance with his sociology of forms, Simmel, by contrast, analyses fashion as a *form*, in connection with the process of association (*Vergesellschaftung*). As we remember from the previous chapter, for Simmel society is actualized to a greater or lesser degree in each and every social form, and thus in fashion Simmel is also interested, among other things, in how it enacts society.

When analysed as a form, fashion appears for Simmel as a duality between two antithetical tendencies in which our life finds the poles of its oscillations: a tendency towards uniformity and conformity to the demands of society, on the one hand; and a tendency towards individual differentiation and departure from the claims of society on the other (Simmel, [1904] 1957, pp. 542–3).[2] The tendencies are antagonistic in that they tend to annul or refute one another: pure or absolute distinction allows no uniformity, and complete uniformity is bound to erase all differences.

From the point of view of the individual, the tendency towards uniformity manifests itself as a psychological tendency towards *imitation* (p. 543). By imitating others, the individual is able to become part of a bigger whole and gain social acceptance. The community on whose support the individual relies provides legitimacy for one's action:

> Whenever we imitate, we transfer not only the demand for creative activity, but also the responsibility for the action from ourselves to another. Thus the individual is freed from the worry of choosing and appears simply as a creature of the group, as a vessel of the social contents. (pp. 542–3)

Imitation, then, 'gives to the individual the satisfaction of not standing alone in his [sic] actions' (p. 542). One perceives oneself as part of a larger community. Thereby fashion possesses certain powers of integration. Through imitation, fashion creates and nourishes a sense of community between the ones obeying it.

The tendency towards *individual differentiation* presents the other pole of the duality. Simmel notes that especially in the modern metropolis, which is the breeding ground of fashion, individuals have a need to express their difference from others amidst the abundance of people and stimuli (Simmel, [1903] GSG 7, p. 129; 1971, p. 337). In rural settlements and small towns, this need is not nearly as strong. In the metropolis, by contrast, the temptation 'to appear to the point, clear-cut and individual' appears 'with extraordinarily greater frequency' and higher urgency ([1903] GSG 7, p. 129; 1971, p. 337).

Fashion provides a safe and socially accepted means to individual differentiation. It succeeds in producing a feeling of individual difference in a manner that is socially acceptable, for while the individual does what others do, fashion is never assumed by all, but only some people obey it. As Simmel puts it:

> By reason of its peculiar inner structure, fashion furnishes a departure of the individual, which is always looked upon as proper. No matter how extravagant the form of appearance or manner of expression, as long as it is fashionable, it is protected against those painful reflections which the individual otherwise experiences when he [sic] becomes the object of attention. ([1904] 1957, p. 553)

According to Simmel, the 'fashionable person is regarded with mingled feelings of approval and envy; we envy him [sic] as an individual, but approve of him [sic] as a member of a set or group' (p. 548). Thanks to fashion, we may thus simultaneously both express 'our obedience to the standards established by our time, our class, and our narrower circle' (p. 554) and stress our individuality. By the aid of fashion a person may accentuate one's individuality by relying on a general model, and thereby fashion even provides a 'mask' of some sort behind which one can hide (p. 552). Simmel writes that fashion allows people to 'save their inner freedom all the more completely by sacrificing externals to enslavement by the general public' (p. 553). Slightly pompously, he notes that:

> sensitive and peculiar persons [...] consider blind obedience to the standards of the general public in all externals as the conscious and desired means of reserving their personal feeling and their taste, which they are eager to reserve for themselves alone, in such a way that they do not care to have it enter in an appearance that is visible to all. (p. 552)

Thus, fashion itself provides a solution to the antinomy that it presents: while fashion is an antagonism of imitation and individual differentiation, or of society and the individual, it is *also* a 'third' that reconciles them. Though being based on subjective and personal preferences, it manages to create a socially binding form of action (Gronow, 1997, p. 91). Thereby 'social life' which otherwise 'represents a battle-ground', because the adherence to the group and the will to act and be like others is opposed to the striving towards individuality, finds a reconciliation in fashion (Simmel, [1904] 1957, p. 543). Fashion offers a possibility of at once appearing as different and nevertheless remaining obedient to the community. To quote Simmel:

> Fashion furnishes this very combination in the happiest manner, for we have here on the one hand a field of general imitation, the individual floating in the broadest social current, relieved of responsibility for his [sic] tastes and his [sic] actions, yet on the other hand we have a certain conspicuousness, an emphasis, an individual accentuation of the personality. (pp. 550–1)

However, the reconciliation that fashion provides is no final synthesis – rather, it is *disjunctive* by nature. Every fashion tries to extend the dynamics of conformity and individuality beyond all limits, but the moment fashion gains complete social acceptance it can longer satisfy the striving for difference, and consequently it must die as a fashion. And that is when the play of imitation and differentiation begins anew. Fashion is thus characterized by the 'ever renewed strife' between the two tendencies (p. 553): their balance is sought 'by means of ever new proportions' (p. 552). They are bound to lack permanent reconciliation.

The transient, fleeting character of fashion results precisely from here, from the very 'logic' of fashion. According to Simmel, there is an inherent striving towards expansion underlying in fashion, as if everybody should submit to the group. However, as soon as fashion becomes widely accepted, 'it must die as *fashion* of the logical contradiction against its own essence' (Simmel, [1911] GSG 14, p. 196), because at that point it can no longer produce distinction. Accordingly, Simmel suggests that the:

> very character of fashion demands that it should be exercised at one time only by a portion of the given group, the great majority being merely on the road to adopting it. As soon as an example has been universally adopted, that is, as soon as anything that was originally done only by a few has really come to be practiced by all [...] we no longer speak of fashion. ([1904] 1957, p. 547)

Fashion is able to provide an arena for the co-existence of imitation and differentiation only when it has not yet been assumed by everyone. The collective of people collected by the circulation of the imitable examples and ideals presented by fashion is therefore bound to remain a kind of 'cloud of community', to borrow a notion employed by Jean-Francois Lyotard (1988, p. 38). It is a community that needs to be built and rebuilt time and again (Gronow, 1997, pp. 90, 99). The being of fashion is therefore in the *striving* for its goal, not in the actual fulfilment of that goal. Fashion is characterized by simultaneous 'to be and not to be' (*Sein und Nichtsein*) (Simmel, [1905] GSG 10, p. 17): when fashion 'is', it no-longer-is, but has already perished. It *is* only by not-yet-being; that is, it is only as long as it has not reached fulfilment.

Fashion as a metaphor for modernity

Simmel observes that in the fashions of his day the struggle between social and individuating forces was mostly class-based, and the distinctions produced by fashion were class distinctions (Simmel, [1904] 1957, p. 544). While fashion appealed to all social strata, the latest fashion was nevertheless according to him limited to the upper classes. This is to say that 'the fashions of the upper stratum of society are never identical with those of the lower; in fact, they are abandoned by the former as soon as the latter prepares to appropriate them' (p. 543). Thorstein Veblen ([1899] 1992) called this the 'trickle down' effect, which means that the fashions adopted by the upper classes tend to trickle down in the social hierarchy.[3] There is therefore a constant race between the upper and the lower classes about good taste and the latest fashion: the elite deserts the prevailing fashion and escapes into a new one as soon as the lower classes adopt the former. More exactly, according to Simmel the mechanism of class differentiation is the following:

> Just as soon as the lower classes begin to copy their style, thereby crossing the line of demarcation the upper classes have drawn and destroying the uniformity of their coherence, the upper classes turn away from this style and adopt a new one, which in its turn differentiates them from the masses; and thus the game goes merrily on. ([1904] 1957, p. 545)

However, in his pieces on fashion Simmel is not merely trying to depict class fashion, but he already has his eye on something else. First of all, the form of fashion – the dualism of imitation and differentiation – is not confined within the class structure, but may also operate beyond and irrespective of it. Second, when speaking of the ever-increasing tempo of fashion and of how products had become cheaper because of the increased wealth of the lower classes, Simmel appears to be describing precisely modern mass fashion. In *The Philosophy of Money*, he writes:

> the social changes of the last hundred years have accelerated the pace of changes in fashion, on the one hand through the weakening of class barriers and frequent upward social mobility of individuals and sometimes even of whole groups to a higher stratum, and on the other through the predominance of the third estate. [...] If contemporary fashions are much less extravagant and expensive and of much shorter duration than those of earlier centuries, then this is due partly to the fact that it must be made much easier for the lower strata to emulate these fashions and partly because fashion now originates in the wealthy middle class. Consequently, the spreading of fashion, both in breadth as well as speed, appears to be an independent movement, an objective and autonomous force which follows its own course independently of the individual. ([1900/7] GSG 6, p. 640; 2004, p. 461)

Thereby, Simmel already seems to anticipate a more open mass fashion that does not necessarily bear any immediate relation to class hierarchy. The tempo of modern mass fashion is faster, and the products presented are not only cheaper but also standardized enough to serve the taste of the masses. In the mass fashion, differentiation is no longer class-based, but primarily amounts to *difference from the past* (with the past being epitomized by the old fashion).

The transitory character of fashion is linked to the modern experience. Fashion is transitory in the sense in which Baudelaire understood aesthetic modernity. The transitoriness of fashion makes it a downright *metaphor for modernity*: it epitomizes the inner movement and dynamics of modernity. It is important to note, however, that the transience of fashion is not absolute.

Transience is accompanied by the striving of each fashion to make the transitory and the fleeting into something eternal. Simmel remarks that although fashions come and go, each and every individual fashion still presents itself 'as though it intended to live forever' ([1904] 1957, p. 556). This is another feature that makes fashion modern to the highest degree. According to Simmel, 'the great problem of the modern spirit [...] [is] to find a place for everything which transcends the givenness of vital phenomena within those phenomena themselves, instead of transposing it to a spatial beyond' ([1923] GSG 20, p. 185; 1997a, p. 243). The eternal is sought in the transient.

Through the play of expansion and destruction fashion directs our consciousness to the *present* (Simmel, [1904] 1957, p. 547), mentioned above as one of the three meanings of the word modern besides 'transient' and 'new'. As Simmel puts it: 'Fashion always occupies the dividing-line between the past and the future, and consequently conveys a stronger feeling of the present, at least while it is at its height, than most other phenomena' (p. 547). The heightened feeling of the present is born in the hinge of the expiring and the upcoming fashion: the becoming of the new fashion and the fading of the old are present simultaneously. Because of this, fashion provokes the ambivalence and attraction of 'a simultaneous beginning and end, the charm of novelty coupled to that of transitoriness' (p. 547). With its ambivalence, fashion succeeds in embodying in its form the nature of the present, since the present, too, is a paradox. As Niklas Luhmann (1987, p. 167; trans. Lichtblau, 1995, p. 43) puts it, the present is 'the excluded *tertium quid* included in time, neither future nor past, but at the same time also the one and the other'. The present is thus at the same time both a '*past future*' and a '*future past*' (Lichtblau, 1995, p. 43). Both features are simultaneously present in fashion: the past future being manifest in the old fashion, and the future past in the new replacing the old while always also returning to the past in a cyclical manner and being destined to become outdated sooner or later.

Besides the transient and the present, fashion also embodies the third meaning of the term modern explicated above, the 'new'. Fashion lives off its constant renewal, its ability to present itself as new time and again. What is fashionable is always new, and the new equals 'modern'. The attraction of fashion is based on the attraction of novelty: we follow fashion precisely because it is something new. In relation to this, Colin Campbell (1987, p. 158) has suggested that fashion 'expresses a fixed and agreed aesthetic standard by which beauty is determined: it is the criterion of stimulative pleasure as achieved through novelty'. The contents of fashion appear as desirable because of being new. However, against Campbell it is easy to argue that the standard of taste provided by fashion is anything but fixed (Gronow, 1997, p. 92) – it is rather in constant alteration. In fact, the desirability or beauty of what is fashionable seems to be derivative from and thus secondary to the form of fashion; as long as it is new and fashionable, it is seen as desirable and beautiful. What is more, instead of proceeding towards an ever more refined aesthetic standard of taste, fashion makes no linear progress, but it goes around in circles: 'fashion repeatedly returns to old forms – as is repeatedly illustrated particularly in wearing-apparel – so that the course of fashion has been likened to a circle' (Simmel, [1904] 1957, p. 557). In a sense, then, fashion embodies the Nietzschean eternal return of the same: even though each fashion presents itself as 'new', fashion in fact repeats itself in cycles. Simmel observes that '[a]s soon as an earlier fashion has been partially forgotten there is no reason why it should not be allowed to return to favor' (p. 557). In other words, fashion always contains some reference to past fashions. This is already due to the fact that in the sphere of consumption products are deliberately *produced* as fashionable to make profit. Too progressive and unfamiliar products would not be likely to sell.

As a final note, Simmel's treatment succeeds in showing that, despite its seeming superficiality, the phenomenon of fashion is highly important for the understanding of contemporary life and the modern experience. In modernity, novelty has even become something of an obsession, and fashion is a token of that. Things may be desired, valued, praised, and adopted for no other obvious reason than because of being new, and then again they may also suddenly appear undesirable, ugly, degraded, and repugnant, even, just because they no longer satisfy our craving for novelty and distinction. What is more, fashion exercises a wide influence. As said, its mechanism is not restricted to clothing alone, but it has spread to various spheres and domains of life, from cosmetics to design, home furnishing, music, hobbies, food, literature, and academic theories and theorists as well as, even, to administration and politics.

The metropolis and the intensification of nervous life

Simmel's essay 'Die Grossstädte und das Geistesleben', published in 1903 and better known as the 'metropolis essay' from the title 'The Metropolis and Mental Life' of its English translation, is perhaps the single most famous and most influential sociological text ever written on the city and urban life (Wirth, 1925, p. 219). The essay is a revised version of a lecture Simmel gave in Dresden as part of a lecture course organized in winter 1902–3 in connection with a municipal exhibition on the metropolis held in the city in 1903. Despite the plural form '*Grossstädte*', 'metropolises', in the title, Simmel does not carry out any comparison between different cities (unlike many of the other lectures in the lecture course). The essay is distinctively marked by Simmel's relational approach. In it, he examines the metropolis sociologically, as a web of relations of reciprocal interdependence woven by the circulation of money and characterized, for example, by punctuality, fleeting social contacts, increased division of labour, enlargened social circlers, and individual freedom. The key question of the essay is the influence of the metropolis on the freedom and psyche of the individual. In the text, Simmel explores the psychological foundation of urban individuality and tries to disclose how that foundation is created by the modern metropolis and money economy.

For Simmel, the metropolis is the seat and focal point of modernity, money economy, consumption, and fashion. It is also characteristically a place of several contrasting tendencies, a kind of *coincidentia oppositorum*, coincidence of opposites. For example, according to Simmel the metropolis both consists of anonymous and impersonal contents and promotes mental individualization; it makes individuals both dependent on numerous people and, thanks to the enlargement of social circles, independent to highest degree; and it also provides an arena for the strife between two contrasting historical forms of individualism, the 18th-century individualism of liberalism and rationalism, on the one hand, and the 19th-century individualism of romanticism and modernity on the other.

The modern metropolis also simultaneously displays utmost order and disorder. Simmel remarks that the web of relationships in the space of the metropolis is so complex and involves so many people with divergent interests that the activities, transactions, and relations need to be coordinated and organized in the most punctual way: 'the lack of the most exact punctuality in promises and performances would cause the whole to break down into an inextricable chaos'. Simmel invites us to imagine a situation where all clocks and watches in Berlin suddenly went wrong in different ways. This would result in the disruption of its entire economic life and communication for quite some time (Simmel, [1903] GSG 7, p. 120; 1971, p. 328). Yet it is also precisely these punctual, calculated, and matter-of-fact intersecting interactions that in their sheer amount, diversity, and rapidity produce the turmoil of the metropolis.

Simmel highlights several threats that the metropolis poses to the individual subject trying to cope in the modern world and maintain independence and individuality against the sovereign powers of society, history, and culture. As Simmel puts it, the modern individual is constantly in danger of being 'swallowed up in the socio-technological mechanism' ([1903] GSG 7, p. 116; 1971, p. 324). The sheer amount of people, the steep increase in impersonal, objective cultural elements which tend to suppress personal interests and colourings, as well as the multitude of transitory, chance, and contrasted social contacts and the wealth of stimuli of urban life are all prone to reduce the individual to a 'negligible quantity', to nothing but 'a single cog as over against the vast overwhelming organization of things and forces' ([1903] GSG 7, pp. 129–30; 1971, p. 337). Nevertheless, instead of moralizing about the negative features and hazards of the metropolis, Simmel's approach is above all that of a neutral sociological observer. He concludes the metropolis essay with a credo declaring that 'our task is not to complain or to condemn but only to understand' ([1903] GSG 7, p. 131; 1971, p. 339; translation altered).

Indeed, what distinguishes Simmel from many of his contemporaries is that he does not view urban life with sour antipathy. The perception of the German economic historian Werner Sombart, for example, was exceedingly negative. Sombart contends that the modern metropolis is dominated by mass phenomena, quasi-independent technology, and rapid change, and that together they produce a wholly new culture, which he terms 'asphalt culture'. For Sombart, the modern metropolis is an utterly impoverished landscape, with people living in great stone canyons and upon hills of stone, glass, and iron. Furthermore, he laments that the urbanites lack any real relationship to nature; they are a completely 'artificial species' (Sombart, 1903). Like Sombart and many other contemporaries of his, Simmel, too, observes the metropolis in comparison with the countryside or small towns. For him, the characteristics of urbanism become discernible above all in contrast to life in rural settlements. But instead of romanticizing the bliss of rural life and being dismayed by the urban environment, Simmel sees life in the city as not at all unnatural; for him the metropolis rather comprises the natural habitat of the urbanite.[4] He suggests that the urbanite would not simply feel at home in a small town. In fact, Simmel assumes that for urbanites the countryside may appear so alienating and suffocating that it becomes even difficult to breathe there:

> Small town life in antiquity as well as in the Middle Ages set such barriers upon the movements of the individual and his [sic] relationships with the outside world as well as upon individual independence and differentiation that under such conditions the modern person could not even breathe. Even today an urbanite who is placed in a small town feels a restriction very similar in kind. ([1903] GSG 7, pp. 124–5; 1971, p. 333; translation altered)

Indeed, while the metropolis threatens individuality, it also nourishes individual freedom to an unforeseen extent. Whereas the small and closed agrarian community guards and controls its members jealously, the metropolis 'assures the individual of a type and degree of personal freedom to which there is no analogy in other conditions' ([1903] GSG 7, pp. 123–4; 1971, p. 332). The metropolitan atmosphere is tolerant to individual peculiarity, and thereby one is relatively independent from pettiness and prejudices which would set barriers upon individual freedom in smaller and more enclosed settlements.

According to Simmel, life in the metropolis is significantly different from that in small towns and in the countryside. In rural settlements, the inner life of individuals is conditioned by deeply felt stable relationships and by lasting, only slightly varying impressions, the course of which is regular and habituated. Metropolitan life, by contrast, is characterized by rapid change of nervous stimuli:

> The psychological foundation, upon which the metropolitan individuality is erected, is the *intensification* of nervous life [*Steigerung des Nervenlebens*] due to the swift and continuous shift of external and internal stimuli. Man [sic] is a creature whose

existence is dependent on differences, i.e. his [sic] mind is stimulated by the difference between present impressions and those which have preceded. Lasting impressions, the slightness in their differences, the habituated regularity of their course and contrasts between them, consume, so to speak, less mental energy than the rapid telescoping of changing images, pronounced differences within what is grasped at a single glance, and the unexpectedness of violent stimuli. To the extent that the metropolis creates these psychological conditions – with every crossing of the street, with the tempo and multiplicity of economic, occupational and social life – it creates in the sensory foundations of mental life, and in the degree of awareness necessitated by our organization as creatures dependent on differences, a deep contrast with the slower, more habitual, more smoothly flowing rhythm of the sensory-mental phase of small town and rural existence. ([1903] GSG 7, pp. 116–17; 1971, p. 325; translation altered)

Shock experience and blasé attitude

Simmel's understanding of the intensification of nervous life within urban space bears a striking affinity with the tradition of aesthetic modernity. The nerves had come into fashion in European literature around the middle of the 19th century. The vogue was manifest especially in the aesthetic of the present, which emphasized the shortening of lived time and space and the way they were squeezed into each other in experience, as it were. Time and space were considered in terms of the conditions of individual psyche. The aesthetic of the present, grounded in real urban experience, is expressed elegantly by the notion of *shock*, derived from the French word *la choque*, which originally meant the tip of a sabre. In the tradition of aesthetic modernity, shock became the emblem of nerve impulses. Walter Benjamin, for example, has examined the shock experience in relation to the motifs of Baudelaire's poetry in a most illuminating manner. He shows how 'Baudelaire placed shock experience [*Chockerfahrung*] at the very center of his art' (Benjamin, [1940] 2003, p. 319): in Baudelaire's work, there is a 'close connection [...] between the figure of shock and contact with the urban masses' (p. 320). For Benjamin, Baudelaire's poetry centres on 'an experience [*einer Erfahrung*] for which exposure to shock [*Chockerlebnis*] has become the norm' (p. 318). This is because in the modern metropolis, so Benjamin suggests, shock has become the normal form of experience: in the urban space, events and chains of events typically present themselves to our consciousness as shocks.

Simmel, too, refers to the shock experience in this sense briefly in *Sociology* in the excursus on the sociology of the senses. He writes: 'Modern man is shocked [*chokiert*] by so many things, and many things that appear to his senses as unbearable less differentiated, more robust modes of sensing take in without any kind of reaction' ([1908] GSG 11, p. 734). In the metropolis essay, Simmel maintains that to be able to adapt him/herself to the wealth of stimuli and to the bombardment of the senses, the urbanite needs to develop a specific way of reacting to external stimuli, a psychological 'protective organ

[*Schutzorgan*] [...] against the threatening fluctuations and discrepancies of the external environment which would otherwise uproot him [sic]' ([1903] GSG 7, p. 117; 1971, p. 326; translation altered). In contrast to small towns, where relationships are more deeply felt and therefore 'rooted in the unconscious levels of the soul and develop most readily in the steady equilibrium of unbroken customs' ([1903] GSG 7, p. 117; 1971, p. 325; translation altered), the bustle of metropolitan life demands heightened intellectualism of its habitants. Instead of reacting emotionally, the urbanites need to react with their intellect, favouring a distanced, indifferent relationship to phenomena.

The idea of the need to protect oneself against stimuli bears fascinating affinities with the hypothesis Sigmund Freud was later to present in *Beyond the Pleasure Principle* ([1922] 2010; orig. *Jenseits der Lustprinzips*, 1920) with regard to the relation of memory and consciousness. For Freud, consciousness has an important function as protecting against stimuli. To quote him at length:

> For the living organism protection against stimuli is almost a more important task than reception of stimuli; the protective barrier is equipped with its own store of energy and must above all endeavour to protect the special forms of energy-transformations going on within itself from the equalising and therefore destructive influence of the enormous energies at work in the outer world. (Freud, [1922] 2010)

The threat of these energies is conceptualized explicitly by both Freud and Benjamin and implicitly by Simmel as the threat of shocks, against which consciousness functions as a protective shield, normalizing them into unharmful and safe experiences and thus making them controllable. Benjamin writes: 'The more readily consciousness registers [...] shocks, the less likely they are to have a traumatic effect' (Benjamin, [1940] 2003, p. 317). When discussing consciousness as a protective shield against shocks, Freud himself does not have especially the modern urbanite in his mind, but he is speaking of 'the living organism' in general. The specific contribution of Simmel and Benjamin vis-à-vis Freud is thereby based on formulating this idea that Freud was to apply to all living organism in connection with the modern metropolis to explore the psychological foundation of urban life. However, while there are similarities between their views, there are also crucial differences between Simmel and Benjamin in how they picture the reaction to external stimuli. Simmel, as we saw, thinks that the change brought about by the metropolis is manifest especially in that people react with their intellect instead of emotions. For Benjamin, by contrast, the protection against the overwealth of stimuli does not manifest itself as heightened intellectualism. Unlike Simmel, he does not juxtapose the intellect and emotions, but considers the change into modern experience in terms of a transformation in the structure of experience, from *Erfahrung* to *Erlebnis* (Benjamin, [1940] 2003). Whereas *Erfahrung* is for him a matter of continuity and the product of things flowing together in memory and leaving a trace, *Erlebnis*, by contrast, is an 'isolated experience', less anchored in memory (Benjamin, [1940] 2003, pp. 314, 318).

With regard to the massification and swift change of sensuous images Simmel suggests that there may be no other psychic phenomenon as exclusively reserved to the metropolis as the so-called blasé attitude (*Blasiertheit*). To the blasé person things appear 'in an evenly flat and gray tone with no one of them deserving preference over any other' ([1903] GSG 7, p. 121; 1971, p. 330; translation altered). Simmel perceives the blasé attitude, as with many other phenomena, in a highly ambivalent manner, viewing it both as a means to adapt to the metropolitan life and as a pathology produced by the metropolis. On the one hand, it is a normal response provoked by the metropolitan reality; and yet, on the other hand, it is a detrimental consequence of metropolitan life.

According to Simmel, the blasé attitude stems from the very same factors which increase the impersonal and objective aspects of life. He identifies two sources to it. First, the blasé attitude is a result of the intensification of nervous activity provoked by metropolitan life. In Simmel's words, it is a 'consequence of those rapidly shifting stimulations of the nerves which are thrown together in all their contrasts and from which [...] the intensification of metropolitan intellectuality seems to be derived' ([1903] GSG 7, p. 121; 1971, p. 329). The external stimuli violently excite the nerves to the point at which they exhaust their last reserves of strength and are finally unable to produce any kind of reaction at all. Second, in addition to this 'physiological source', Simmel regards the blasé attitude also as a consequence of the modern money economy. He depicts money as 'the most frightful leveller' that 'hollows out the core of things' and deprives things of 'their individuality, their specific value, and their incomparability' ([1903] GSG 7, pp. 121–2; 1971, p. 330; translation altered). The blasé attitude is a subjective or psychic correlate of the levelling of values produced by money. In the modern money economy, all things 'rest on the same level' and differ from one another only in quantitative terms ([1903] GSG 7, p. 122; 1971, p. 330).

To sum up, in the metropolis essay Simmel is interested above all in the changes in individual psyche brought about by the modern metropolis. His perception of the city is reminiscent of other early views of urban life in that, like many of his contemporaries, Simmel identifies the characteristic features of the city by relying on the urban–rural divide, which possessed great mythological force at the time. The contrast is mythological because it is not devoid of value judgements and romanticism. However, unlike, for example, Sombart and Tönnies, Simmel does not use the dichotomy to project nostalgic longing of a lost harmonious community of the past, but only to delineate more sharply what is *new* in the metropolis and what it requires of the individual psyche. However, the urban–rural divide is mythological and problematic also because in reality there is perhaps no city without any rural features. The dividing line between real, empirical urban and rural settlements is anything but absolute and clear. Thus also the difference between the urban and rural psyche is perhaps not as radical as Simmel assumes;

besides dissimilarities there may also be similarities and continuities between them.[5] Interestingly, Simmel, too, softens the contrast, though not by referring to how urban life bears certain features of rural life, but by suggesting that cities tend to overflow their tangible borders. He remarks that in the same way as a 'person does not end with the limits of one's body' or with the place to which one's physical activity is confined, 'the city exists in the totality of its effects which extend beyond its immediate confines' ([1903] GSG 7, p. 127; 1971, p. 335; translation altered). For Simmel, 'The most significant aspect of the metropolis lies in this functional magnitude beyond its actual physical boundaries' ([1903] GSG 7, p. 127; 1971, p. 335). Consequently, to paraphrase Simmel's take on boundaries, the city needs to be understood not as a spatial entity with sociological consequences, but as a sociological entity that is formed spatially (cf. [1908], GSG 11, p. 697; 1997a, p. 143). It is also precisely the transcending of its physical confines that makes the metropolis the seat of cosmopolitanism, allowing an unprecedented degree of individual freedom.

Conclusion

In this chapter, I have focused on Simmel's sociological diagnoses of modernity. His analyses of fashion and the modern metropolis invite one to read his approach as a sort of *phenomenology of modernity* (Frisby, 1992, p. 66), aspiring to explore the mode of experience characteristic of modernity and the world of novel phenomena that entangle people in their everyday lives.[6] In modernity, so Simmel thinks, the mechanism of fashion and its emphasis on rapid change is spread to various spheres of life. What is more, the transitory character of fashion is intimately connected not only to the cult of 'novelty' that can be said to be characteristic of modern culture, but also to the modern experience as a vertigo in the face of the fleeting present. And it is, according to Simmel, above all in the metropolis that modern fashion flourishes, since urban inhabitants need to emphasize their individuality in the midst of the fleeting masses of people and stimuli. The metropolis is for Simmel the soil and focal point of modernity and also the main site of the modern experience. It is in the metropolis that modern phenomena develop and appear in their most pronounced form.

With his analyses of phenomena like fashion and the bustle of the metropolis, Simmel's work is suggestive of the worth in paying attention to the subtleties of everyday life. It is typical of Simmel not to avoid engaging with even the seemingly most insignificant or superficial phenomena in his work. This is because he is convinced that a deeper meaning can always be found in them. Simmel insists that daily occurrences and mundane objects provide us with fascinating leads to the profundities of life. 'It is possible to relate the details and superficialities of life to its most profound and essential movements', as he suggests in *The Philosophy of Money* ([1900/7], GSG 6, p. 13; 2004, p. 56). Or, as Simmel writes in a passage of the metropolis essay, he thinks that:

> from each point of the surface of being, however much it may appear to have merely grown in and out of this surface, a plumb line can be dropped into the soul's depth such that all of the most banal superficialities are in the end bound to the final determinations of the meaning and style of life via indications of direction. ([1903] GSG 7, p. 120; trans. Scott & Staubmann, 2005, p. xiii)

The idea of 'the possibility [...] of finding in each of life's details the totality of its meaning' ([1900/7], GSG 6, p. 12; 2004, p. 55) guides almost all of Simmel's studies (Kracauer, 1995, p. 252; Goodstein, 2002, p. 211). In the preface to his book *Rembrandt*, Simmel even names the dropping of a plumb line as the main task of philosophy: 'What has always seemed to me to be the essential task of philosophy [...] [is] to lower a plumb line through the immediate singular, the simply given, into the depths of ultimate intellectual meanings' ([1916], GSG 15, p. 309; 2005, p. 3). Simmel sets himself this task in his studies of fashion and the modern metropolis, too. Fashion tells him about a lot more than just whims and decoration. It provides us with a prism to investigate the process of association (*Vergesellschaftung*), the modern experience, and, ultimately, the metaphysical depths of human life. And the metropolis is connected for Simmel to the sensory foundations of the individual psyche and to the vital impulses of individuals. Punctuality, calculability, and exactness, which condition and characterize metropolitan life are, according to Simmel, not only 'most intimately connected with its capitalistic intellectualistic character but also color the content of life and are conductive of those irrational, instinctive, sovereign human traits and impulses which originally seek to determine the form of life from within' ([1903] GSG 7, p. 120; 1971, pp. 328–9). While the metropolis tends to foster most impersonal structures, it however also nourishes individual differentiation and highly subjective phenomena. Metropolitan life is characterized by the rapid crowding of changing images and by sharp contrasts, discontinuity, and unexpectedness of onrushing impressions. Such bombardment of the senses by the overabundance of rushing physical and social stimuli requires certain adaptive mechanisms from the individual, such as the blasé attitude and mental reserve.

Notes

1 Literally, 'shell as hard as steel' (see Baehr, 2001).
2 For Simmel, fashion is only one of the many forms of life where this dualism is actualized. Ultimately, he understands the dualism in an ontological sense, placing it in the foundations of what it is to be human. According to Simmel, there are two antagonistic forces at play in every human being, and thus humans have 'ever had a dualistic nature' ([1904] 1957, p. 541).

3   Grant McCracken (1988, pp. 93–4), who erroneously puts the trickle down mechanism in Simmel's name, has criticized the notion by emphasizing that the lower classes do not simply passively adopt the fashion that assumedly trickles down to them, but they actively imitate the upper classes and *seek* fashion. In other words, the lower classes, too, pursue distinctions.

4   Georges Perec ([1974] 1999, p. 62), French author and filmmaker, later wrote of this in a fitting manner: 'We shall never be able explain or justify the town. The town is there. It's our space, and we have no other. We were born and raised in towns. It's in towns that we breathe. When we catch the train, it's to get from one town to another town. There's nothing inhuman in towns – unless it's our own humanity.'

5   In 'Urbanism as a Way of Life' (1938), Luis Wirth makes a similar point. He writes: 'To a greater or lesser degree [...] our social life bears the imprint of an earlier folk society, the characteristic modes of settlement of which were the farm, the manor, and the village. This historic influence is reinforced by the circumstance that the population of the city itself is in large measure recruited from the countryside, where a mode of life reminiscent of this earlier form of existence persists. Hence we should not expect to find abrupt and discontinuous variation between urban and rural types of personality. The city and the country may be regarded as two poles of reference to one or the other of which all human settlements tend to arrange themselves. In viewing urban – industrial and rural – folk society as ideal types of communities, we may obtain a perspective for the analysis of the basic models of human association as they appear in contemporary civilization' (Wirth, 1938, p. 3).

6   Gary Backhaus (1998; 2003a; 2003b) has emphasized Simmel's affinities with Husserl and phenomenology, and Elizabeth Goodstein (2002; 2016) has interpreted Simmel's work as a 'phenomenology of culture'. François Léger (1989, pp. 36–42) discusses the similarities and differences between Simmel's and Husserl's thoughts, and he claims that although in many respects they could empathize with each other's projects of dealing with the Kantian heritage and of defending the independence of philosophy as a field, a fundamental difference remained in their epistemological positions: whereas Husserl developed phenomenology as 'rigorous science', Simmel cultivated a relationalistic philosophy. In relation to this, Backhaus (2003a, p. 207) argues that in contrast to Husserl, Simmel 'arrives at the parameters of phenomenology through discovery; that is, by concrete applications, rather than through a highly self-reflective stance of the principles of phenomenology prior to its practice'.

5

Money

Simmel's *The Philosophy of Money*, originally published in German in 1900 – the same year as the first volume of Edmund Husserl's *Logical Investigations* and Sigmund Freud's *The Interpretation of Dreams* – is to this day not only the most refined and comprehensive treatise of money, but also among the greatest philosophical works of the 20th century. It discerns, on the one hand, the preconditions that give money its specific meaning and role in our culture; and, on the other, the effects of money on culture, on individual psyche, and on the whole modern mode of life. In its own right, the book also challenges the long-prevailing perception of Simmel's work as particularly unsystematic, essayistic, and impressionistic. The book, thick as a brick, is built with architectural symmetry; while its content is driven mostly by philosophical and sociological motives, its structure expresses explicit aesthetic motives. In his essay '*Soziologische Ästhetik*' from the year 1896, Simmel notes that '[t]he origin of all aesthetic motives is to be found in symmetry' ([1896] GSG 5, p. 201). And *The Philosophy of Money* presents a carefully crafted symmetrical and harmonious whole: the book is divided into two parts, 'analytical' and 'synthetic',[1] with each of the parts consisting of three chapters, and each and every chapter being in itself further divided into three sections marked by the Roman numerals I, II, and III.

For the study of money and the economy, *The Philosophy of Money* is of utmost importance, especially in that it opened up a radically new way of thinking about money and economic phenomena by stressing their philosophical and sociocultural dimension. Simmel insists that money and the economy are not topics to be left to economics alone. Buying and selling, exchange and the means of exchange, value and value creation, possession, and the functioning of money, for example, are by no means only economic facts, but they can also be studied, for instance, from a philosophical, sociological, historical, or psychological perspective. To make sure that his reader understands that the book that they have in their hands is a philosophical treatise, as its title *The Philosophy of Money* also announces, Simmel insists on its opening pages that '[n]ot a single line of these investigations is mean to be a statement about economics' ([1900/7] GSG 6, p. 11; 2004, p. 54).

It is of particular interest to sociology that in the book Simmel treats the social and the economic as deeply intertwined, thus stripping the market and its laws of an autonomous existence. This idea has been one of the starting points of latter-day economic sociology, though more often than not without reference to Simmel. For example, Karl Polanyi, who is commonly regarded as one of the founding fathers of economic sociology,[2] famously proposes in his book *The Great Transformation* (1944) that economic phenomena are 'embedded' in a social context (meaning by 'social context' ultimately 'society'). However, while Polanyi, basically, merely substitutes an already-established structure (society) for another one (the economy), what makes Simmel's contribution original even compared to much modern economic sociology is that he does not examine money as being embedded in society or social institutions. On the contrary, his approach invites us to dissolve all assumedly fixed and static structures; not only that of the pure and perfect market but also that of society. Instead of assuming the prior existence of society, as we saw in Chapter 3 in relation to Simmel's processual relationalism, Simmel examines in his sociology of forms how society is something constantly produced and connected rather than being always already there. He rejects any pre-established unities as valid starting points for sociological enquiry and dissolves them into dynamic relations and processes. What makes this approach significant for the study of the economy is, of course, that along with the dissolution of society, all Polanyian metaphors of embeddedness, too, evaporate.[3] This is the original contribution Simmel potentially *could* have made to economic sociology had scholars paid more attention to it – for a long time, *The Philosophy of Money* remained largely neglected, little understood, and without significant scholarly impact.[4]

In this chapter, I explicate Simmel's theorizing on money. It bears a close connection with his analysis of the modern metropolis discussed in the previous chapter. Besides treating the metropolis as the seat of the mature money economy, Simmel also regards the metropolis and money as reflecting two different yet interrelated sides of modernity: if the metropolis designates the focal point and *intensification* of modernity, the mature money economy *extends* its structures and forms across the modern world (Frisby, 1992; 2001). What is more, while the metropolis presented, above all, a key spatial dimension of modernity, money, like fashion, is also connected to its temporal facet, as with its constant circulation it accelerates the pace of modern life. The chapter follows the structure of Simmel's book in that I will first focus on the preconditions of money, and after that discuss its cultural role and effects.

Value, desire, and exchange

One of the key motives of *The Philosophy of Money* is to construct a theory of value. For Simmel, values are an integral part of what it is to be human: it is a psychological necessity that our life runs in 'experiencing and judging values' (Simmel, [1900/7] GSG 6, p. 25; 2004, p. 60). Without valuations, reality would be devoid of any sense or significance (*Sinn*) altogether. Like neo-Kantians, Simmel, too, thought that when being conceived as plainly 'real' there is no significance or value at all included in reality. Simmel considers the role of philosophy as highly significant in examining the value and meaning of our life or the world. He suggests that the purpose of philosophy is to 'elevate our sense of the value and the interconnectedness of the world as a whole into the sphere of abstract concepts' ([1906] GSG 10, p. 125; 2007, p. 162).[5] For Simmel, value and being (reality) represent two different worlds or primary categories: being is the primary form of our perception (the being of objects cannot be deduced logically, but it can only be sensed, experienced, perceived, and thought), and value the primary form of creativity and demand (Simmel, [1900/7] GSG 6, pp. 27, 38–9; 2004, pp. 61, 69).

The basis of Simmel's explorations of economic value in *The Philosophy of Money* is the notion of 'exchange' (*Tausch*). For Simmel, exchange is not solely or even primarily an economic concept to be understood within the framework of utility, but economic exchange is only one specific type of exchange ([1900/7] GSG 6, p. 67; 2004, p. 87). Simmel understands exchange ultimately as a basic form of association (*Vergesellschaftung*). Thereby it is linked to the concept of *Wechselwirkung* and Simmel's relational mode of thinking. For him, in human relationships reciprocal effects appear in forms that can be regarded as forms of exchange: 'Every interaction can be regarded as an exchange: every conversation, every affection (even if it is rejected), every game, every glance at another person' ([1900/7] GSG 6, p. 59; 2004, p. 82). Accordingly, Simmel notes: 'Exchange is the purest and most developed kind of interaction' ([1900/7] GSG 6, p. 59; 2004, p. 82), a 'sociological phenomenon *sui generis*' ([1900/7] GSG 6, p. 89; 2004, p. 100). The notion of exchange goes to the heart of Simmel's relational worldview. Accordingly, *The Philosophy of Money* is in the last instance an attempt to lay out the real as relational. Ultimately, money stands for him as merely an example or means to accomplish this. For Simmel, the great philosophical significance of money lies in it being the ultimate symbol of the relativity of all being. Money, Simmel suggests, 'represents within the practical world the most certain image and the clearest embodiment of the formula of all being, according to which things receive their meaning through each other, and have their being determined by their mutual relations' ([1900/7] GSG 6, p. 136; 2004, pp. 128–9).

Exchange becomes economic by nature when we exchange *values*. Accordingly, in the first part of *The Philosophy of Money*, Simmel sets out to develop a theory of value. His take bears a polemic but close relation especially to Marx and his thoughts in *Capital*. However, here it is possible to cover the issue only briefly and superficially, to outline Simmel's point of departure.[6] On the one hand, Simmel aims at supplementing Marx's theory of value by 'constructi[ng] a new storey beneath historical materialism'. He understands economic forms as 'result[s] of more profound valuations and currents of psychological or even metaphysical pre-conditions'. However, instead of simply reducing the economic basic structure to ideas and conceptions, Simmel establishes a dialectical relation between historical materialism and idealism. As he puts it himself at more length:

> Every interpretation of an ideal structure by means of economic structure must lead to the demand that the latter in turn be understood from more ideal depths, while for these depths themselves the general economic base has to be sought, and so on indefinitely. (Simmel [1900/7], GSG 6, p. 13; 2004, p. 56)

On the other hand, Simmel's theory of value can be understood as a critical response to Marx. What the two authors have in common is that both denounce the idea that value would inhere in the things themselves. But whereas Marx proposes a labour theory of value, Simmel expands upon an exchange theory of value. While for Marx value is based on production and labour, Simmel regards the human subject as the origin of values. This links Simmel's theory ultimately much more closely to the marginal utility theory of value than to Marx (Frisby, 2004a, p. 24). The subjective basis of Simmel's theory of value means, above all, that he sees value as a result of subjective *valuation*. Since people may regard one and the same object as of a different value, and since objects with very different properties may receive the same value, value cannot be a property of the objects themselves ([1900/7] GSG 6, pp. 23–5, 29; 2004, pp. 59–60).

Simmel suggests that we regard something valuable on the basis of *desire*. We do not desire objects because they are valuable, but objects come to possess a value in the first place only because we desire them. The constitutive element of desire, Simmel contends, is the *distance* that separates us from the object of our desire: we desire objects only insofar as and as long as they are not in our immediate use and enjoyment ([1900/7] GSG 6, p. 34; 2004, p. 66). 'Objects are not difficult to acquire because they are valuable, but we call those objects valuable that resist our desire to possess them' ([1900/7] GSG 6, p. 35; 2004, p. 67). The moment of enjoyment, in which the separation of subject and object is won, consumes value. With his emphasis on the dialectics of desire and distance Simmel also happens to draw a very accurate picture of more recent modern consumerism and its accent on the anticipation of enjoyment and possession rather than on the actual possession of commodities itself.

Nevertheless, notwithstanding all the emphasis Simmel lays on distance as a precondition of desire, he acknowledges that of equal importance for desire is a promise that the distance can be overcome. The distance that constitutes desire is never insurmountable or invincible, but it is experienced as something that postpones enjoyment, thus making the object of desire appear as something 'not-yet-enjoyed' (*Nochnichtgenießen*) ([1900/7] GSG 6, p. 34; 2004, p. 66). Therefore, '[t]he longing, effort and sacrifice that separate us from objects are also supposed to lead us towards them' ([1900/7] GSG 6, p. 49; 2004, p. 75). In the essay 'Money in Modern Culture', Simmel suggests that the greatest yearning, craving, and desire are not created by some absolutely remote and unattainable thing, but one which is not yet ours though the possibility of possessing it seems constantly to lie ahead of us, on the verge of realization. Desire is thus based on the paradox of simultaneous distance and proximity: while desire arises only at a distance it tries to overcome, the promise that the distance will be overcome already presupposes that objects are in our vicinity.

Thus, as was noted above, Simmel suggests that value is ultimately based on subjective valuations.[7] Things can acquire an economic value only provided that they are first valuable for someone. And, for the subject, value is determined in relation to the effort that overcoming the distance separating the subject from the object of one's desire requires. The sacrifices and all the effort made to obtain an object are invested in its value ([1900/7] GSG 6, p. 335; 2004, p. 256). Therefore Simmel thinks that a value can only be obtained by sacrificing another value.[8] It is only because of a sacrifice that satisfying a desire comes to have a price. Consequently, Simmel considers economic exchange in terms of an 'exchange of sacrifices' ([1900/7] GSG 6, p. 61; 2004, p. 80). Unlike, for example, the French historian, philosopher, and literary critic René Girard (1979), who conceives desire as mimetic by nature and also sees mimetic desire as the source of all human conflicts, Simmel thinks that we enter into exchange not because we want what the other has, but because of a *lack*: 'exchange is not conducted for the sake of the object that the other person possesses, but to gratify one's personal feelings which he [sic] does not possess' ([1900/7] GSG 6, p. 60; 2004, p. 79). The sense in economic exchange lies in that both parties, paradoxically, receive more than what they give away in return. Exchange is thus able to generate and produce value.[9]

Nevertheless, while ultimately based on subjective valuations, economic value according to Simmel also overcomes the purely subjective forms of valuations. This is so because it is based on exchange. Economic value means 'to be exchangeable for something else' ([1900/7] GSG 6, p. 124; 2004, p. 121). In exchange, an object is offered for another, and therefore the value of each object is determined in relation to other objects and not solely in relation to the desiring subject anymore: 'The fact that the object has to be exchanged against another object illustrates that it is not only valuable for me, but also valuable independently of me' ([1900/7] GSG 6, pp. 58–9; 2004, p. 81). By being exchanged, each object acquires a measure of its value through the other object ([1900/7] GSG 6, pp. 52–3; 2004, p. 78). This makes economic value in principle an objective social fact; the 'decisive fact in the objectivity of economic value' is according to Simmel 'that its validity transcends the individual subject'.

Money as a means of exchange and measure of value

From the investigation of value and exchange Simmel proceeds to exploring what money adds to the picture: what is monetary value and monetary exchange? Simmel suggests that for the exchanged valuations money provides an objective measure, as it allows them to be compared objectively. While in the exchange of gifts, for example, one can never be sure of getting possessions on a fair price, due to its nearly unlimited divisibility money makes possible the exact equivalency of the exchanged values. By mediating subjective valuations and providing the exchanging parties an objective measure of value, money forges a metamorphosis: via money, value becomes an objective, measurable, and reified social fact. Exchangeability is materialized in money. And because money can be used for whatever economic purposes ([1900/7] GSG 6, p. 268, 436), both parties of exchange get a chance to acquire precisely what they desire: while the one receives an object that one aspires, the other receives in exchange what everyone wants – money ([1900/7] GSG 6, p. 388; 2004, p. 292). Money is that which everyone appreciates, because with it one can acquire whatever one desires. Simmel suggests that money is thus 'the pure form of exchangeability' ([1900/7] GSG 6, p. 138; 2004, p. 130). It has no meaning outside exchange relations, but its sole purpose is to be passed around, to be exchanged for other objects and measure their value. Money has no significance and value in itself, but only in relation to other objects.

Money acts both as a means of exchange and as a measure of value. This makes it ultimately a double, not only in the sense of having a dual role, but also in having two contradictory characteristics. On the one hand, as a means of exchange, it does not remain unaltered through its various uses but presents and preserves its identity only in and via 'the greatest and most changing variety of equivalents' ([1900/7] GSG 6, p. 301; 2004, p. 234). Simmel observes the convenience of the expression 'liquid' (*flüssig*) money: like a liquid, money 'lacks internal limits and accepts without resistance external limits that are offered by any solid surroundings' ([1900/7] GSG 6, p. 691; 2004, p. 495). Money is indeed analogous to a fluid, keeping its shape for only a relatively short period of time. What is decisive for money is its flow. It has to circulate and remain in motion in order to function as money: 'The meaning of money lies in the fact that it will be given away. When money stands still, it is no longer money according to its specific value and significance' ([1900/7] GSG 6, p. 714; 2004, p. 510). Besides being in motion itself, money also dissolves and bursts solids into movement: 'Money is nothing but the vehicle of movement in which everything else that is not in motion is completely extinguished' ([1900/7] GSG 6, p. 714; 2004, p. 511).

Yet, on the other hand, money is not only that which is mobile and constantly mutable, but also that which remains stable and immutable. Simmel conceptualizes the latter characteristic by calling money in Aristotelian terms an 'unmoved mover' (*unbewegte Beweger*) ([1900/7] GSG 6, p. 204; 2004, p. 171): it presents a stabilized, trustworthy, and objective measure of things. Money provides exchange with continuity and evenness that are largely missing in barter, for example. In measuring values, the value of money value persists even if the value of objects alters: 'money, as the stable pole, contrasts with the eternal movements, fluctuations and equations of the objects' ([1900/7] GSG 6, pp. 124–5; 2004, p. 121). So, here money appears as something other than an object; while objects are constantly in motion money stands still.

Consequently, what is at issue in the contradiction described above is perhaps the difference between money as an object, on the one hand, and as an abstract idea on the other. As a tangible object, money is 'the substance that embodies abstract economic value' ([1900/7] GSG 6, p. 122; 2004, p. 120). Money is relationality or relativity reified; it is 'nothing other than a special form of the embodied relativity of economic goods that signifies their value' ([1900/7] GSG 6, p. 716; 2004, p. 512). In among objects, money presents a special case in that it is not so much a thing as a relation and abstract idea. Simmel holds that money appears *ante rem*, *in re*, and *post rem* ([1900/7] GSG 6, p. 123; 2004, p. 120) – that is, 'before the thing', 'in the matter of a thing', and 'after the thing', without itself being a thing. The object used as money is merely 'a symbol of money' ([1900/7] GSG 6, p. 246; 2004, p. 198). Of course, as a piece of paper, plastic, or metal, money can be cut, torn, and even burnt or eaten, but what makes it money is ultimately not its physical properties. On the contrary, Simmel contends that it is precisely because 'its qualities are invested in the social organizations and the supra-subjective norms' that money is capable of doing the things it does. He insists that money is a form of social interaction, a reified social function ([1900/7] GSG 6, p. 209; 2004, p. 175). The essential thing in money is *trust*. Without trust in the fact that the money once accepted can be spent again at the same value, monetary transactions would 'collapse' ([1900/7] GSG 6, pp. 214–5; 2004, pp. 178–9). The exchanging parties need to be able to have confidence in the fact that money passes for a general means of exchange and preserves its value.

For Simmel, that money appears as a pre-thing, in-the-thing, or post-thing rather than as a thing itself is a result of a historical development. Money has not always been as 'immaterial' as the modern money is. According to Simmel, the development of money is characterized by the dissolution of its substance into functions. In the Middle Ages, the substance of money dominated its effects. In the modern money economy, by contrast, there is 'a tendency to eliminate substance entirely' ([1900/7] GSG 6, p. 201; 2004, p. 169). Today, the function of money no longer necessitates that it be a valuable object: 'The more it is really money in its essential significance, the less need there is for it to be money in a material sense' ([1900/7] GSG 6, pp. 203–4; 2004, p. 171). Hence, Simmel distinguishes between the material sense of money and its function or 'essential significance'. One justification for this is that money has no inner relation to its material value: 'Money has value not on account of what it is, but on account of the ends that it serves' ([1900/7] GSG 6, p. 251; 2004, p. 201). As we know, the material value of paper money is close to nothing in itself, and Simmel notes that it is also secondary whether the value of money is based upon metal ([1900/7] GSG 6, p. 214; 2004, p. 178). In the light of the phenomenon of trust, the development of money from substance and use-values to credit and, more recently, electronic money, appears not that radical at all. The latter stages in the development are merely more strongly and independently based upon the dimension of trust already present in material money when what were exchanged as money were utility values.[10]

Nonetheless, money cannot cast off its materiality completely. Although money is becoming less and less tied to a physical substance, it can never attain the state of amounting to a pure symbol ([1900/7] GSG 6, pp. 181–2; 2004, p. 157). According to Simmel, this has to do not so much with the nature of money as with 'certain shortcomings of economic technique' ([1900/7] GSG 6, p. 182; 2004, p. 158). One of these shortcomings concerns the use of money as a means of exchange. As long as the equation between the measured value and the standard remains imprecise, the measuring process requires support by and a reference point in substance, such as in precious metal. The second reason why money cannot entirely free itself from matter has to do with its possible misuse. A necessary limit has to be set on the amount of money in circulation (and/or money has to be linked to a substance of a limited supply) in order to prevent inflation ([1900/7] GSG 6, pp. 184–6; 2004, pp. 159–60). To some extent, money has to remain scarce.

Money and modern lifestyle

What is particularly fascinating from a sociological perspective in *The Philosophy of Money* is how Simmel manages to depict the characteristic features of the modern mode of life by focusing on money as an object. Money appears as an excellent tracer of social relationships. Simmel uses it as a means to study society's 'movements' and 'transformations' (Papilloud, 2002, p. 97). For Simmel, money is a bearing structure and crucial symbol of modernity, weaving together the network of modern society:

> On the one hand, money functions as a system of articulations in this organism, enabling its elements to be shifted, establishing a relationship of mutual dependence of the elements, and transmitting all impulses through the system. On the other hand, money can be compared to the bloodstream whose continuous circulation permeates all the intricacies of the body's organs and unifies their functions by feeding them all to an equal extent. ([1900/7] GSG 6, p. 652; 2004, p. 469)

By following the motion and circulation of money we can grasp the formation of the relational network of society money is entangled in. One's image of society would remain hopelessly abstract and vague were one to start from an all-encompassing, reified, and holistic notion of society. In fact, one would not 'see' anything were one to just stare at 'society' in itself. However, by following the movement and circulation of money, Simmel notes, 'the unity of things [...] becomes practical and vital for us' ([1900/7] GSG 6, p. 13; 2004, p. 56). By drawing on Arjun Appadurai's (1988, p. 5) formulation, one could thus say that Simmel's approach in *The Philosophy of Money* is imbued by a sort of 'methodological fetishism', that is, by a conviction that things-in-motion not only illuminate but also participate in generating the relations they are entangled among. It is perhaps by following the circulation and stabilization of objects that we are best able to observe what kind of relations exist between us, what happens in our collectives, and how our social aggregates are made stable (see e.g. Serres, 2007; Pyyhtinen, 2014; 2015).

Due to its functioning as a general measure of value, in the modern world money has, according to Simmel, become the 'the centre in which the most opposed, the most estranged and the most distant things find their common denominator and come into contact with one another' ([1900/7] GSG 6, p. 305; 2004, p. 236). To some extent even incommensurable and singular realities like artworks, fine wines, personalized skills, and particular kinds of expertise are made commensurable by means of money. And when things are valued in money, their unique individual qualities are in a sense 'devalued', so Simmel thinks, as money is interested only in what is common to them all: their exchange value. Therefore money presents for Simmel 'the most frightful leveller', as was already noted in Chapter 4. The levelling accompanies the growth of the web of money transaction and the increasing significance of money. If anything is purchasable, everything lies ultimately on the same level, regardless of the qualitative differences of things, because nothing is valuable except in terms of money. In the modern money economy, Simmel suggests, things differ from one another only in quantitative terms: all other differential features but price are excluded. This furthers the reduction of qualitative and individual values to quantitative ones. According to Simmel ([1900/7] GSG 6, p. 340; 2004, p. 259): 'With reference to money, we do not ask what and how, but how much.'

Money economy is thus responsible for a pervasive change in the very way we value and perceive things (Sassatelli, 2000, p. 208). Simmel asserts that the 'how much' rationality of money socializes us into calculative reasoning, as a result of which constant mathematical calculations have become an integral and necessary part of our everyday life ([1900/7] GSG 6, pp. 612–3; 2004, p. 444). Money tends to turn the world into an arithmetic problem: many of our mundane practices involve frequent evaluations, calculations, summing ups, and reductions. What is more, the rapid increase in the supply of commodities and the devaluation and loss of quality that objects undergo in the modern money economy make the individual object utterly insignificant or almost worthless. Simmel takes the pin as his example. While 'one particular pin is just as good or as worthless as any other', we are highly dependent on pins in general, to the extent that 'the modern civilized individual could not manage without pins'. The same applies to the significance of money. Whereas specific amounts of money are less important, we are more increasingly reliant on money as such, in general ([1900/7] GSG 6, p. 401; 2004, p. 301).

While money measures more and more things, it becomes more and more colourless and neutral itself. As a general equivalent, it expresses all the values and meanings and has none itself. Lacking any inherent individuality or qualities, it is neutral, a blank figure. Money is any object and no object. No other value is more detached from concrete valuable objects than economic value, and no other object 'is more completely the abstract bearer of value' than money ([1900/7] GSG 6, p. 181; 2004, p. 157). As money can be used for basically any economic purpose and to serve any imaginable ends, it is not tied to any of these uses and ends in particular. This makes money a 'purely abstract means' ([1900/7] GSG 6, p. 269; 2004, p. 214), 'the purest form of the tool' ([1900/7] GSG 6, p. 263; 2004, p. 210). It is exchangeable for basically anything whatsoever.

More recently, Viviana Zelizer (1994) has challenged Simmel's idea of the impersonal and colourless nature of money. According to Zelizer, money has all kinds of meanings for people. Consequently, money is not one, but there exist multiple moneys: inherited money differs from money earned through hard labour, just as a sum of money won in the lottery differs from the money one has made by picking winning stocks. Nor is loaned money the same as stolen money, which in turn differs from money received as a grant, as a donation, or as, say, unemployment benefit (Zelizer, 1994, pp. 2–3). However, Zelizer's criticism of Simmel is not entirely accurate or justified. This is because, first, Simmel seems to acknowledge the fact that money may have various meanings. For instance, he notes in *The Philosophy of Money* how the same amount of money may differ in nature, depending on whether it belongs to a poor or wealthy person ([1900/7] GSG 6, pp. 277–81; 2004, pp. 219–21). Further, a bit later in the book, Simmel tells how 'the same amount of money in the hands of a stock exchange speculator or a renter, or the State or the large industrialist produces extraordinarily different returns' ([1900/7] GSG 6, pp. 277–81; 2004, pp. 293–4). Second, while he admits that it is possible to attach for instance personal, practical, and aesthetic value to money, he stresses that these are renounced or they at least recede to the background when money is used as money ([1900/7] GSG 6, pp. 173–4; 2004, p. 151). As soon as these extra-economic values prevail, money is in a sense withdrawn from circulation and no longer operates as money. Just as 'the unsold commodity is merely a possible commodity, which becomes a real commodity only at the moment of sale', money that is not used for the purpose of buying is money only potentially. It becomes 'real money only at the moment when it buys something' ([1900/7] GSG 6, p. 150; 2004, p. 136).

Accordingly, Simmel emphasizes that money is just a *means*. It receives its significance as money only from being used. However, he argues that it is precisely because money has become the absolute means that for many it has in fact become the absolute *end*, a purpose in itself. As the absolute means seems to promise 'unlimited possibilities for enjoyment' ([1900/7] GSG 6, p. 313; 2004, p. 243), money becomes the fixed point of activities and the ultimate object of desires. This breeds phenomena like greed and avarice. Simmel suggests that the 'ultimate craving for money must increase to the extent that money takes on the quality of a pure means' ([1900/7] GSG 6, p. 298; 2004, p. 232). As most people have to dedicate most of their lives to the acquisition of money, it seems as if all the happiness in life and all real satisfaction was dependent on a certain amount of money (Simmel, [1896] GSG 5, p. 188; 1991a, p. 25). This is perhaps one of the main reasons why people keep buying, for example, lottery tickets, even though they are aware that the chances of their ticket winning are minutely small.

For Simmel, the transformation of money from a means to an end in itself is a key factor in the restlessness and dissatisfaction of our times. According to him, it is characteristic of the modern sensibility that we feel like 'the core and meaning of life slips through our fingers again and again, that definite satisfactions become ever rarer, that all effort and activity is not actually worthwhile' ([1896] GSG 5, p. 186; 1991a, p. 23). While money seems to bring all the happiness and all the joys of life within reach, it also creates ungratified desire, resulting in one disappointment after another. This is because money is merely a means, a mediator, a link leading to actual enjoyment and purpose without being able to offer it itself. In other words, money is 'only the bridge to definitive values, and one cannot live on a bridge' ([1896] GSG 5, p. 189; 1991a, p. 25). In modernity, the absolute has been relativized. Even when money presents itself as the absolute purpose and fixed point, it is nothing but movement and liquidity, nothing but an expression of the value of other objects. Accordingly, Simmel maintains that the constant circulation of money accelerates the modern pace of life ([1900/7] GSG 6, pp. 696–7; 2004, pp. 498–9): 'The modern view of life rests upon money whose nature is fluctuating' ([1900/7] GSG 6, p. 301; 2004, p. 234). With its constant circulation, money is an ever-rolling wheel making modern life as a whole restless and feverish, akin to a '*perpetuum mobile*' (Simmel, [1896] GSG 5, p. 191; 1991a, p. 27).

Conclusion

Simmel conceives the modern style of life as intimately tied up with money transactions. In modernity, more and more things find their value expressed in money: money functions as a general means of exchange that weaves a web of mutual connections between things. Via money, we are also connected – directly or indirectly – with numerous people. Money establishes incomparably more connections between people than ever existed before modernity. Our lives are marked by unprecedented connectivity, extending well beyond our niche. Thus money also makes people more and more dependent upon the services of others; every intersection in the web of relations is connected to multiple others.

However, while money is able to overcome distance by bringing more and more things within our reach and by forging ties even between complete strangers (to some extent it even socializes us into strangers), it also increases distance not only between subjects and objects, but also among subjects. As far as things are attainable only via money, money places itself between us and the objects of our desire. Nothing is immediate in money, but it is all about mediation. In stands in-between, in the position of a 'third'. And, as far as relations between subjects are concerned, while linking individuals with different interests, needs, and desires, money also tends to make the persons who perform the services irrelevant and interchangeable behind and apart from them. It makes no difference to us who delivers our mail, who operates our train to work, and who serves us at the checkout of a supermarket – as long as someone competent enough does. So, we are interdependent not in terms what we are but what we do, in relation to our tasks and performances.

All in all, following the circulation of money allows us to grasp the process of association (*Vergesellschaftung*) in a most concrete manner. As an object generated by relations, money also generates relations. Its functioning is not only dependent on relationships and social institutions, but with its circulation money is also able to weave relationships. Via money, we are dependent not only on each other, but also on the whole of society. Money spreads over our relationships and life in general. As Simmel puts it in *The Philosophy of Money*: 'At present [...] the whole aspect of life, the relationships of human beings with one another and with objective culture are coloured by monetary interests' ([1900/7] GSG 6, p. 305; 2004, p. 236). This makes money a perfect means for Simmel to develop and present his relational mode of thought as well as put forth a diagnosis of modernity in *The Philosophy of Money*. As Simmel writes in one of his journal aphorisms:

> Money is the only cultural formation that is *pure power*, that has fully eliminated material supports from itself, in that it is absolutely pure symbol. To this degree it is the most characteristic among all the phenomena of our time, when *dynamism* has gained command of all theory and practice. The fact that it is *pure relationship*

(and this likewise characteristic of our time) without including any of the content of the relationship does not contradict this. For in reality, power is nothing but relationship. (GSG 20, p. 295; 2010, p. 186)[11]

As an object, money is more a relation than a thing, at once both engendered by relations and able to engender relations. Simmel's notion of the relationality of money invites us explore the relationality of being, that is, to study entities in their relations rather than as separate and static substances. Objects are intermeshed in relations: in many cases they are not only enactments of relations but also participate in weaving them. Simmel's account of money has thus considerable methodological relevance as regards the study of the share of objects in social relations.

Notes

1 The two notions derive from Kant.
2 William Stanley Jevons had coined the term 'economic sociology' in 1879, and some scholars identify the birth of economic sociology with Alexis de Tocqueville's books *Democracy in America* (1835–1840) and *The Old Regime and the Revolution* (1856).
3 Bruno Latour and Vincent Antonine Lépinay (2009) credit Gabriel Tarde for making a similar move.
4 With regard to the last point, Rammstedt (2005, p. 9) states that 'no scientific discipline has regarded *The Philosophy of Money* as one of its classic texts' and the book has not 'been […] accepted by any discipline as fully belonging to its field of analysis', either.
5 The motif behind this view becomes clear against the background of the rise of the natural sciences in the latter half of the 19th century: philosophers felt it as crucial to preserve meaning and value to life against the attack of naturalism. In the worldview of the natural sciences, as Simmel presents in *Kant and Goethe*, there is no room for ideas, values, ends, religious convictions, or ethical freedom. On the contrary, from the days of Galileo and Copernicus natural science has explained and interpreted the world in terms of causal mechanisms and with an increasing mathematical precision ([1910] GSG 10, p. 122; 2007, p. 160).
6 For a detailed account of the affinities and differences between Simmel's and Marx's theory of value, see e.g. Frisby (2004a, pp. 22–8).
7 Or, more exactly, this holds only for values as valuations. Analytically, Simmel distinguishes between values of specific objects and values as such. The values of objects are not intrinsic and objective qualities of the objects themselves but based on valuations by human subjects, yet values as such present for Simmel a category independent of both the subject and the object.
8 This also applies to situations lacking explicit exchange. For example, our common, everyday experience of responsibility is that we can be responsible towards someone only by sacrificing others (see Derrida, 1995, p. 68). If I was to devote myself completely to writing books, it is likely that I would fail to fulfil my responsibilities to students as a teacher, and when I am working I can't be there for my children,

but when I am playing with my children I often get the nagging feeling that I really should be at my desk writing.
9 Simmel goes as far as to claim that 'exchange is just as productive and value-creating as is production itself' ([1900/7] GSG 6, p. 63; 2004, p. 81).
10 With regard to this, see Dodd (2016) on Simmel and Bitcoin.
11 In use of italics I follow the German original; in the translation by Andrews, the words 'power' and 'dynamism' italicized by Simmel himself do not appear in italics.

6

Studying Social Forms

Beyond the programme of the sociology of forms that Simmel sketches in *Sociology* he also contributed to sociological thought with his several concrete investigations of a whole variety of social forms. In the previous chapters I have already discussed Simmel's examinations of fashion, the metropolis, and money, and this chapter will look into some of his sociological analyses to be found in the books *Sociology* and *Grundfragen der Soziologie*.[1] I will begin by exploring what Simmel regards as the key dimensions of social forms: time (*Zeit*), space (*Raum*), and number (*Zahl*). After that I will turn to friendship, love, and relations to the stranger as examples of the particular forms of relations analysed by Simmel in his work. They are chosen as examples to illustrate how for Simmel all social relations are structured along the axis of proximity and distance. From there the chapter proceeds to a discussion on sociability (*Geselligkeit*). Sociability is included here especially for the reason that it exemplifies the distinction of form and content that is of crucial importance to Simmel's sociology and to his manner of perceiving social phenomena. For Simmel, sociability is a pure form that has no purpose outside itself. I will conclude with a note on how there is nothing formalistic in Simmel's investigations even though he is interested in the form of interrelations.

Time, space, and number

Simmel's sociological writings cover a remarkably large variety of social forms. He does, however, identify certain key dimensions that in his view apply to all social forms: temporality, spatiality, and number. Simmel does not consider time as much as the other two aspects. In his sociology, he gives space primacy over time, and in *Sociology* he devotes a whole chapter to discussing the significance of the number of participants for social formations. With regard to the priority of space over time, Matthew Lipman (1959, p. 121) has noted that 'if Bergson repeatedly asks that we admit the importance of time, Simmel is just as insistent in stressing the significance of space'. This is not all that surprising, given Simmel's emphasis on relationality. Each relation sets and assumes a space of betweenness, a space in between what is related. When two people look at each other, engage in conversation, or exchange letters, for example, their interaction presupposes and creates a space in-between, a midway across and through which the reciprocal influences must pass, though in its spatiality the between is more like a non-site rather than a particular localizable place with exact coordinates. It refers to the movement from pillar to post.

Contrasting temporalities of life and form

While Simmel did not treat time as extensively and explicitly as space and number, he nevertheless did pay some attention to it.[2] We have already noted that especially in his early work Simmel was preoccupied with the problem of history. In *The Problems of the Philosophy of History*, Simmel suggests that history is a temporal sequence into which the knowing subject orders singular events according to certain apriorities of knowledge. What is more, temporality is also implied in the language of flows and fluxes of life-philosophy. In his life-philosophy, where the contrast and interplay between timeless form and fleeting, restless, and ever-renewing life occupies the centre stage, Simmel also addresses time and temporality in very explicit terms. In *The View of Life*, he contends that: 'Time is real for life alone' ([1918] GSG 16, p. 221; 2010, p. 8). It is only in the life of the individual that the no-more of the past is united in the present with the not-yet of the future. It is in large part through memory (besides objects that persist) that our past is able to continue to exist in the present, and thus personal identity for Simmel ([1918] GSG 16; 2010) is to be understood in a temporal sense.

The idea of the divergent rhythms of life and forms is without doubt developed to the fullest in Simmel's life-philosophy in such books as *Rembrandt* and *The View of Life*, but it is already present in *Sociology*. Towards the end of the book, Simmel remarks that 'a basic dualism [...] pervades the fundamental form of all association': 'a relation, which is a fluctuating, constantly developing life-process, nevertheless receives a relatively stable external form'. The two, 'relation and form, have different tempi of development'; forms, '[w]hether they are the forms of individual or social life, [...] do not flow as our inner development does, but always remain fixed over a certain period of time' ([1908] GSG 11, p. 659; 1971, pp. 351–2; translation altered).

What is more, according to Simmel, it is possible to consider social forms – just as concepts, technologies, works of art, moral imperatives – with respect to their objective meaning, which they possess in themselves irrespective of historical actualities. In their timeless validity, they are independent of whether they are actualized a thousand times or not even once, or when and by whom they may be actualized. However, social forms are no Platonic Ideas, but they appear only in and through historically mutable and changeable contents. The eternal aspect of forms is thus considered by Simmel as something that dwells within the transience of life and human experience.

Aside from the contrast of the eternal and the transient, it is in particular in relation to modernity that Simmel addresses temporality in his sociology. He understands modernity as the 'temporal dissolution of everything substantial, absolute, and eternal into the flow of things, into historical mutability, into merely psychological reality' (Simmel, GSG 20, p. 304). And he associates modernity with a 'transformation of our experience of time' (Frisby 2004a, p. xxiv). It was already noted in Chapter 4 that according to Simmel fashion stands at the dividing line between past and future, thus giving us an especially strong feeling of the present. For Simmel, fashion also embodies and speeds up the ever-increasing tempo of modern life.

Sociology of space

While Simmel also paid some attention to time, his sociology of forms clearly stresses the spatial aspects of social forms over their temporality. Simmel published two essays on space and spatiality, 'Sociology of Space (orig. 'Soziologie des Raumes')' and 'On the spatial projection of social forms' (Über räumliche Projektionen socialer Formen), both of which came out in 1903. Together they constitute in a reworked form Chapter 9 'Space and the Spatial Ordering of Society' (*'Der Raum und die räumlichen Ordnungen der Gesellschaft'*) of *Sociology*. In the chapter, Simmel examines space in a twofold manner. On the one hand, he explores the sociologically relevant aspects of space and, on the other, he considers the effects of social forms on space.

As his starting point Simmel refers to Kant's definition of space as 'the possibility of being together', that is, of co-existing side by side. But this does not mean that the social is materially determined. Rather, according to Simmel, space is a *wirkungslose Form*, a form without effects ([1908] GSG 11, p. 687): while space appears as an inevitable context for social relations – because *Wechselwirkungen* are inevitably located somewhere, contained in some space and also assuming a spatial form – Simmel stresses that space determines neither the social form that relations take nor their course. It merely provides conditions of possibility for the emergence of social relations, and thus its effect remains only 'formal'. For Simmel, space is a sociological phenomenon in that only social relations – and mental activities and phenomena like language – make space legible and meaningful to us. Yet he admits that space also has a reality of its own that is irreducible to the social. Simmel's overall position with regard to space, as Frank Lechner (1991, p. 196) has suggested, lies thus 'somewhere between spatial determinism and social constructionism'.

Simmel identifies all in all five relevant aspects of space for social relations. The first is the *exclusivity* of space ([1908] GSG 11, p. 690). Simmel suggests that social configurations vary in the extent to which they require exclusive occupation of 'their' space. He uses nation-states and the Catholic church as examples of opposite sides of the spectrum, with nation-states as an example of spatially exclusive communities, organized as clearly demarcated self-enclosed territorial units, and the Catholic church of a more or less indifferent relation to a particular area or place.

As the second relevant aspect of space for social relationships Simmel mentions the *boundary*. By setting boundaries space can be divided and partitioned for practical needs and uses. Simmel emphasizes the socially produced nature of boundaries: 'The boundary is not a spatial fact with sociological consequences, but a sociological fact that forms itself spatially' ([1908] GSG 11, p. 697). In addition, Simmel suggests that, sociologically, a boundary expresses a unique kind of interaction: the parties involved affect each other by setting a boundary, but at the same time this very boundary keeps them from affecting each other. Establishing a boundary is thus an effect-preventing effect. According to Simmel, the significance of spatial boundaries for a community or group is analogous to the significance of the picture frame for a work of art: much like the frame makes the work of art a self-enclosed whole separated from the surrounding world, boundaries constitute the group closed within them as self-dependent and subject to its own laws ([1908] GSG 11, p. 694). Simmel claims that the extensity of the space framed by boundaries has a positive relation to the intensity of social relations; boundaries render any social order into a more integrated and more strongly experienced whole. Order is created by establishing boundaries. A borderline needs to be set to establish order within and close it off from the disorder of the outside. Therefore society or, more exactly, a nation-state, for example, can be 'characterized as inwardly homogeneous because its sphere of existence is enclosed in acutely conscious boundaries; and conversely, the reciprocal unity and functional relationship of every element to every other one gains its spatial expression in the enclosing boundary' ([1908] GSG 11, p. 694; 1997a, p. 141). However, besides being a prerequisite of order, spatial boundaries also lend 'greater clarity to conflictual relations. Partitioning thus influences relations within and across boundaries' (Lechner, 1991, p. 197).

The third spatial variable of social relations examined by Simmel is *fixity* ([1908] GSG 11, p. 705). Space has the capacity to fix the contents of social formations. Simmel suggests that the extent to which groups or some of their individual members are spatially fixed or remain spatially indeterminate has an effect on the structure of the groups. And he notes that fixity may assume several forms:

(1) It may vary from configurations tying individuals to a particular place (e.g. a prison cell) to configurations that make the actual simultaneous presence of individuals in a particular place more or less indispensable (e.g. science).

(2) Activities may be centred on a specific place (e.g. the marketplace as the physical central point of commerce and trade).
(3) Spatial fixedness may also occur by momentarily gathering otherwise independent and separate elements together in a certain place (e.g. into a train, supermarket, hotel, or church).
(4) The individuation of places, for example by naming and numbering streets and houses.

The fourth relevant spatial aspect is *distance* ([1908] GSG 11, p. 716). According to Simmel, all social relations could in principle be arranged on a scale according to the extent of spatial proximity or distance that a configuration either tolerates or demands. For example, such emotional relationships as friendship and love that come with sensuous closeness tend to require and manifest physical proximity (see next section), whereas objective, rational, and impersonal relations demand and display greater distance (in both the spatial and mental sense). The latter are relatively indifferent to that which is spatially close, or they may not even tolerate closeness at all, though they may also bring spatially distant matters and people close to each other (we can think of the ability of money to connect and span distance, for example). The contrast and mixture of bodily proximity and mental distance reaches its culmination in the space of the metropolis, where one may not recognize by sight even one's neighbours (Simmel, [1903] GSG 7, p. 123; 1971, p. 331).

Fifth, and finally, *movement* through space is sociologically significant as well ([1908] GSG 11, p. 748). Mobile groups differ considerably from groups and communities that are fixed to a certain place. Groups vary also with regard to whether the whole community or only some of its members are mobile. As two typical communal forms of being on the move, Simmel mentions nomadism and migration. While for nomadism 'wandering is part of the substance of life, as marked by the endlessness and the circularity of the return to the same place again and again', for mass-scale migrations of people, moving is only an intermediate state between more or less stable or static states. Simmel notes that mobility tends to be coupled with low internal differentiation and high integration of the group. He also mentions the strange momentary closeness felt by fellow travellers, when one is away from home.

In the latter part of the chapter 'Space and the Spatial Ordering of Society' Simmel explores the effects of *Wechselwirkungen* on space and how groups use space. He distinguishes between four different aspects of spatial configurations of social formations. The first is the *organization of space according to social organization*. Simmel suggests that social ordering usually also involves spatial organization. Political and economic organizations, particularly, rely visibly on the ordering of space. The organization of space reflects the aim of these organizations to organize things in a more mechanical, rational, and political manner; and, in the process, space itself becomes mechanically, rationally, and politically organized. Second, the *control of space* is an essential part of domination of the people located in that space. Let us only think of a factory, a school, or a state. Yet another example is provided by the model of the 'panopticon' by the British reformist Jeremy Bentham (and famously discussed by Michel Foucault in his book *Discipline and Punish* ([1975] 1991)). Bentham's panopticon was a design of a prison that would allow total surveillance of its inmates. Architecturally, it was a machine of visibility: large, panoramic windows of the central tower gave a view to the cells, situated in a circular building surrounding the tower. Because of having both an inner and an outer window each cell would be backlit to enable constant visibility and observation of the inmates. As the third aspect Simmel explores *localization* as an expression of social bonds. Such social formations as a family, club, administration, university, and religious community are housed in particular buildings. Besides offering a visual representation for the existence of these communities, the buildings also provide them with solidity and stability. The existence of more free-floating associations, by contrast, is much more feeble and precarious. Fourth, and finally, *empty space* appears as a mediator or expression of social relations: it can serve as a neutral territory for commerce or for solving conflicts; it may appear as a protective wilderness or desert; and it may also designate an area not yet seized but which is potentially up for grabs. Simmel also mentions that within a crowd an empty space may offer one a protective reserve.

The dyad and the triad

Simmel has shown more explicitly than perhaps any other author that the nature of social formations is dependent on the number of elements involved. In the second chapter of *Sociology*, 'The Quantitative Determination of Groups' ('Die quantitative Bestimmtheit der Gruppe'), he suggests that there exists an explicit correlation between the form and size of social configurations. While a clear distinction can be detected also between the forms of small groups and those of large groups, Simmel contends that it is only in the *Wechselwirkung* between two elements, which he terms the 'dyad' (*Zweizahl*), and that of three, the 'triad' (*Dreizahl*), that the quantitative determination can be specified in numerical terms. And thus they are of primary significance.

Sociologically, the interplay and dynamics between the dyadic relation and the 'third' is highly interesting and important in that it provides us with the elementary algebra of social relations.[3] Simmel regards the 'society of two' (*Gesellschaft zu zweien*) as the beginning of sociality ([1908] GSG 8, p. 348). (It should be noted that the term 'society' does not refer here to a societal whole, but it designates a relation, the 'unity of one human being with another' ([1908] GSG 11, p. 44). The dyad is for him the most rudimentary and basic constellation of social relations.[4] As a sociological unit, the dyad is, according to Simmel, even simpler and more basic than a unit consisting of just one person (*Einzahl*) ([1908] GSG 11, p. 124). This is because connectedness via relations always precedes the ostensible non-relation of 'being-alone'. And therefore even being-alone is essentially 'being-with-others'. Being-alone is not the sheer absence of social relations but their presence which is then removed: in being-alone, the presence and influence of others is merely turned from actual into 'ideal'.[5] Simmel himself does not mention this explicitly, but past face-to-face interactions may echo in the present, for example when one has internalized the voice of the other (e.g. parent, PhD supervisor, therapist, critic) and engages in semantic interaction with it within the self. Being-alone is thus not a way of being without any relations to others, like in being the only person on the face of the earth. On the contrary, being-alone is a relation in itself, a form of interaction in which the other party is no longer actually present after having real effects on the person ([1908] GSG 11, p. 96). Being-with constitutes the being of individuals. It is nothing added to being; it is no supplement, but being is always already given as being-with.

However, while emphasizing the primacy of the dyad, Simmel also insists that we can fully understand the dynamics of social relations only when we add a third element to the dyad. And, for Simmel, a third element also completes the whole picture; in a way it saturates the sociological universe in the sense that no further additions are necessary to depict the dynamics of sociality; one can manage with just three. According to him, any further expansion to the formations of four, ten, 100, 100,000, and so on does not modify our relations to the same extent ([1908] GSG 11, pp. 117–18). Therefore, the contrast between the dyad and the third is fundamental for Simmel. In their interplay, the spectrum of social relations is played out in its full complexity.

Importantly, Simmel stresses that the difference between the dyad and the triad is not only quantitative, meaning that it does not have to do only with the fact that the latter involves more participants, but it is also qualitative. The triad differs from the dyad significantly by its degree of objectivity and also in terms of stability and dynamics.

As regards the difference in the degree of objectivity, the addition of the third produces 'a completely new formation' ([1908] GSG 11, p. 121): a supra-individual social whole ([1908] GSG 8, p. 349), an 'independent, supra-individual unity' ([1908] GSG 11, p. 101). Whereas in the twosome the individuals are confronted only by one another (I encounter a you to whom I am a you), with the arrival of the third they may have a relation also with the relation itself. The third is thus a source of objectivity that indicates the threshold of a social fact in the Durkheimian sense – that is, of a formation independent of the individual. The greater independence makes the triad, in principle, much more objective and durable than the dyad. It provides the twosome a wider, solidifying 'social frame' ([1908] GSG 11, p. 115).

By looking at the dynamics of bivalent and trivalent constellations, Simmel is thereby able to account for how the social as a 'thing', both collective and objective, emerges. (This is clearly what Durkheim fails to explain with his notion of the social. For him, the social, as external to individuals and endowed with coercive power, appears as already made.) The third also marks the threshold of group dynamics.[6] The arrival of the third produces at least five types of constellations that are not possible in the relations between two individuals:

(1) Alliance: unlike in the triad, in the dyad no majority can be built up to 'outvote' an individual (Krackhardt, 1999, p. 185).
(2) Supra-individuality: vis-à-vis the dyad, the triad means reduced individuality. The dyad is able to preserve the individuality of the partners to a much greater extent, as it does not build up 'any higher unity above its individual elements' (Simmel, [1908] GSG 11, p. 106), but 'relies immediately on the one and the other' ([1908] GSG 11, p. 101).
(3) In the case of a conflict between the two parties, the third can play the part of an 'impartial' (*Unparteiische*) or act as act as a 'mediator' (*Vermittler*) helping them to negotiate ([1908] GSG 11, p. 125).[7] Conflicts are thus more readily managed and resolved in triads than in dyads (Krackhardt, 1999, p. 185). While the dyad presents the first embodiment, not only of synthesis and unification, but also of separation and antithesis, Simmel contends that the third brings a 'crossing, reconciliation, rejection of absolute contrast' (Simmel, [1908] GSG 11, p. 124). It is, according to him, precisely the third that presents the 'type' and the 'schema' of the mediator; all the other cases of mediation are in the final analysis reducible to it.[8] And, as for the position of the 'mediator', Simmel holds that there is no social formation of more than two participants in which mediation would not play a part ([1908] GSG 11, pp. 125–9).
(4) While the impartial and the mediator appear as benevolent, in the sense that they wish to contribute to the cohesion of the parties, the third may also seek egoistic interests and try to benefit from the conflict among the two. For Simmel, the third appears in this constellation as a *tertius gaudens*, 'rejoicing third' (Ger. *der lachende Dritte*), who takes advantage of the conflict between the two parties ([1908] GSG 11, p. 134).
(5) Finally, the fifth type of constellation could be described as a situation of *divida et impera*, 'divide-and-conquer' ([1908] GSG 11, p. 143). Like in the constellation involving a *tertius gaudens*, in that of *divida et impera* the third appears as malevolent and benefits from the disunion of the other two. The difference between the rejoicing third and the divide-and-conquer, however, is that whereas the former pertains to situations where the two parties already stand in conflict, in the latter they are disunited precisely by the effect of the third.

Accordingly, it is not surprising that many commentators have argued that it is only just the triad and not yet the dyad that marks the threshold of the social in Simmel's work (e.g. Litt, 1926, p. 114; Freund, 1976, p. 9). However, things are not quite as simple as that. While the third marks the threshold of the societal milieu, to which the dyadic relation between the I and the you is always connected and which bears on the relation, the third may carry its effects only in relation to the relationship between the two. Hence, neither simply the dyad nor the triad can be regarded as the basic unit of the social or as the most elementary relation, since each appears mutually dependent on the other: the possibility of the dyad is conditioned by the third, and the actions of the third, in turn, always already presuppose the dyad. Or, the dyad may be the simplest social formation, as Simmel suggests, but only insofar as it is made possible and produced by the exclusion of the third.

So, the paradox of the dyad (and this is a paradox that Simmel, as I see it, does not fully recognize) is that the dyad is simultaneously made possible and impossible by the third. As he assumes that the third automatically takes a personified human form, Simmel fails to notice that already the relation in-between the associated two elements presents a third. In order for there to be two, there has to be a relation connecting them, yet as soon as it connects it becomes a middle term between the partners through which their reciprocal give-and-take must pass. What is more, when two people communicate they never merely interact with one another, but the event of communication is grounded in accepting and relying on a complex network of rules and other kinds of presuppositions. If I disregarded, say, grammatical rules, my speech would quite likely be simply incomprehensible to the other. However, as soon as a third is present, it intervenes. For example, a channel that is used to transmit messages works properly only as long as it disappears into immediacy. It becomes visible only when it does not work. As Michel Serres writes about it: 'If it is there, if it exists, that means that it failed' (Serres, 2007, p. 79). The example suggests two significant things. First, there are many more thirds out there than just our fellow humans. Non-human or more-than-human thirds are implicated in every relation. Second, in order for the dyad to be possible, the 'between' must at the same time be included (for there to be I and/with you) and excluded as a third (for there to be two and only two). The only way two can be together is via a third *and* simultaneously excluding that third. Thus, the bivalent algebra of relations is always already trivalent. For the dyad, the third is its condition of possibility and impossibility.

Friendship, love, and the stranger

The 'between' necessarily inscribed in the dyadic relation (for otherwise the parties would fuse together and form a common substance, and in a situation like that there could not be any relation between them, but they would literally be 'one') also refers to a key dualism of all relations: that between *proximity* and *distance*. Donald N. Levine (1959, p. 23) has correctly pointed out that, for Simmel, 'distance is the main dimension in social life': in topics like secrecy, the stranger, value, the pauper, and super- and subordination, as well as in the sociology of space, distance plays a significant role as a theme. The relevance of distance/proximity is thereby not restricted to the sociology of space alone, but it is a key dimension structuring all human relations. Simmel ([1908] GSG 11, p. 717) stresses that, in principle, all social relations can be analysed in terms of spatial and psychological distance/proximity.[9] This is most evident in the knowledge of one another required in relationships. According to Simmel, 'our relationships [...] develop upon the basis of reciprocal knowledge' ([1908] GSG 11, p. 385; 1950, p. 309). All our relations with fellow humans are thus based on the fact that we know something about one another. Without such knowledge many of our relations would be utterly impossible; in order to be able to interact with someone one needs to know with whom one is interacting. ([1908] GSG 11, p. 383; 1950, p. 307) Yet at the same time '[o]ne can never know another person *absolutely*' ([1908] GSG 11, p. 384; 1950, p. 308). The you whom I face is bound to remain to some extent distant and separate from me. This places high significance on 'confidence' (*Vertrauen*).[10] Simmel depicts trust or confidence as 'intermediate between knowledge and ignorance about a man [sic]' ([1908] GSG 11, p. 393; 1950, p. 318). It is needed only in a situation of incomplete knowledge: a 'person who knows completely need not trust'. At the same time, however, trust assumes at least a minimum of knowledge, since a 'person who knows nothing can, on no rational grounds, afford even confidence' ([1908] GSG 11, p. 393; 1950, p. 318). Simmel suggests that modern life is based upon trust and confidence to a much larger extent than is usually realized. He takes up the economy and science as his examples: the former has increasingly become a 'credit economy', and in the latter scholars need to trust the results of others, for they must use their studies without always being able to examine in the minutest detail how they have been produced ([1908] GSG 11, p. 389; 1950, p. 313).

While all relations are structured along the axis of proximity and distance, they differ to the extent of how strongly they are articulated in relation to it. Natàlia Cantó-Milà (2016, p. 87) makes a very useful distinction between forms for which proximity/distance is merely one axis among others and those which are 'primarily articulated in relation to this axis'. The forms mainly structured along the axis of proximity and distance include, for example, friendship, love, and the stranger.

Friendship and love are located at a different end of the continuum between proximity and distance than the stranger. The ideal of friendship, at least to the extent that it is received from antiquity, and the notion of romantic love both strive for absolute psychological (*seelische*) closeness. Simmel remarks that this closeness may in fact be more easily attainable in friendship than in love, for it is not centred so one-sidedly on a certain dimension of the relationship as love tends to be. Yet he also admits that for many people erotic enjoyment may clear the way for sides of the relationship and personality which otherwise would have remained latent or hidden: in love, a person can give oneself entirely and unreservedly, as it were. Nevertheless, due to increased differentiation among people, absolute closeness may be ever more difficult to attain. Simmel suggests that modern personalities may be too uniquely individualized to allow for complete intimacy, and thus modern sensibility favours differentiated friendships, which cover only a part of the personality. Our friendships 'connect us with one individual in terms of affection, with another, in terms of common intellectual aspects, with a third, in terms of religious impulses, and with a fourth, in terms of common experiences'. Modern friendship is thereby a 'very special type of friendship', in which the tension between proximity and distance is very much present (Simmel, [1908] GSG 11, p. 401; 1950, p. 326).

While in friendship and love the relationship seeks to overcome all distance, the stranger presents a relation in which distance is dominant over proximity (Cantó-Milà, 2016). Simmel discusses the stranger in one of his best-known texts, 'The Stranger' ('Exkurs über den Fremden'). It appears in *Sociology* as part of a chapter on the sociology of space. With the help of the figure of the stranger Simmel examines movement through space. The stranger is a 'third' between wandering and fixation to a given point in space. Unlike the wanderer, 'who comes today and leaves tomorrow', the stranger is, as it were, 'the *potential* wanderer: although he [sic] has not moved on, he [sic] has not quite overcome the freedom of coming and going' ([1908] GSG 11, p. 764; 1950, p. 402). As long as the stranger who has arrived among us remains a stranger, s/he does not shed this in-between position.

The position of the stranger in whatever community or group is determined by the fact that s/he does not belong to it originally, but comes from the outside, from elsewhere, and thereby 'imports qualities into it which do not and cannot stem from the group itself' ([1908] GSG 11, p. 765; 1950, p. 402). And, as long as one remains a stranger, one is imbued with otherness and difference despite all similarity and hospitality. There is always something disturbing, alien, and thus also intrusive in the stranger. Intrusiveness cannot be extracted from the being of the stranger. If disturbance and intrusion are excluded, the stranger either stops being a stranger or becomes excluded.

Nevertheless, importantly, the figure of the stranger is characterized not so much by distance in itself, but by a particular 'unity of nearness and remoteness' ([1908] GSG 11, p. 765; 1950, p. 402). The stranger presents a tension and paradoxical synthesis between proximity and distance; strangeness is the proximity of someone remote. The stranger does not simply stand outside the community, but being a stranger is a 'specific form of interaction' ([1908] GSG 11, p. 765; 1950, p. 402).[11] The stranger is at once within and outside the community, included only in as far as being excluded. S/he belongs only by not belonging. Thereby the figure of the stranger makes visible the boundary between the inside and the outside of the community. Against much cherished Western political utopias no community can be absolutely inclusive. The constitution of community relies on drawing a dividing line between the inside and the outside. A border needs to be set up to establish order within and close it off from the disorder of the outside; a completely open, inclusive community without any exclusion could not survive. Order is possible on the condition that chaos is excluded, while chaos, of course, exists only in relation to order and exclusion. To maintain order, the gesture of exclusion has to be repeated incessantly, again and again.

For Simmel, it was above all the Jew who embodied the figure of the stranger. Throughout economic history 'the stranger everywhere appears as the trader, or the trader as stranger' ([1908] GSG 11, p. 765; 1950 p. 403). A trader is required when the social circles grow, accompanied by the rise of industrial production and markets: when products originate outside the spatially narrow group, an intermediary is needed to make them available. The stranger-merchant differs from the landowner in that his or her property is not tied to a place, but it is of the most mobile kind: money. However, the state of being a stranger might also be said to form the general mode of being in the city. Being urban amounts to sharing mutual strangeness. Lynn H. Lofland (1985) has suggested that life in the city is life shared with strangers. In a city, people know personally nothing about the vast majority of others with whom they share this space. While one is aware of the existence of numeral others as an aggregate, as it were, one does not know their names, personal histories, hopes, dreams, or fears. The city, then, is a world of strangers, a world populated by persons who are personally unknown to one another (p. 3).

In our contemporary world, the figure of the stranger is embodied, sadly, by refugees. Refugees are not perceived as singular individuals, but more or less as a non-individuated homogeneous mass. Simmel maintains that a person is categorized as a stranger not due to his or her individual properties, but from outside, in relation to 'us'. As regards the position of the refugee in relation to us, the category is most homogeneous. However, from within it is utterly heterogeneous insofar as it contains the most varied fates and life-histories. Strangers have in common merely the fact that they are others, not-us. Being (classified as) a stranger is based merely on 'the strangeness of origin', that is, on the fact that the person does not belong to the community originally ([1908] GSG 11, p. 770; 1950, p. 407).

One way of presenting the difference between anti-immigrant hate groups and individuals and groups who express hospitality by welcoming the refugees is to focus on their relation to refugees on the axis of proximity and distance. In the relation of the latter to the refugee-strangers proximity dominates over distance. The former, by contrast, perceive the refugees primarily under the category of distance and also seek to preserve distance to them, whereas those who are willing to give refugees a place hold that we need to be responsible, express solidarity, and care also for those whom we may not know personally and not only for those who are familiar and the closest to us, because universal human rights belong to all. Nativist and vigilante individuals and groups, by contrast, tend to deny refugees all universal human properties. It is also not uncommon that in public media discourse refugees are spoken of by using such negative naturalistic metaphors as the 'flow of refugees' or the 'flood of migrants' that liken the people to uncontrollable natural phenomena. For the anti-immigrant groups the strangeness of migrants renounces all commonness between 'us' and 'them'. Because the stranger is not considered to be one of 'us', the groups refuse all contact with him or her.

Nevertheless, it is important to understand that ultimately strangeness is no fixed quality of this or that person, such as refugee or foreigner, nor even a fixed position, but it is context-dependent. One is defined as a stranger not by oneself, but from the outside and by others, in relation to an in-group, 'us'. However, Simmel suggests that strangeness is not merely a relative state of affairs or a social construction, but it can also be understood in an ontological sense as an integral part of what it is to be human. Strangeness is present even in our most intimate relationships and is part of what constitutes subjectivity. As Simmel writes in one of his most beautiful and tragic formulations:

> The fact that the human being is, in one's most passionate needs, dependent on the being from whom one is separated by perhaps the deepest metaphysical gap is the purest, possibly even the archetypical form of the loneliness which makes the human being ultimately a stranger [*Fremdling*] not only amongst all the beings in the world, but also amongst those who are the closest to him or her. ([1909] GSG 12, p. 48)

The insolvable tension between proximity and distance that is characteristic of being a stranger is thus constitutive of our relations both to others and to ourselves.

Sociability

As I have already noted, Simmel sees it as the task of sociology to study the principles on which the unity of society rests. This is to focus on the relations between individuals and on their various forms of being with, for, in, against, and through one another. To the end of analysing association (*Vergesellschaftung*), 'sociability' (*Geselligkeit*) presents itself it as an ideal object. At the first meeting of the German Sociological Association held in October 1910 in Frankfurt, Simmel gave a talk titled 'Soziologie der Geselligkeit', which appeared in print in the following year in the conference proceedings and was later translated by Everett C. Hughes into English as 'The Sociology of Sociability' in *The*

American Journal of Sociology in 1949. Simmel also incorporated the piece in a slightly revised form into the book *Grundfragen der Soziologie*, published in 1917, where it appears as its third chapter, titled 'Die Geselligkeit (Beispiel der Reinen oder Formalen Soziologie)' ('Sociability (An Example of Pure or Formal Sociology)'). As the part of the chapter title placed within parentheses suggests, for Simmel sociability stands above all as an example of his sociology of forms. It also offers a symbol of the art of conducting sociological research fashioned by Simmel with his programme of sociology (Simmel, [1917] GSG 16, p. 84).

By sociability Simmel means a sociable gathering that serves no exterior purposes but is its own end. In sociability, 'that which is otherwise pure form of interaction is its own self-sufficient content' (Simmel, [1911] GSG 12, pp. 188–9; 1971, p. 137). Sociability is driven by an impulse to be with others for the sake of sociability itself, and it is characterized 'by a feeling for, by a satisfaction in, the very fact that one is associated with others, and that the solitariness of the individual is resolved into togetherness, a union with others' ([1911] GSG 12, p. 178; 1971, p. 128). Sociability is thus a *pure form* that is self-purposive; it 'has no ulterior end, no content, and no result outside itself' ([1911] GSG 12, p. 180; 1971, p. 130). Out of the realities of social life it 'distils' association as such. However, it is not that the content of sociable conversation, for example, would be completely irrelevant; on the contrary, 'it must be interesting, gripping, even significant' ([1911 GSG 12, p. 188; 1971, p. 136). Nevertheless, a sociable conversation is had not for the sake of some external goal (e.g. the task of producing truth or reaching an agreement on a decision), but only for the sake of the relation, for the purpose of interaction. The whole value and significance of whatever topic lies in how it feeds the play of sociable conversation.

This also means that whenever people engage in interaction for the sake of objective content, as in the case of, say, business transaction, sociability is not the guiding principle of the relation. In content-driven relationships, contact, exchange, and conversation become instrumental, means to achieve some external end, while in sociability they are ends in themselves. Besides excluding external, objective purpose, in sociable interaction the participants also need to renounce purely and deeply personal qualities. 'It is tactless to bring in personal humour, good or ill, excitement and depression, the light and shadow of one's inner life' ([1911] GSG 12, p. 181; 1971, p. 131). According to Simmel, sociability thus has two boundaries or thresholds, an upper and a lower one: the participants need to abstain both from purely objective contents and goals and from overly personal qualities, egoistic interests, and individual impulses ([1911] GSG 12, p. 182; p. 132). Simmel suggests that sociability offers a refuge or safe haven from the overburdening objectivity of modern life: while 'modern life is overburdened with objective content and material demands' ([1911] GSG 12, p. 184; 1971, p. 133), in a sociable gathering we are able to rid ourselves of this burden.

Simmel contends that its focus on form, dissolved of all specific contents, makes sociability comparable to art and play, both of which draw their form and essential themes from the contents of reality but nevertheless leave the reality of those contents behind them ([1911] GSG 12, p. 177; 1971, p. 128). Much as art reduces the realities of life into symbols and play receives its cheerfulness by being freed of all substance and the seriousness of life, sociability draws its substance from numerous varieties of serious relationships among individuals and yet elevates that substance to the level of symbolic playfulness. For Simmel, 'Sociability is, then, the *play-form of association*. It is related to the content-determined concreteness of association as art is related to reality' ([1911] GSG 12, p. 180; 1971, p. 130). Importantly, sociability is a play form that is not only played *in* society, but what is played in sociability is precisely *society itself* ([1911] GSG 12, p. 185; 1971, p. 134): it is a *form of forms* that draws from, employs, and plays at various forms of association. According to Simmel, 'only the sociable gathering is "society" without qualifying adjectives' ([1911] GSG 12, p. 180; 1971, p. 129).

Besides having aesthetic motives, for Simmel sociability is also of ethical significance. In his view, sociability presents 'an ideal sociological world, for in it [...] the pleasure of the individual is always dependent upon the joy of others' ([1911] GSG 12, p. 183; 1971, p. 132; translation altered). In sociability, no one can have his/her satisfaction at the cost of others, but one can win sociable values such as joy, relief, and vivacity only provided that and insofar as others win them as well. Sociability has thus a 'democratic structure' ([1911] GSG 12, p. 183; 1971, p. 132): the rights of others require that the participants regulate their egoistic interests and individual impulsiveness. The democratic structure also leaves aside the participants' social position. As Simmel writes of this:

> In sociability, whatever the personality has of objective importance, of features which have their orientation toward something outside the circle, must not interfere. Riches and social position, learning and fame, exceptional capacities and merits of the individual have no role in sociability or, at most, as a slight nuance of that immateriality with which alone reality dares penetrate into the artificial structure of sociability. ([1911] GSG 12, p. 181; 1971, p. 130)

So, Simmel suggests that in sociable interaction the participants are equal, for no one can benefit in it at the expense of others. Or, more exactly, he writes that sociability 'is a game in which one "acts" as though all were equal' ([1911] GSG 12, p. 184; 1971, pp. 133–4). The participants may not be equal in the real world, but they nevertheless need to appear as such; any differences in wealth and class, for instance, must be disregarded and denounced *in situ*.

From the various social forms analysed by Simmel in his work, two in particular bear an intimate relationship to sociability. One is coquetry or flirtation. According to Simmel, it 'finds in sociability its lightest, most playful, and yet its widest realization' ([1911] GSG 12, p. 185; 1971, p. 134). Flirtation is a form of 'ironic play with which eroticism has distilled the pure essence of its interaction out from its substantive or individual content'. While sociability plays at and with the forms of association, flirtation 'plays out the forms of eroticism'. ([1911] GSG 12, p. 187; 1971, p. 135) Flirtation is a play of simultaneous consent and denial, yes and no. In flirtation, one lets the other hang on the verge of getting what he or she wants without letting it become too serious.

Another Simmelian social form actualizing itself as a sociable gathering is the meal (or, literally, 'meal-time' (*Malhzeit*)). The meal connects the sheer the physiology of eating with sociality, that is, 'with a frequency of being together, with a habit of being gathered together' (Simmel, [1910] GSG 12, p. 140; 1997a, p. 130). The sociality of the meal thus designates a triumph over the naturalism of eating ([1910] GSG 12, pp. 142, 147): in the meal, people are not gathered together merely for the purpose of eating, but togetherness is sought also as a value in its own right ([1910], p. 144; 1997a, p. 133). Thereby, the meal 'permits the merely physical externality of feeding […] to rest upon the principle of an infinitely higher ranking order' ([1910] GSG 12, p. 142; 1997a, p. 131). Simmel suggests that the more the meal is about being together, the more the naturalism of eating loses its significance vis-à-vis sociable and aesthetic values. Stylization and aesthetics are crucial for the meal, as we can detect in the well-ordered setting, ornamentation, and table manners, for example. Simmel contends that 'in so far as the meal becomes a sociological matter, it arranges itself in a more aesthetic, stylized and supra-individually regulated form' ([1910] GSG 12, p. 142; 1997a, p. 131). The sociable aspect of the meal brings in aesthetic stylization which affects how we set the table, use knife and fork, gnaw the food, and even what are considered as appropriate topics for conversation at a meal.[12]

The meal also illustrates well that while sociability presents a self-purposive, pure form, distilled out of specific contents, it cannot completely cut off the threads that connect it to *life* and out of which it draws its materials. While the meal elevates us beyond the naturalism of eating, we simply cannot have a meal without any food to eat. In a like manner, when sociability is completely purified of all contents and disconnected from reality, it 'turns from play to empty farce, to a lifeless schematization' ([1911] GSG 12, p. 191; 1971, p. 139). Just as art may in and by its form reveal the depth and wholeness of life, sociability would not be able to produce the joy, relief, and satisfaction that it does if it was a sheer empty form of custom and ritual and a momentary flight from life and its seriousness.

Conclusion

Philosopher Isaiah Berlin (1953) once divided thinkers playfully into two categories: hedgehogs and foxes. While hedgehogs have one grand idea that they apply to every phenomenon, foxes refuse to boil the diversity of the world into a single defining idea, but instead come up with a new idea for each object.

To me Simmel presents a sort of 'third', a strange fox-hedgehog or hedgehog-fox hybrid, that does not fit in either one of these categories, but rather combines elements from both groups and swings between both positions. He is a hedgehog in that there is most certainly a basic formula to Simmel's manner of thinking in that he perceives phenomena in terms of contrasts and 'thirds'. What is more, the notion of form is an organizing principle that runs throughout his work. Yet Simmel does not remain the same; along with continuity his thought also shows modulation and change, and this would make him a (spiny?) fox. While he perceives the world largely through the form–content or form–life distinction, his concrete investigations do not simply bring out this one general rule or big idea, time and again, but they stay true to the surface of existence and express what is specific in and characteristic of each phenomenon. Thereby each of his analyses is also able to teach us something new and surprising.

The topics discussed in this chapter should also make it clear that Simmel's concrete sociological investigations are anything but formalistic. On the contrary, they are lively, free, and highly creative. Simmel is an adventurer in thought and an innovator of ideas. Further, importantly, contrary to the common misunderstanding of his programme of sociology, Simmel does not examine social phenomena completely irrespective of their content, but he only explores them from the perspective of their form instead of that of their content. Thereby the allegations that Simmel's own concrete sociological analyses violate his programme of sociology – which the critics lament for being too narrow (e.g. Small, 1909, p. 544; Abel, 1929, p. 44; Timasheff, 1955, p. 102) – are clearly misguided. The contents do play an active part in the forms of *Wechselwirkung*, since they often give rise to and modify the forms, and in reality the forms appear only in conjunction with contents. 'Forms can be demonstrated only in an arrangement of contents', as Tenbruck (1959, p. 75) notes. What is more, while Simmel emphasizes that forms are valid irrespective of the fact of whether they are actualized or not, he also pays attention to how certain forms have undergone changes in modernity. Friendship serves as one example. Modern friendship, as we saw, is different to previous forms of friendship. Instead of being given in advance and staying unaltered, social forms emerge and change in a process that could be termed *morphogenetic*, in which contents matter to and affect the process of formation.

Notes

1 While his analyses of fashion and money most certainly also contain sociological aspects, Simmel himself intended them above all as *philosophical* studies, as a look at just the titles of the books *Philosophie der Mode* ('Philosophy of Fashion') and *The Philosophy of Money* suggests.
2 For a detailed investigation of Simmel on time and temporality, see Scaff (2005).

3 The expression 'elementary algebra of social relations' is from Michel Callon (1998, p. 10).
4 In *Sociology*, Simmel suggests that '[t]he numerically simplest formations which in general can still be called social interactions seem to express themselves between two elements' ([1908] GSG 11, p. 96). And, a few pages later, he further elaborates on this by stating that the relation 'between two elements' is 'the methodically simplest sociological formation': 'It offers the schema, the germ and the material for innumerable formations of more members' ([1908] GSG 11, p. 100).
5 To me, what Simmel seems to intend here with the term 'ideal' approximates to the concept of the 'virtual', in the sense specified by Deleuze: 'real without being actual, ideal without being abstract'. That is, the virtual is not less real or simply a simulation of the real, but it already 'possesses a reality'. Deleuze further elaborates the notion of the virtual by distinguishing it from the 'possible'. Whereas the possible is according to him 'the opposite of the real', the virtual is not opposed to the real but only to the actual. The possible is something that either will or will not be realized. Whereas the real is in the image of the possible, to which realization only adds existence, the actualization of the virtual is creative: it invents something new. (Deleuze, 1991, pp. 96–7)
6 In a manner not dissimilar to this, Gesa Lindemann (2006) has stressed how the third marks the threshold of emergence.
7 The German term 'Vermittler' translates also as 'arbitrator', 'conciliator', 'intermediary', and 'middleman', for instance. I have chosen the translation 'mediator' for its generality; it covers all of the mentioned terms.
8 When in an impartial position, the third appears equally distant from the two parties: it may either be completely beyond and untouched by their interests and opinions or participate in both sides to the exact same extent. As for the impartiality that is required in arbitration, the third may reconcile the conflict between the two parties either by leaving the decision in their hands to reach an independent solution or by becoming a 'referee' (*Schiedsrichter*) who makes the judgement. When playing the part of a mediator, the third may either reinforce the bond between the two parties, as in the case of a common enemy against whom the two are sided (in the dyad, of course, no majority can take form that could subjugate the individual) or in that of a newborn child who consolidates the parents' relationship. Or, it may change the relation between the two parties into an indirect one, so that it is mediated by the third (again, a child may serve as an example here).
9 Or, as Simmel puts it in *The Philosophy of Money* ([1900/7] GSG 6, p. 397; 2004, p. 299), 'every human relationship consists of elements of closeness and distance'.
10 I follow here Wolff's translation, although it might be more apt to translate the German term *Vertrauen* as 'trust'. In more recent sociological scholarship, it is common to make a conceptual distinction between 'trust' and 'confidence'.
11 The dialectic of inclusion and exclusion is at play in the position of the poor, too. From a sociological perspective, as Simmel suggests in the chapter 'The Poor' in *Sociology*, poverty is essentially defined in relation to assistance. According to him, the poor are not those in destitution, but those who are given aid because they are considered to be destitute: 'The poor, as a sociological category, are not those who suffer specific deficiencies and deprivations, but those who receive assistance

or should receive it according to social norms' ([1908] GSG 11, p. 551; 1965, p. 138). The poor are thus simultaneously included in and excluded from the community. They are included insofar as assistance is given to them, and yet excluded insofar as the assistance they receive degrades them, keeps them at a distance, in an inferior position.
12 Thomas Kemple (2013a) employs and develops Simmel's ideas of the meal in a fascinating and creative manner when discussing what he calls 'the table of conviviality'.

7
Philosophy of Culture and Life

In his mature work, Simmel was primarily preoccupied with metaphysical studies. And it is above all on the notion of *life* (*Leben*) that they are centred; life amounts to his basic metaphysical principle. As Simmel notes in one of the aphorisms to be found in his journal, for him life stands in-between 'Ego and idea, subject and object, person and cosmos'. Examining life is for Simmel not only a way of thinking of the dynamics of becoming and being, but also a way of tackling the subject–world relation: 'I locate myself in the concept of life as though in the center – from there the path goes in one direction towards soul and Ego, in the other towards the Idea, the cosmos, the absolute.' (GSG 20, p. 264; 2010, p. 163)

Metaphysics may be said to have become Simmel's major interest around the year 1908, when his sociological magnum opus *Sociology* was published, though he begins to discuss metaphysical themes as early as 1902. That year he published the essay 'Tendencies in German Life and Thought Since 1870', which seeks to unify different threads of German philosophy in a new theory of life expressed in the work of Schopenhauer and Nietzsche. However, as Josef Bleicher (2007, p. 139) suggests, it is above all Goethe who stands as an important signpost in Simmel's intellectual journey from the discipline of Kant's philosophy and from parallels with neo-Kantianism to developing his metaphysics of life. According to Bleicher, Simmel's own notion of life owes much to his 'interpretation of Leben as it manifested in Goethe, as a "lived polarity"'. Besides providing an object of study, for Simmel Goethe was also 'an exemplar of a life where Leben has come to its fullest expression' (p. 140).

The crowning achievement of Simmel's metaphysics is *The View of Life* (2010; orig. *Lebensanschauung*), published posthumously in 1918, a couple of weeks after Simmel's death.[1] Simmel considered the book as his philosophical testament. Already aware of his imminent death – he had been diagnosed with liver cancer and the doctors had given him only a few weeks to live – Simmel knew that the book was definitely going to be his last one. He also felt that the book would bring his oeuvre and wisdom to completion; whatever would have followed it could not have added anything more to his work substantially (see GSG 23, pp. 1007, 1024). The title of the book, literally, 'lifeview' (*Lebensanschauung*), which is a variant of Wilhelm Dilthey's notion of *Weltanschauung*, 'worldview' (Kemple, 2007, p. 15), has to be understood in the most literal sense. Instead of presenting his personal view of life, for instance of a good or happy life, or investigating specific contents of life, in the book Simmel sets out to *view* life in the bare, that is, not only the life of the individual, but life itself, as an incessant, continuous flux.

Of course, while being an age-old philosophical question that derives at the latest from Aristotle, any speculation about 'life itself' is immediately met with extreme difficulties. Life is on the one hand the most equivocal and elusive of concepts and, on the other, far too readily reduced to genes, DNA, or organism, for instance. Accordingly, as argued by Eugene Thacker (2010, p. xv), today the notion of life has come to be caught between (quasi-)religious mysticism and scientific reductionism. It is being both fervently defended by religious groups (such as evangelical Christians and Roman Catholics objecting to abortion and stem cell research) as something 'sacred'[2] and increasingly seized by technoscience (for example with scientists exploring the human genome as well as trying to synthesize and design life). Simmel's life-philosophy (*Lebensphilosophie*) sides with neither one of these camps. While he refutes scientific reductionism – Simmel insists that life itself is irreducible to specific forms of life – his work suggests that it is equally important and necessary to abjure the mysticism and irrationalism that considers life in terms of a soul or a personalized life-force.

The importance of exploring life philosophically becomes perceptible, for instance, against the pervasive bio-political techniques of governing that take the natural life, life itself, as a target of (ontological) politics, thus breaking down, as Giorgio Agamben (1998) shows, the old distinction between *zoe* and *bios*, 'bare life' – or 'life in general' – and the political form that life takes. The chapter discusses Simmel's philosophy of life and culture in relation to the debates and problems Simmel draws his inspiration from. However, to a get a better grasp of Simmel's philosophical thought, it is first important to briefly examine his conception of philosophy. As my primary sources in this task I will use the books *Hauptprobleme der Philosophie* ('Main Problems of Philosophy') and *The Philosophy of Money*. The first is an exceptional philosophical text by Simmel in that in it he does not merely discuss particular questions of epistemology, metaphysics, aesthetics, or ethics, but examines the very nature of philosophy itself, and he touches on the matter also in the preface to *The Philosophy of Money*. After that I will engage with Simmel's life-philosophy, first in relation to its influences and then by summing up its key ideas. Simmel's life-philosophy also provides a necessary point of passage to Simmel's philosophy of culture, with which the rest of the chapter deals, as for Simmel the contrast of life and form is the motive for all cultural transformation and the ultimate grounds for culture to have a history (see [1918] GSG 16, pp. 183, 226). For Simmel, culture is above all else about the cultivation of the human being (*Mensch*). However, the cultivation of subjects is according to him only possible by cultivating objects. Objects are essential materials for the making of ourselves, and yet in modernity, so Simmel thinks, we are increasingly dominated by the objects and forms of our own creation. He conceptualizes this as the 'tragedy of culture', which refers to the widening gap between subjects and objects. I will conclude the chapter by examining how Simmel does not, however, end up in cultural pessimism, but goes beyond the tragic view with his notion of the 'individual law'.

Philosophy

While Simmel is most widely appreciated as a sociologist, he thought of himself first and foremost as a philosopher. As he expresses in his letters, he was also troubled by the fact that he was perceived especially outside Germany only as a sociologist (see e.g. GSG 22, p. 342). Reading Simmel's sociological works detached from his philosophical concerns, as has been common throughout the entire reception history, is distortive in at least two respects. First, the sociological and philosophical aspects of his thought were closely connected. As Simmel's student Albert Salomon once noted, his 'sociological studies [...] were never separated from his philosophical concerns. He became a philosopher sociologist, one and indivisible' (Salomon, [1963] 1997, pp. 93–4). Second, the separation hampers our understanding of Simmel's sociology. Bevers (1985, p. 21), for example, has argued: 'Who does not pay attention to Simmel's philosophy easily ends up in a one-sided account on form-sociology: it appears as purely ahistorical and evinces no unity.' Indeed, we cannot understand Simmel's sociology properly without paying attention to his philosophy. For example, his emphasis on process in his sociology resonates with his metaphysics of life. In many places the notion of life hovers about Simmel's conception of the social; ultimately, as we have seen, the social amounts for him to a continuous, fluctuating, and dynamic life-process.

In his early work, Simmel perceived philosophy as merely a pre-stage of scientific enquiry, a preliminary form of science (*Vorwissenschaft*) (see, e.g., Simmel, [1892] GSG 2, pp. 267–8). However, from *The Philosophy of Money* onwards he comes to provide philosophy with a much more autonomous position, and endows to it two tasks that distinguish it from specific disciplines. We could call the first task *analytical*. Simmel insists that only philosophy has as its goal to 'think without preconditions'. Therefore, as he writes in the preface to *The Philosophy of Money*, philosophy is the 'last point of cognition' ([1900/7] GSG 6, p. 9; 2004, p. 51). According to him, all knowledge is conditioned by something else, by something that orients and frames thought and defines its degree of independence. Individual disciplines can – and must – be free of some of these conditions, but only philosophy is characterized for

Simmel by the striving to go beyond all of them and study them. Of course, among others sociologists, historians, anthropologists, and physicists, too, may explore the preconditions of their disciplines. In fact, one may even argue that it is precisely *their* business and not so much that of a professional philosopher, for it is they whom the questions within their discipline primarily concern. Nevertheless, whenever scholars undertake such explorations, they momentarily abandon their roles as 'scientists' and begin to philosophize ([1910] GSG 14, p. 14). Simmel is also aware that a complete freedom from preconditions is impossible already in principle: wherever thinking begins there is necessarily already something presupposed. Each point of view appears by necessity limited; if it were not, it would not be a point of view and our consciousness would have immediate access to the world as such in its totality. However, the significance of the goal to think without preconditions is for Simmel not diminished by the impossibility of reaching it. The main thing is the striving, the orientation to transgress these preconditions ([1910] GSG 14, p. 14).

While the effort to think without presuppositions is placed, as it were, below the 'lower boundary' of other disciplines, the second task of philosophy, which can be termed *synthetic*, relates to what is located beyond the other disciplines' 'upper boundary' ([1900/7] GSG 6, p. 9; 2004, p. 51). Empirical research is striving towards exact knowledge of particular contents of the world. Yet this knowledge can never be summed up into a totality, as it is necessarily always bound to a specific viewpoint. It is, according to Simmel, the task of philosophy to supplement, with the help of its concepts and categories, scientific understanding by offering a comprehensive overall perspective – a 'world picture' (*Weltbild*) ([1900/7] GSG 6, p. 9; 2004, p. 53). Philosophy cannot therefore be separated from a certain conception of totality for Simmel. He argues that even when concerned with a 'special problem of logic or ethics, or aesthetics or religion', a philosopher thinks about these problems as a philosopher 'only if the relationship to the totality of being is a living element in his [sic] discussion' ([1910] GSG 14, p. 17). A philosopher is thus not primarily concerned with single items or states of the world, but with the totality of existence.

In *Hauptprobleme der Philosophie*, Simmel emphasizes yet another distinctive feature of philosophy. What distinguishes philosophy from other disciplines is that while physics, for example, hardly takes physics as its first object, and philology does not ask primarily the nature of philology, one of the main and primary concerns of philosophy is philosophy itself:

> Alone in philosophy, every original thinker determines not only what he [sic] wants to answer but also what he [sic] wants to ask – not only in the sense of asking particular questions but in that of asking what he [sic] altogether has to ask in order to match the concept of philosophy. ([1910] GSG 14, p. 15)

For Simmel, this is the root of philosophy's dispersal – both the incompatibility of schools and the strong attachment to philosophers' personalities. However, from the fact that philosophical problems and, even more essentially, philosophy itself as a problem are defined again and again within the practice of doing philosophy follows that philosophy cannot be defined from outside and before engaging in practising philosophy. Instead, what philosophy is can be specified only from within. This endows philosophy with a certain inner freedom: philosophy is characterized by 'the inner autonomy of a thinking process' ([1910] GSG 14, p. 14). Simmel considers philosophy as living thought or thinking life – philosophy is thinking becoming life and life assuming the form of thinking. Although the various doctrines in philosophy may differ as to their contents, what they have in common is for him the fact that their results are born in and through an autonomous process of thought. Accordingly, in *Hauptprobleme der Philosophie*, Simmel examines the practice of philosophy as an 'inner process'. He sees that only rarely has the nature of philosophy as practice been acknowledged, let alone examined philosophically. It is much more common to focus on the sublime results of philosophy – that is, to crystallized ideas and systems that, in their logically enclosed form, keep the widest possible distance to the living process of thought ([1910] GSG 14, p. 11). In contrast to such an approach, Simmel sets out in *Hauptprobleme der Philosophie* to 'enliven' philosophical systems, to show their 'inner life' ([1910] GSG 14, p. 12). This is to 'turn from the metaphysics as dogma to the metaphysics as life' ([1910] GSG 14, p. 165) – an endeavour intimately connected with his own life-philosophy.

The background of Simmel's life-philosophy: Goethe, Schopenhauer, Nietzsche, and Bergson

Simmel extracts the notion of life for his own work from the German tradition of life-philosophy (*Lebensphilosophie*) as well as from French vitalism. For Simmel, life is the key category of the modern worldview. Life-philosophy and vitalism are 'imbued with a modern sense of life' ([1918] GSG 16, pp. 198–9; 1997a, p. 85). In the essay 'Eros, Platonic and Modern', he states:

> [T]he dynamic vital character of the modern life-feeling [...] is manifest to us as a form of the movement of life, consumed in a continuous flux in spite of all persistence and faithfulness, and adhering to a rhythm that is always new. ([1923] GSG 20, p. 179; 1971, p. 238; translation altered)

The actual *Lebensphilosophie* movement saw its birth in Germany between 1900 and 1910, but for Simmel the modern notion of life begins to take form already in Goethe's (1749–1832) lifetime. For Goethe, both nature and human soul emerge from life. He regards both of them as manifestations of the unity of being – with nature as its external dimension and the human soul as its internal dimension ([1906] GSG 10, p. 131). Yet, in Simmel's view, the prehistory of the modern notion of life dates back much further than this. It can be situated in a historical succession of basic categories characteristic of each cultural epoch. For Simmel, each epoch is crystallized into a single basic category that does not characterize so much the reality of life in a period as its 'failures, its longing and its salvation' and the scope of its thought ([1900/7] GSG 6, pp. 301; 2004, pp. 233–4).

According to Simmel, Greek philosophy was premised on the concept of *substance*. All changeability of phenomena was based on static essences and fixed forms reflected in eternally valid concepts ([1912] GSG 12, p. 386; [1914] GSG 13, p. 53). The Greeks were able to conceive 'the continuity of life only if the fleetingness of time was supplemented by a solid and constant content' ([1900/7] GSG 6, p. 301; 2004, p. 233).[3] For Simmel, the Middle Ages only gave Greek philosophy a Christian-theological colouring by replacing the notion of substance with *God* and the divine order of things. Later, the thought of the late Renaissance dissolved the static reality into motion. The world was no longer perceived as eternal, static, and fixed, but as constantly changing in accordance with the laws of mechanical movement. In the Renaissance, the decisive form of existence is thus found in *mechanism*. Knowing the world was no longer a matter of revealing logically binding concepts and the metaphysical eternity of substances but of calculating the laws of motion governed by causality ([1912] GSG 12, p. 386; [1914] GSG 13, pp. 53–4). Events were perceived in terms of 'to-and-fro of matter and energy determined by natural laws' ([1906] GSG 10, p. 122; 2007, p. 160). According to Simmel, Kant's philosophy did not alter this in any significant way, even though it conceived the external world as a representation within the representing subject. For Kant, the world amounted to mechanical movement ([1912] GSG 12, pp. 386–7), something 'external, consisting exclusively of spatial and mechanical relationships' ([1906] GSG 10, p. 131; 2007, p. 166).

Finally, the 'philosophy of life' (*Philosophie des Lebens*) represents for Simmel the fourth and most recent stage of Western thought. Retrospectively, the historical trajectory from the category of substance to life via God and mechanism can, in Simmel's view, be conceptualized as a process of 'enlivening' (*Verlebendigung*) thought. Simmel suggests that, notwithstanding all its incompleteness, the philosophy of life may so far be the purest expression of the 'enlivening' of thought and the world it studies ([1912] GSG 12, p. 387). Both surprising and unsurprising, it is the names Schopenhauer, Nietzsche, and Bergson that Simmel mentions here. On the one hand, it is surprising in that the life-philosophical movement sprang up only during 1900–10 and, in addition to Simmel, it is his contemporaries such as Max Scheler, Hermann Keyserling, and Theodor Lessing who are usually named as its key representatives.[4] So, of the authors mentioned by Simmel, it is only Bergson who – as the chief representative of French vitalism – belongs to the same era as the life-philosophical movement. Schopenhauer and Nietzsche were not life-philosophers themselves, but only precursors of life-philosophy. Yet on the other hand it is not the least bit surprising that Simmel foregrounds especially the names Schopenhauer and Nietzsche over his contemporaries, for the latter belong to his usual suspects: it is only the 'greats' of philosophy that Simmel mentions by name in his works, while references to contemporaries are almost completely absent.

But why does Simmel choose to emphasize Schopenhauer, Nietzsche, and Bergson? There must be more to it than the sheer fact that Schopenhauer and Nietzsche were renowned in his day, and that Bergson was very fashionable at the time. And there is. Although the modern notion of life already finds expression in the work of Goethe, according to Simmel it was only Schopenhauer who was the first philosopher to philosophize on life as such ([1912] GSG 12, p. 384) – Goethe's writings lack even the basic intention of philosophy ([1906] GSG 10, p. 26; 2007, p. 162). Schopenhauer's significance for life-philosophy lies in the fact that he did not examine the value and meaning of this or that experience or aspect of life but the meaning and value of life itself, purely as life ([1912] GSG 12, p. 384; [1918] GSG 16, p. 188). Simmel thinks that this yearning to a final goal and meaning of life is connected to the preponderance of means over ends that he sees as characteristic of modern culture. According to him, in modernity individuals are surrounded by a whole multiplicity of means 'in which the most important means are constituted by other means and these again by others' ([1907] GSG 10, p. 176; 1991b, p. 3). The individuals are 'born into a teleological system composed of many links' – that is, into 'an ever-increasing infrastructure of means' ([1900/7] GSG 6, pp. 297–8; 2004 p. 231). Our strivings in life take the form of long and complex teleological chains in which it becomes ever more difficult to keep the ultimate goal in sight. And, consequently, our consciousness is focused on the means, whereas the final ends lose in significance correspondingly ([1907] GSG 10, pp. 176–7). Money serves as a good example here, but Simmel feels that not even philosophy has remained unaffected by this general tendency of means gaining preponderance over ends. He takes as his example Kant's philosophy, which redirected the attention of philosophers from objects – the contents of the world and their being, essence, meaning, and purpose – to our means of knowing them ([1912] GSG 12, p. 381). It is in this cultural situation of the growing significance of the means and the corresponding loss of final goals and definite values that there appears the desire for an absolute goal. And, as Schopenhauer places life at the heart of his work, his philosophy is for Simmel 'the absolute philosophical expression for this inner condition of modern man [sic]' ([1907] GSG 10, p. 178; 1991b, p. 5).

Schopenhauer rejected the possibility of finding any absolute purpose or value outside of life. For Schopenhauer, life cannot obtain any meaning and purpose beyond itself since everywhere it finds nothing but itself as willing. This folding of life back on itself is for Simmel the source of Schopenhauer's deep pessimism. As in Schopenhauer's view life has no absolute purpose outside itself, 'the inner rhythm of life appears as an unremitting monotony' ([1907] GSG 10, p. 183; 1991b, p. 8). This monotony leads to 'the pain of ennui': 'If we are occupied by nothing, [...] then we feel, solely and purely, life itself – and exactly this experience causes an unbearable situation' ([1907] GSG 10, p. 183; 1991b, p. 9). Thus, for Schopenhauer, so Simmel's argument goes, the only redemption from this ennui and meaninglessness of life can be the negation of life, *Nicht-Leben*.

Importantly, Simmel maintains, Nietzsche's unlimited optimism stems from the exact same source as Schopenhauer's pessimism: the negation of any absolute goal or purpose outside life. However, Nietzsche manages to escape the pessimism of a life without meaning through finding redemption within life itself. He sees the ultimate purpose and absolute value of life in its augmentation. This allows 'the possibility for saying "yes" to life' ([1907] GSG 10, p. 179; 1991b, p. 5). Hence Nietzsche operates with a very different notion of life than Schopenhauer. Instead of running in monotony, for Nietzsche life appears as a constant drive towards 'more life' (*mehr Leben*) ([1907] GSG 10, pp. 377–8). In Nietzsche's philosophy, Simmel claims, life is seen as 'an immeasurable sum of powers and potentials which, in themselves, are aimed at the augmentation, intensification, and increased effectiveness of the life process' ([1907] GSG 10, p. 180; 1991b, p. 6). Nietzsche's concept of life presents for Simmel nothing but 'a poetical-philosophical absolutization of the Darwinian idea of evolution' ([1907] GSG 10, p. 179; 1991b, p. 6); 'between Schopenhauer and Nietzsche lies Darwin' ([1907] GSG 10, p. 179; 1991b, p. 5).

Whereas Goethe appears in Simmel's work as an exponent of organicism that opposes mechanicist thought, Nietzsche's influence is clearly traceable in Simmel's notion of life.[5] Simmel subscribes to the Nietzschean view of life constantly transcending itself. According to Simmel, 'life is that which at all points wants to go beyond itself, reaching out beyond itself' ([1916] GSG 15, p. 385; 2005, p. 57). However, Simmel dispenses with the Nietzschean axiological interpretations: he does not value the augmentation of life in any explicit manner. For him, life's striving for more-life is a simple fact: life simply cannot exist otherwise than by producing more life. The epithet of 'more-life' is in other words essential to life: 'It can only exist by virtue of its being more-life' ([1918] GSG 16, p. 229; 1971, p. 369). Already sheer self-maintenance inevitably involves regeneration for Simmel.

Besides Nietzsche, another important source of influence for Simmel's life-philosophy is Bergson. Simmel's preoccupation with Bergson's philosophy begins around 1908. Simmel wrote two essays on Bergson, but rather than being interested in the inner composition of Bergson's work or its method Simmel interprets Bergson's key concepts – duration, memory, and élan vital – above all from the perspective of his own life-philosophy, for example by equating élan vital with life (Schwerdtfeger, 1995, p. 92).

What separates Bergson's vitalism from Nietzsche's notion of life as more-life is that whereas in Nietzsche's work the category of life appears as 'anthropomorphized and anthropocentric' (Bleicher, 2007, p. 152), concerning only human existence and its values,[6] in Bergson the idea of life as constantly striving for more-life becomes something cosmic: for Bergson, as Simmel interprets it, all existence, whatever its content, is a particular development of the vital force, élan vital. Not only does this imply that evolution is devoid of any external goal, but it also suggests that life does not consist only of its maintenance. If it did, the process of evolution would have already stopped with the most elementary organisms capable of adapting themselves to external conditions. For Bergson, as Thomas A. Goudge argues, life has kept on evolving because élan vital is constantly 'driving it towards higher levels of organization. This impulse constitutes the unique nature of all that is animate' (Goudge, [1949] 1999, p. 17).

The extension of the notion of life to the cosmic level is what Simmel appropriates from Bergson. That is, Simmel does not consider life only in anthropomorphic terms, but he understands it ultimately as a 'cosmic fact'. In Simmel's life-philosophy, the creativity that for anthropocentric approaches to life seems 'the innermost essence' of the human subject 'no longer stands in contrast to unconscious, numb, nature-like being, but rests in its great order' (Kantorowicz, [1923] 1959, p. 4). In the piece 'Der Fragmentcharakter des Lebens' (trans. 'The Fragmentary Character of Life', 2012), Simmel proposes that we have to understand the spatial and temporal existence of all nature in terms of continuity, as 'a constant stream of energies interacting with everything, in an unending unity of elements in ever different combinations' ([1916/17] GSG 13, p. 203; 2012, p. 238). So, unlike Schopenhauer and Nietzsche, Simmel does not consider the process of self-transcendence as being restricted to the activity of the will. On the contrary, in his view it 'holds for all dimensions of life's movements' ([1918] GSG 16, p. 229). Simmel thus establishes a continuum between physiological-vital life and spiritual or mental life. As Gertrud Kantorowitz ([1923] 1959, p. 4) has noted, Simmel sees the 'spirit' (*Geist*) merely as 'the strongest expression of the metaphysical power which led to the formation of organisms; it is mere symbol or embodiment of total cosmic reality'. With the notion of life Simmel thus explores the position of humans in the 'totality of being', in relation to 'the whole extra-human sphere' (p. 4).

Keeping in mind Kant's substantial influence on Simmel's work, especially on its middle, sociological period (and let it be remembered that Simmel had been engaged with Kant's philosophy at least ever since the essay that had won him the academic prize in 1880), the distance of his mature work from Kant – and simultaneous proximity to Schopenhauer, Nietzsche, and Bergson – is striking.[7] The radical break with the Kantian preoccupation with knowledge is expressed for example in occasional remarks such as this one: 'A philosophy which has as its object just knowing itself seems to be like someone who constantly polishes his knife and fork and studies their usability but does not eat a thing' ([1912]

GSG 12, p. 382). All in all, in Simmel's life-philosophy epistemology becomes subordinate to ontology. Instead of converting the problem of the world to one of how it is that we can know it, Simmel the life-philosopher advances a full-blown metaphysics that centres on the problem of *life*.

Life as pre-individual flux and dynamic inter-subjectivity

Notwithstanding its influence on his own life-philosophy, Simmel's conception of life differs considerably from Bergson's. Unlike Bergson (see, e.g., 1999, p. 30), Simmel does not think that we should renounce rigorously defined concepts in favour of 'intuition'. This separates Simmel significantly not only from Bergson but in fact from the majority of life-philosophers. He is well aware of the logical difficulty involved in the attempt to come to grips with life with the help of concepts, since fixed and static concepts inevitably obliterate life's characteristics of flux and processuality ([1918] GSG 16, p. 235; 2010, p. 18). Nevertheless, rather than insisting on the necessity of grasping life via intuition, Simmel rejects the very possibility of viewing 'life proper'. He thinks that we are denied access to life as such. According to him, we can experience and know life only in some form, never as an absolute flow: 'Life is the opposite of form, but obviously an entity can be conceptually described only if it has a form of some sort' ([1918] GSG 16, pp. 205–6; 1997a, p. 107).

Overall, Simmel considers the process of life on a quite different basis than Bergson. Unlike Bergson, he does not model it in accordance with the process of evolution. While Bergson regards the biological processes of evolution as paramount, Simmel, by contrast, grounds his notion of life on two foundations – or perhaps it would be more accurate to say that he employs two different notions of life.

The first notion that Simmel introduces in his work presents life as a *pre-individual flux*. Simmel contrasts life to static being. As he notes of life in the book *Rembrandt*, 'It never *is*, it is always *becoming*' ([1916] GSG 15, p. 321; 2005, p. 11). Hence, becoming is the essence of life, its peculiar way of being. With the notion of life, Simmel gets at conceptualizing becoming in positive terms. Life is not movement from non-being to being but a potentiality or virtual, a course of becoming that determines the actuality of phenomena (see [1916] GSG 15, pp. 377–8; Lash, 2006, p. 325). It is a potentiality insofar as life is always not yet, always in the making, and virtual insofar as it creates its own lines of actualization.

Even though it appears everywhere as the life of the individual, Simmel maintains that in itself, as a continuous, unrestricted flow, life is opposed to the self-enclosed form of the individual (see Pyyhtinen, 2012). Life not only exceeds but also produces all individual forms and, as such, it refers in Simmel to a more profound dimension beneath the surface of phenomena. Namely, for Simmel, as he puts it in *Rembrandt*, 'Life [...] is a basic fact that cannot be constructed' ([1916] GSG 15, p. 314; 2005, p. 6). Life amounts to dynamic becoming that is 'the architect [*Bildner*] of our traits' ([1916] GSG 15, p. 319; 2005, p. 10). Given Simmel's conviction that life proper constantly eludes our grasp, it follows that if we want to access it, we have to approach it indirectly. This emphasizes the centrality of form in Simmel's work. He believes that it is by examining concrete forms or objects that we gain an access to a deeper reality, ultimately that of life itself. He thinks that forms present the surface level of reality that is nonetheless connected to the deep metaphysical currents of life. Ultimately even 'the sociological forms' are for Simmel 'themselves accomplishments of deeper lying, more general mental [*seelischer*] basic functions' ([1908] GSG 11, p. 492). Thereby, sociology, too, is a matter of studying *life* in its social forms. As Simmel suggests in *Sociology*, 'society' is just one category 'in the series of concepts which methodically order the study of life' ([1908] GSG 11, p. 862; 1971, p. 40).

When examining human life, Simmel pays special attention to *Erlebnis*, 'lived experience'. Thus he considers human life largely in terms of inner subjectivity (*Innerlichkeit*) (Lash, 1999, p. 131). This emphasis connects him to Dilthey. According to Dilthey, *Erlebnis* is an immediate, lived experience, the smallest phenomenon of life; life appears as a stream of lived experiences. By means of the notion of *Erlebnis*, Simmel strives to overcome Kant's intellectualism (see [1904] GSG 9, pp. 75–6): like 'will' in Schopenhauer and the 'will to power' in Nietzsche, for Simmel, life and lived experience precede reason. That is, he does not see 'consciousness' (*Bewußtsein*) as being dependent on the apriorities of reason but on those of lived experience (Bevers, 1985, pp. 48–9). It is only through being first experienced that an object becomes known. For Simmel, lived experience is thus the expression of our primordial relation to the world, the response of our 'total existence' (*Gesamtexistenz*) to the being of things:

> In lived experience [*Erleben*], life, the most intransitive of all concepts, sets itself in an immediate functional connection with objectivity and, indeed, in it, in a unique mode, the activity and passivity of the subject, regardless of their mutual logical exclusiveness, are connected to the unity of life. ([1917/18] GSG 13, pp. 321–2)

In his philosophy of lived experience, Simmel is largely in unison with the tradition of life-philosophy.

The other concept of life that Simmel employs does not emphasize the inner sphere of the individual, but rather the *relations* between two or more individual elements (Lash, 1999, p. 131). It rests on the notion of *Wechselwirkung*, reciprocal action and effect. Simmel draws here in particular on biology. Life, in its biological form, is for him 'nothing but the sum of interacting forces among the atoms of the organism' ([1900/7] GSG 6, p. 210; 2004, p. 175). In *Einleitung in die Moralwissenschaft*, he states that it would be a mistake 'if one posited, beyond the individual effects and interactions of organic cells, some specific force of life [*Lebenskraft*]' ([1892/3] GSG 3, p. 275). Further, in *Die Probleme der Geschichtsphilosophie*, Simmel maintains that 'there is no law of life' nor any 'force of life' ([1892] GSG 2, p. 344). It would thus amount to something of a tautology to say that the interaction between atoms brings about life or that life animates these atoms – for their interaction already *is* life.

We can thus see that the difference between the two notions of life presented above is quite radical. While the first notion views life as a force of becoming over and above entities and their relations, the latter denies of life any such qualities. According to it, by contrast, life has no existence apart from the interactions between entities, but precisely amounts to such interactions. It is also above all in the sense of the latter notion that Simmel speaks of the social in terms of life. Simmel contrasts the 'living reciprocation' (*lebendige Wechselwirkung*) ([1907] GSG 8, p. 280) among individuals to the structures of higher order into which interaction may crystallize ([1908] GSG 11, p. 32; [1917] GSG 16, pp. 68–9). For example, in the piece 'Soziologie der Sinne' ('Sociology of the Senses') he asserts that:

> aside from the connecting forms that are elevated to the level of those comprehensive organizations, this pulsating life which links human beings together displays countless other ones, which, as it were, remain in a fluid, transitory condition, but are no less agents connecting individuals to social existence. ([1907] GSG 8, p. 277; 1997a, p. 109)

In the quotation, the social is pictured in terms of life; it is equated with 'this pulsating life which links human beings together'. In general, the notion of life can be interpreted in Simmel's sociology as a way of addressing and stressing the dynamic processuality of living reciprocity over substantialist conceptualizations of social formations. In any case, life is part of Simmel's analysis of the social. He stresses social process by pleading to the *living reciprocation* as the starting point for the study of all social formations. However, life figures in bonds between living individuals also with regard to finitude. It is as living beings characterized by an immanent and imminent death that individuals participate in social relationships (see Pyyhtinen, 2009; 2010). The dyad, in particular, is fundamentally limited and shaped by death. The communion revealed in the dyad does not outlive the existence of the partners, but manifests itself first and foremost as the being-with of two finite beings.

Life as more-life and more-than-life

Despite the fact the Simmel gives precedence to process and life, he does not simply champion fluency and variation at the expense of the permanent and the fixed. On the contrary, in his work Simmel explicitly sets out to bridge that gap between becoming and being that, beginning from Parmenides and Heraclitus, runs throughout Western thought. For Simmel, the failure of what he calls the modern version of Heraclitean worldview is that it dissolves all substantiality and solidity into movement and thereby ignores stability and permanence ([1916] GSG 15, p. 445; 2005, p. 105). In result, it tends to make time strictly atemporal. Whereas the mechanistic worldview of Kant's philosophy eliminates time by making it something ideal and abstract (see [1918] GSG 16, pp. 219–21), the neo-Heraclitean worldview, too, obliterates it, but in a completely different manner. As modern Heracliteanism perceives life as an 'absolute flow', it abandons 'all solidity in which a before and after – that is, time – could mark itself'. It makes the identification of singular moments or events impossible; absolute becoming is therefore just as atemporal as absolute non-becoming ([1916] GSG 15, pp. 445–6; 2005, pp. 105–6).

In the end of his essay on Bergson, published in 1914, Simmel speculates on the possibility of connecting becoming and being. He suggests that perhaps the next steps in the enlivening of philosophy will occupy a notion of life that would include both sides of the contrast of processuality and stability ([1914] GSG 13, p. 69). And it is especially to his own work that he is alluding. In his life-philosophy, Simmel proposes the idea of 'absolute life' (see [1916] GSG 15, pp. 403, 419; [1918] GSG 16, p. 232) as a wider concept of life that 'embraces the relative contrast between life in the narrower sense and content independent of life' ([1918] GSG 16, p. 232; 2010, p. 16). Similarly, in the small book *Das Problem der historischen Zeit* ('The Problem of Historical Time'), Simmel insists that also that which stands against life is still a form of life ([1916] GSG 15, p. 304). So, instead of having unrestricted life on the one hand, and restrictive form on the other, the notion of absolute life integrates both being and becoming into a unified worldview. Importantly, however, absolute life is not a synthesis or final reconciliation of the opposition of life and form. In it, neither one of the poles is 'degraded' or 'compromised', but both 'maintain their absolute character' (Kantorowicz, [1923] 1959, pp. 3–4): life *is* both becoming and being, dynamic fluency and its opposite, fixed unchangeability. The notion of absolute life is thus a Simmelian third which appears only in and through the contrast of the two opposite principles. The contrast between life and form is 'the very way in which [the] unity [of life] exists' ([1918] GSG 16, p. 233; 2010, p. 372). Or, As Simmel writes a few pages earlier in *The View of Life*:

> If we wish to express the unified character of life in abstract terms, our intellect has no alternative but to divide it into two [...] parts, which appear as though they were mutually exclusive and only subsequently merge to form that unity. ([1918] GSG 16, p. 230; 2010, p. 14)

Simmel conceptualizes this duality of absolute life by employing the concepts *more-life* (*Mehr-Leben*) and *more-than-life* (*Mehr-als-Leben*). More-than-life designates the 'transvital' or 'transcendent' element of life that is still part of life:

> Just as life's transcendence, within the plane of life itself, of its current, delimited form constitutes more-life (although it is nevertheless the immediate, inescapable essence of life itself), so also its transcendence into the level of objective content, of logically autonomous and no longer vital meaning, constitutes more-than-life, which is inseparable from it and is the essence of spiritual life itself. ([1918] GSG 16, p. 232; 2010, p. 16)

In other words, for Simmel, life is a constant movement that continually produces not only more-life but also something independent of and irreducible to the process of life. And, importantly, Simmel suggests that life is more-life and more-than-life precisely *because* life exists by producing more-life; life's creativity is 'both the dissipation and culmination of its own force and the reach beyond itself', as Kantorowicz ([1923] 1959, p. 3) puts it.

The notions of more-life and more-than-life also mark in Simmel's work an analytical distinction between physiological-vital life and mental life, or corporeal and cultural existence. For Simmel, life, as a cosmic fact, amounts to process and continuous flux, yet the 'picture changes dramatically [...] as soon as life's process is seen to be something mentally conscious' ([1916/17] GSG 13, p. 203; 2012, p. 238), whereby it ascends above the level of 'sheer animality' (*bloß Animalische*) ([1918] GSG 16, p. 183). Conscious human life is not sheer absolute flow but manifested in the self-enclosed, limited form of the individual. It gives the world a new centre: the individual 'I' (*Ich*) who connects what is separate and separates what is connected, creates accentuations and shifts perspective ([1916/17] GSG 13, p. 203; 2012, p. 238).

Whereas physiological or organic life has only the quality of more-life, with more-than-life life becomes conscious and cultural:

> Just as life is a continuous begetting on its physiological level, so that, to use a compromised expression, life is always more-life – so too on the level of the spirit it begets something that is more-than-life: the objective, the construct, that which is significant and valid in itself. ([1918] GSG 16, p. 295; 2010, p. 60)

Human life is always pitted against itself in the objects or forms that originate from life. It can realize and manifest itself only in forms: 'Forms are inseparable from life; without them it cannot be itself' ([1918] GSG 16, pp. 183–4; 1971, p. 375). These forms range from words and deeds to images, laws, social formations, technology, works of art, philosophical doctrines, and scientific findings, for example ([1918] GSG 16, pp. 183–4), and they have an objective validity and significance in their own right, independent of the lives of the individuals who have created them ([1918] GSG 16, p. 230; 2010, p. 14). It is with them that life becomes cultural. Mental and cultural life are always entangled for Simmel: subjects do not exist solely in and by themselves, but the development of subjectivity always involves 'something external' to the subject ([1908] GSG 8, pp. 367–8).

Life and boundary

Besides connecting becoming and being, what is original in Simmel's notion of life is that he deduces the striving towards more-life from the same formal structure that restricts life (Fitzi, 2002, p. 271). Accordingly, the key to Simmel's life-philosophy is the concept of 'boundary' (*Grenze*). In the process of more-life, every boundary and fixed form is transcended, but only insofar as there exists something to be transcended. As a boundary, form is a necessary element of life: boundaries are indispensable in that they create order and help us to orient ourselves in the world; by setting boundaries, we are able to find our place and a place for our feelings, deeds, experiences, and thoughts. Yet every single boundary can also be stepped over. Consequently, Simmel notes that we are boundary beings who have no boundaries ([1918] GSG 16, pp. 212–14; 2010 pp. 1–2). For Simmel, life is thus defined ultimately in terms of transgression. In the act of self-transcendence, breaking through boundaries and establishing boundaries are united: each step over a boundary also finds and creates a new one ([1918] GSG 16, p. 213; 2010, p. 2).

However, it is precisely in its self-transcendence that remains immanent to life that life is absolute: life is at once centripetal and centrifugal, a bounded form and a flux without boundaries.[8] Even when transcending itself life remains itself. Simmel clarifies this idea in the following manner:

> [A]s soon as 'something' exists as a unity unto itself, gravitating toward its own center, then all the flow from within its bounds to beyond its bounds is no longer agitation without a subject; rather, it somehow remains bound up with the center, so that even the movement beyond its boundary belongs to the center; it represents a reaching out in which this form always remains the subject, and yet which proceeds nonetheless beyond this subject. ([1918] GSG 16, pp. 222–3; 2010, p. 9)

However, life, in the absolute sense, does not belong to a subject any more than it refers to an object. As the 'metaphysical foundational principle' it rather absorbs everything and 'generates subject and object from itself' ([1912] GSG 12, p. 387; trans. Bleicher, 2007, p. 150). What Simmel writes in *Schopenhauer and Nietzsche* with reference to Nietzsche's notion of life also holds for that of his own:

> Life, in its primary sense, beyond the opposition of corporeal and spiritual existence, is seen here as an immeasurable sum of powers and potentials which, in themselves, are aimed at the augmentation, intensification, and increased effectiveness of the life

process. It is impossible to describe this process through analysis, however, because *its unity constitutes the ultimate and basic phenomenon of ourselves.* ([1907] GSG 10, p. 180; 1991b, p. 6; italics added)

Life here stands as the ultimate foundation or boundary beyond which Simmel does not strive to go in his life-philosophy. Simmel does not reduce life to anything else, but treats it as 'a basic fact that cannot be constructed'. There is no 'outside' to life and no transcendent dimension that would determine it. In his life-philosophy Simmel does not try to locate phenomena in any realm beyond lived experience and life, but he views them from the perspective of life. Much in the vein of Baudelaire's modernism, Simmel sees it as 'the great problem of the modern spirit [...] to find a place for everything which transcends the givenness of vital phenomena within those phenomena themselves, instead of transposing it to a spatial beyond.' In other words, he does not aspire for any '*synthesis* of the finite and the infinite, but a grown unity of life' ([1923] GSG 20, p. 185; 1997a, p. 243). The eternal (i.e., form) is considered by him as something that dwells within the transient (i.e., life). As Simmel puts it in *Rembrandt*, he is 'following the structure of the concepts with which we divide up the idea of the world [*Weltbild*] not beyond that point at which the polarity of form and life underpin at all the even unity of substance' ([1916] GSG 15, p. 387; 2005, pp. 58–9). Life is the disclosure of subject and the world. Standing at the same time both 'within' and 'outside' our experience, life constitutes the ultimate horizon of thought: it is something that needs to be thought and yet constantly escapes thought. Simmel acknowledges that there is already in principle no philosophical solution at hand to the riddle of life – after all, such a solution would mean the end of life as a tension between more-life and more-than-life. The notion of life is bound to remain 'somewhat vague and logically imprecise', for 'to succeed in giving a conceptual definition of it would be to deny [life] its essence' ([1918] GSG 16, pp. 205–6; 1997a, p. 107).

Culture as cultivation

In his philosophy of culture, Simmel is preoccupied with the dynamics and contrast of subjective creativity on the one hand, and cultural forms on the other. In the essay 'The Conflict in Modern Culture', he writes that '[w]e speak of culture whenever life produces certain forms in which it expresses and realizes itself'. Forms such as technologies, norms, religions, laws, and sciences 'encompass the flow of life and provide it with content and form, freedom and order' ([1918] GSG 16, p. 183; 1971, p. 375). Simmel starts from the idea that subjects and objects come into existence by mutually determining one another. The development of selfhood always involves 'something external' to the subject itself (Simmel, [1908], GSG 8, pp. 367–8). The cornerstone of Simmel's conception of culture is thereby the idea that subjects could not exist as subjects without the creation and assimilation of objects. By these objects or constructs, as was hinted above, he understands social forms, norms, rules and laws, technology, artefacts, religion, the economy, and so on. Forms or objects are obligatory points of passage and essential materials for the making of ourselves. The creation of objects is for Simmel the reverse side of becoming a subject: subjectivity is constituted via giving form to objects. That is, in order to become who one is, the subject has to take a detour through the historico-cultural world. Simmel maintains that it is by cultivating things that we cultivate ourselves ([1900/7] GSG 6, p. 618; 2004, p. 447) or, to put it the other way, that 'we develop ourselves only by developing things' ([1900/7] GSG 6, p. 622; 2004, p. 449). The cultural processes of subjectification and objectification go hand in hand: 'Whatever difficulties metaphysics may find in the relationship between the objective determination of things and the subjective freedom of the individual, as aspects of culture their development runs parallel' ([1900/7] GSG 6, p. 403; 2004, pp. 302–3). Cultural objects play a crucial part in our subjective and social lives: 'culture places life-contents in an incomparably tangled knot of subject and object' ([1908] GSG 8, p. 371; 1971, p. 233; translation altered).

Simmel understands culture ultimately on the basis of *cultivation*. By cultivation he refers to the process whereby the development of natural entities, forces, and energies are taken beyond the point which they would be able to reach by themselves alone ([1908] GSG 8, p. 363; 1971, pp. 227–8). That is, he sees cultivation as an extension of nature and natural development. Nature and culture do not present two entirely separate spheres, but they are closely intertwined. For Simmel, nature is the ground of culture, so to speak. He thinks that the existence of culture necessitates the existence of a prior 'natural state'; the process of cultivation is possible only provided that prior to it there exists something in an uncultivated state. This also means, at the same time, that 'the ensuing transformation' of this uncultivated entity is 'somehow latent in *its natural structural potential*, even though it could not be realized by itself' ([1908] GSG 8, p. 365; 1971, p. 228). Simmel gives the example of gardening a pear tree:

> The wild pear tree bears woody, sour fruit. Such is the end point of its development in the wild. At this point, human will and intellect have intervened and have led the tree by means of a variety of influences to the production of edible pears, that is, have 'cultivated' it. ([1908] GSG 8, p. 364; 1971, p. 227)

However, with the process of cultivation Simmel refers above all to the cultivation of *subjects*, not so much to that of objects. The cultivation of human subjects is the measure of culture for him. Thereby, understood in this context, nature, too, designates 'a particular phase in the development of a subject' ([1908] GSG 8, p. 365; 1971, p. 228). That the cultivation of the human subject gives cultivation its ultimate purpose leads to the paradoxical fact that what are regarded as the highest achievements in several fields, including art, science, and technology, may in fact contribute only little or hardly at all to the cultivation of subjects ([1908] GSG 8, p. 370; 1971, p. 232). Their *cultural* value is measured according to Simmel only in the extent that they contribute to the whole existence of the subject, that is, to 'the development of our inner *totality*' ([1908] GSG 8, p. 370; 1971, p. 232).[9]

Tragedy of culture

While the subject attains a selfhood only through and in relation to cultural objects, Simmel asserts that in modernity subjects are also threatened by objects. He holds that in the modern world the culture of subjects, to which he refers by the term 'subjective culture', and that of objects – or 'objective culture' – are increasingly growing apart from one another. Simmel describes this process with the notion 'the tragedy of culture'. Basically, the concept entails the idea that the objects of our own making gain independence from our needs and may even come to enslave us. As Simmel puts it, they 'follow an immanent developmental logic in the intermediate form of objectivity [...] and thereby become alienated from both their origin and their purpose' ([1911] GSG 14, p. 408; 1997a, p. 70). According to Simmel, 'historical development tends increasingly to widen the gap between concrete creative cultural achievements and the level of individual culture'. Objective culture has 'become substantially [...] independent of subjective culture', because objects 'become more perfect, more intellectual, they follow more and more obediently their own inner logic of material expediency' ([1908] GSG 8, p. 372; 1997a, p. 45). As a result, we become dominated by the objects of our own creation. As examples, we could think, for instance, of bureaucracy, fashion, or the economy. To some extent all of them have become independent of individual subjects and tend to dictate and dominate the lives of subjects.

In his life-philosophy, Simmel conceptualizes the increasing independence of objects from subjects in terms of a 'axial rotation of life' (*Achsendrehung des Lebens*) (see [1918] GSG 16, pp. 244–5; 2010, p. 25). With it, he refers to the process by which forms – all kinds of forms created by individuals, not only the social ones – detach themselves from the vital needs of individuals and gain a life of their own. Instead of forms serving life, life begins to serve forms.

In *The View of Life* Simmel uses science, art, religion, justice, the Kantian categorical imperative, and the economy as examples of such autonomous forms. As regards science, Simmel suggests that all knowledge has probably originally emerged to serve practical needs, but in and for science applicability to practical solutions is secondary. Knowledge that is motivated by practical objectives is for Simmel not yet scientific per se, as we can have practical knowledge of all sorts of matters also without science. In science, truth is sought for truth's own sake ([1918] GSG 16, p. 262; 2010, p. 37). Simmel phrases the development from practical knowledge to science by noting that 'at first men [sic] know in order to live, but then there are men [sic] who live in order to know' ([1918] GSG 16, p. 261; 2010, p. 37).

The same goes, *mutatis mutandis*, for fine arts. Simmel maintains that while 'in general we see to live, the artist lives to see' ([1918] GSG 16, p. 269; 2010, p. 42). In fine arts, seeing becomes an end in itself. It does not serve any practical needs, but adheres only to artistic rules and principles. The relation of poetry to language, according to Simmel, is basically the same kind as that of fine arts to seeing. In poetry, language is not a means of communication but an end in itself.

As for religion, Simmel proposes that we may experience the same kind of feelings that religion makes us feel in other spheres of life as well. For example, we may have faith in a person, we may feel that we belong to a greater whole, such as home country or humanity, or we may have a sense of simultaneous compliance and exaltation, passion and devotion towards a loved one while at the same time feeling highly dependent and responsible in our actions. But religion emerges, according to Simmel, only when these affects and conditions lose their profanely determined contents and become 'absolute', so to speak. This is manifested, for example, in the idea of God as the absolute object of faith and embodiment of transcendence and love ([1918] GSG 16, p. 286; 2010, p. 54). Moreover, religion may have some positive effects on the integration and cohesion of society, but believers presumably do not share the belief in God for the sake of social integration; cohesion is only a possible side effect of their faith, while religious faith is an end in itself.

Similarly, Simmel claims that with their sanctions, norms and rules contribute to the self-preservation (*Sebsterhaltung*) of groups and communities, but if the relation between the group and the individual is to be accordant with justice (*Recht*), people must submit to the norms and rules for their own sake ([1918] GSG 16, p. 289; 2010, p. 56). He suggests that there have indeed existed actions that may be characterized as 'just' by nature even before the notion of justice was created, not to mention the establishment of judicial institutions. However, while in the pre-judicial communities, Simmel claims, what was just was good insofar as it served life, according to the idea of justice life is good insofar as it serves justice ([1918] GSG 16, p. 291; 2010, p. 58). In this respect, Kant's categorical imperative – which advises acting only according to the maxim whereby one can will that which should become a universal law – may be seen as being analogous to the case of justice ([1918] GSG 16, p. 294; 2010, p. 59). According to Kant, it may indeed be worthy and respectable that one fulfils an obligation with joy or because one cares for others, but one acts morally only when one fulfils the obligation for its own sake.

Lastly, the economy is for Simmel a special case. On the one hand, of all the forms that have become independent of the lives, vital needs, and creativity of individuals, perhaps none has been originally so inseparably tied to the practical concerns of life as the economy. In the last instance, people exchange goods and services in order to assuage hunger and take care of other basic needs. However, on the other hand, Simmel notes that perhaps no other form has truly become 'a world for itself' (*eine Welt für sich*) to the extent that the economy has. It seems to operate completely irrespective of what the subjects need or want:

> The violent logic of its development does not enquire after the will of any subject, nor after the sense and necessities of his [sic] life. The economy now goes its necessary way, entirely as though men [sic] were there for its sake, but not it for the sake of man [sic].

In Simmel's view, the economy is thus perhaps the most extreme case of 'demonic violence' done to life in the name of ruthless objectivity and matter-of-fact logic. In the economy, Simmel claims, the tension between life and the 'opposite-of-life' (*Gegenüber-vom-Leben*) reaches its culmination ([1918] GSG 16, 293; 2010, p. 59).

In sum, while they originate in life, cultural forms may occasionally develop in such a manner that they begin to constrain life and even become destructive for life. This presents the tragic side of Simmel's conception of life: what life needs for its subsistence is also what destroys it. Nevertheless, in *The View of Life* Simmel also goes beyond this view with his vitalized and individualized ethical doctrine of 'the individual law'. The notion presents an inversion of Kant's moral philosophy and its categorical imperative. According to Simmel, the individual moral imperative or 'Ought' (*Sollen*) does not confront the subject as an external duty coming from outside as 'a rigid and once-and-for-all', but it stems from the vital process of one's life ([1918] GSG 16, pp. 424–5; 2010, p. 154). Our own life-process, that is, whatever we have been and done, creates the ground for it: 'everything we have ever done and everything we have ever been obligated to is the condition under which our ethical life rises to the crest of what is currently obligated' ([1918] GSG 16, pp. 425; 2010, p. 154). What is more, it applies not only to particular acts, but our entire life is responsible for each act, and each act is responsible for the whole life ([1918] GSG 16, pp. 423; 2010, p. 153). Hence the individualized 'Ought is already our own life': 'the flowing formation of life proceeds as Ought' ([1918] GSG 16, p. 422; 2010, p. 152). The individual law applies to the individual's life in its entirety, to all that one has been, done and been obliged to be and do.

Conclusion

In this chapter I have discussed Simmel's life-philosophy and his philosophy of culture, which conceives culture in a fascinating way in connection with nature. Instead of presenting two separate and disjointed spheres, for Simmel nature and culture are interconnected. As we saw, Simmel considers culture in terms of the knot of subject and object. However, while the development and cultivation of subjects is according to him the ultimate goal of culture, he sees that the gap between the culture of subjects and that of objects is growing wider in modernity. And for Simmel this increasing separation between subjects and objects is largely the cause behind the dissonance of modern life (Simmel, [1908] GSG 8, p. 372; 1971, p. 234). His view of life and culture seems thus utterly tragic: to live we need to produce objects, but those very objects also come to destroy us.

Yet Simmel's life-philosophy also entails optimism, as it stresses the ability of life to break away from constraining cultural forms. Life does not remain trapped within actual forms, but at every moment it has potential to become something different and it also ceaselessly creates new forms, thus amounting to constant renewal.

Importantly, Simmel's sociology of forms, too, can be linked to his life-philosophical concerns. Reformulated in a life-philosophical vocabulary, his sociology is largely about the dynamics of the social as life on the one hand, and the social as self-substantial forms with a logic and lawfulness of their own on the other. In fact, Simmel's sociological work offers quite a refined view on the degrees of the objectification of the social, from the elementary social forms to institutionalized ones, autonomous play forms of society, all the way to the generic form of society itself as a whole (see Levine, 1971, p. xxvii). According to Simmel, only a few interactions, such as the mutual glance between people, do not have any objective content nor produce an objective form that would last.[10] Institutionalized forms, by contrast, are characterized by relative endurance and independence of the individual, and they may also dominate and control the lives of human subjects. The autonomous play forms – as the purest example of which Simmel mentions sociability (see Chapter 6) – present the second degree of autonomization of forms in his work. Due to their vivacity and playfulness they are not particularly stiff and fixed, but they are nevertheless independent of individuals and of practical concerns alike. While being completely oriented to persons, sociability, for instance, is autonomous in the sense that it does not serve any practical purpose external to itself, but is itself its own purpose (e.g., [1918] GSG 16, p. 120). Finally, the third level of autonomization is the generic form of society itself, which has gained a certain amount of independence of particular forms of interaction.

Nevertheless, the fact that the social is *life* should remind us that stability, invariability, and permanence are fragile and precarious; sooner or later, living reciprocity will burst open fixed forms and create new ones. What is more, the permanence of any social formation is based on relations. Society, for example, is no absolute entity in its own right but an assemblage or configuration of several relations of interdependence and interaction. Thereby, Simmel's work executes a shift from the sociology of the social as substance or thing to the sociology of the social as life: it gives primacy not to substances and their properties, but to processes, dynamic relations, fluctuation, and variation.

Notes

1   The book has four chapters, three of which had appeared earlier in the journal *Logos*. It is only the first chapter, 'Life as Transcendence' (*'Die Transzendenz des Lebens'*), that makes its first appearance in the book, though for this volume Simmel also revised chapters 3 and 4 so significantly that he insisted that they should be seen as new works, and he also extended chapter 2.
2   See Bennett (2010) for a critical analysis of the 'culture of life' promoted by these groups and the George W. Bush administration in the United States.
3   Simmel traces substantialism back to Parmenides. Parmenides' philosophy is for Simmel substantialist par excellence. In it, 'being' is not yet an abstract concept, a form, but appears as if as 'matter' (*Materie*), 'stuff' (*Stoffe*): it is an emblem of the emptiest abstraction – being is something common to all beings – which has become perceptible and tangible. ([1910] GSG 14, pp. 46–7)
4   Simmel was in correspondence with Scheler and Keyserling, of which the latter was also a close friend of his.
5   For a more detailed discussion of Simmel's reading of Nietzsche and the latter's role in Simmel's life-philosophical ethics, see Partyga (2016).
6   This is also what, for Simmel, makes Schopenhauer 'without doubt a greater philosopher than Nietzsche': while the latter concerns himself only with moral questions, not metaphysical ones, the first 'has a mysterious relation to the absolute of all things' and to the abyss of existence. Unlike Nietzsche, Schopenhauer is concerned not only with the basis of human beings and their values, but also with that of existence itself ([1907] GSG 10, pp. 188–9; 1991b, p. 13).
7   For example, in a letter to Hermann Graf Keyserling on 31 October 1908 Simmel mentions how the 'epistemological-metaphysical questions' that he was at the time preoccupied with have taken him beyond Kant and into the vicinity of Bergson (GSG 22, p. 666).
8   Simmel hails critical enlightenment for having refuted the idea of the 'transcendent'. The tradition of the transcendent places certain realities, values, objects of belief, and validities – such as 'God' – for which there is no room in the subjectively circumscribed life into the realm of the 'beyond' while, however, letting them act back onto life. However, for Simmel critical enlightenment is flawed by the fact that it jumps to the other extreme: it reduces everything located beyond the subject back within the confines of subjective life. As a line of thinking, it remains completely within the subject, thus failing to recognize anything beyond it ([1918] GSG 16, p. 234; 2010, p. 17).

9 Simmel understands this inner totality of a subject in a rather mystical way, referring with it to 'the harmony' of the subject's 'existence', to 'that mysterious unity that transcends all specific needs and forces' ([1908] GSG 8, p. 370; 1971, p. 232).
10 In *Sociology*, Simmel writes: 'The extremely lively reciprocation [*lebendige Wechselwirkung*] [...] into which the look from one eye to another weaves people together, does not crystallize in any objective constructs, but rather the unity that it creates between them remains directly suspended in the event [*Geschehen*] and in the function' ([1911] GSG 8, p. 280; 1997a, p. 111; translation altered). Its event leaves no objective trace behind.

PART II

INFLUENCE

8

From Fame into Oblivion: Simmel's Early Reception and Influence

Simmel exerted a far-reaching influence on contemporaries. Students crowded his lectures to witness the virtuoso at work; he was widely acknowledged and appreciated both in Germany and abroad especially for having re-established sociology as a discipline and defined its subject matter; and he also wrote bestselling books which were translated into many languages. Given his fame, it is nearly incomprehensible that only two or three decades after his death Simmel was forgotten almost completely. Simmel's widespread influence during his lifetime and the curious oblivion that soon followed his death is the topic of this chapter. The chapter traces the early reception, transmission, and appropriation of his thought. I will not try to be exhaustive; I will only pick some examples to give an idea of the breadth of his influence. First I will depict Simmel's overall position in turn-of-the-century German intellectual culture. After that I will discuss the great influence that Simmel had on his contemporaries in Germany. While his impact was perhaps the greatest in Germany, he had also a much wider following. The subsequent sections deal with the reception of his work abroad during his lifetime, first discussing France and then the United States. Towards the end of the chapter I will examine how triumph was followed by oblivion, as interest in Simmel's work decreased significantly for quite a long time.

Evocative lecturer and bestselling author

In European intellectual culture, Simmel was one of the most renowned thinkers of his time. He was a public intellectual with a significant influence on major cultural and political movements, such as German modernism and the political avant-garde (Leck, 2000). As a sociologist, he was much more famous in Germany than Durkheim, for instance, who remained practically unknown among German sociologists for a long time.¹ Durkheim's *Rules of Sociological Method* did appear in German translation in 1904, nine years after the publication of the French original, but it remained almost totally ineffectual, and *The Division of Labour in Society* was regarded in Germany as a book in economics, not in sociology. It is telling of Simmel's position in German sociology that in 1909 Simmel was being referred to as 'the most important German sociologist'.² What is more, it was acknowledged that he had contributed to German sociology not only discursively but also institutionally: besides providing a new theoretical foundation for sociology, he actively participated in the founding of the German Sociology Association, *Deutsche Gesellschaft für Soziologie* (DGS), at a time when there was not yet a single chair in sociology in the whole of Germany. Simmel was also given the honour of presenting the opening lecture at the first meeting of the Association, held in Frankfurt in October 1910.³

Whereas abroad Simmel was known above all as a sociologist, in Germany he was influential within philosophy as well. In fact, throughout his Berlin years he contributed significantly to the rehabilitation of philosophy, as for example his contemporary Paul Fechter, author, director, and theatre and art critic, suggests ([1918] 1993, p. 157).⁴ Simmel already exerted a great influence especially on the new generation of students in the first years after 1900, before he had managed to secure himself an academic post. To this generation he was the living embodiment of what it is to be a philosopher (Matthias, [1928] 1993, p. 193). In the obituary that he wrote of Simmel, Lukács proposes that

> [Simmel] was so exceptionally fascinating for all the really talented philosophers of the younger generation of scholars [...] that there is almost no one among them who did not for a shorter or longer time fall under the spell of his thought (Lukács, [1918] 1993, p. 171; 1991, p. 145).

But Simmel also had a following among artists and within wider cultural circles. The German-Swiss author Emil Ludwig notes that out of all German academics it was Simmel who was the foremost 'teacher of artists' ([1918] 1993, p. 156).

For many of the young generation of students, Simmel's lectures were a crucial experience that changed their very way of thinking. His student Arthur Salz (1959, p. 235), for example, acknowledges that 'no other teacher has had a stronger and more enduring influence in forming my outlook on life'. When he was about to leave for Strasbourg, Simmel asked his former student, philosopher Martin Buber, what he had given to his students in Berlin. To this Buber replied: 'You have taught them to think' (Buber, [1951] 1993, p. 223). Simmel was a dazzling and inspiring lecturer, whose lectures at the University of Berlin were crowded. There were hundreds of people in the audience, and philosopher Karl Joël mentions a lecture on Kant that was attended by as much as 1000 listeners ([1918] 1993, p. 166). Further, lawyer, author, and dramatist Eckart von Naso reports in a similar vein of a lecture on the philosophy of art, titled 'Rembrandt', that the auditorium just could not possibly fit in all the masses of students, so some of them had to sit on window sills and on the steps of the platform ([1954] 1993, p. 223).

The audience of his lectures sat enchanted and listened to Simmel who managed to breathe life into even the seemingly driest of subjects and make them interesting, exciting, and thrilling (see e.g. Thiess, [1918] 1993, p. 177). In Simmel's gripping lectures, for which he prepared no notes (Landmann, [1958] 1993, p. 13), the listener felt that s/he was witnessing the process of thinking *in situ*, for it appeared as if Simmel improvised the conclusions of his logical reasoning right there on the spot (von Naso, [1954] 1993, p. 223). Simmel's oratorical virtuosity also involved dramatic gesticulation, which according to testimonies by contemporaries brought even the coldest conceptual abstractions to life (Spykman, [1925] 2004, p. li). As Fechter reports:

> Whoever has heard – or better, both seen and heard – him speak has been carried away and been most impressed with his passion for analysis which lived in him. The great, slim figure with peculiar sharp hand gestures when he grabbed a problem with his right hand; with an open hand he lifted something invisible in front of the audience, turned it over on all sides, sometimes intuitively conveying these turns with his whole body and discussing the manner of investigation in his words until the object was clearly and sharply analysed into its components. (Fechter, [1918] 1993, pp. 157–8)

However, it was not only the gripping lecturing style that explains Simmel's popularity, but also his 'Zeitinstink' (Fechter, [1918] 1993, p. 159), his 'seismographic' (Gadamer, [1975] 2004, p. 55) sensitivity to the intellectual currents of the day. Simmel's hearers felt it was as if 'the Zeitgeist itself had come to life' in his lectures, as Joël ([1918] 1993, p. 166) reports. While Simmel seems to have rejoiced in the intellectual attraction that he had for many people,[5] he nevertheless hated the fact that he was fashionable (Salomon in Jaworski, 1997, p. 93). Kurt Gassen ([1958] 1993, p. 300) tells that Simmel:

> became fashionable amongst certain, indeed amongst most West Berlin circles, which out of satiation and snobbery chased each intellectual and artistic sensation and were caught in exaltation precisely in the face of what was difficult to understand, vague, or what they did not understand at all, and like swarms these very hearers filled his lectures, so that the seats were limited also in the largest auditoriums.

Albert Salomon reports of a lecture course by Simmel he attended in 1910 that not even 'the godless time from 2 to 3 P.M.' at which Simmel lectured managed to deter the crowds, but 'even at such an hour there were hundreds of listeners in the largest classroom of Berlin University' (in Jaworski, 1997, p. 93). Gassen's account already gives us a pretty good idea why Simmel might have detested the fact that part of the audience were coming to his lectures just because he was the latest philosophical sensation. Yet Simmel's own analyses of fashion suggest more substantial reasons why it may not always be that desirable to be a fashionable thinker. What is fashionable is opted for and followed only because of it being fashionable, not due to its substance or according to any objective criteria. What is more, for anyone willing to make a lasting contribution and exert an enduring influence being in fashion may be disastrous, for fashion is transitory: what is deemed fashionable today is destined to lose its appeal and vanish. Lukács's obituary of Simmel affirmed this, as Lukács described Simmel 'the most significant and interesting *transitional figure* in the whole of modern philosophy' ([1918] 1993, p. 171; trans. 1991, p. 145; italics added).

Lukács' prediction was accurate in that Simmel's fame was indeed not to last. However, before he fell into oblivion Simmel was not only an immensely popular lecturer, but he was also a very successful author. And without the wide dissemination of his writings Simmel would have probably remained only a local Berlin hero. In academia, it is possible to exert widespread influence only through texts; it is primarily in and through texts that thinking lives and also subsists from generation to another. Simmel's books gained a large audience, and several new editions were published of them. For instance, in just two weeks *Hauptprobleme der Philosophie* ([1910]; 'Main Problems of Philosophy') sold 8,500 copies, and after the fifth edition, published in 1920, a total of 37,000 copies of the book had been printed. Another bestseller was the volume *Philosophische Kultur* ([1911]; 'Philosophical Culture'). Its first edition of 10,000 copies was sold out in six weeks. Many of Simmel's writings also appeared as translations soon after their publication and they found a wide readership especially in the United States, France, Italy, Japan, and Russia. In addition, his books were reviewed internationally. *The Philosophy of Money*, for example, received as many as two reviews in *The American Journal of Sociology*, first by R.H. Meyer in 1901, and followed by a more substantial review by S.P. Altmann in 1903.

Ambivalent influence on contemporaries in Germany

During his life, Simmel's reception in Germany was highly ambivalent. The estimation of Simmel by German Marxist philosopher Ernst Bloch (1885–1977) that he voiced in *Geist der Utopie* (1918) embodies this ambivalence well. While Bloch acknowledges that 'Simmel has the finest mind among all contemporaries', he continues in very a critical tone:

> But beyond this, he is wholly empty and aimless, desiring everything except the truth. He is a collector of standpoints which he assembles all around truth without ever wanting or being able to possess it. He consumes himself in many quick and

occasional fires and is most of the time nothing but dazzling in an ever repeated methodological pyrotechnic display, by which we are rapidly bored. He is coquettish without ever showing his true colors, and is, on the whole entirely unwilling and incompetent to stake his sensitive methodology – which always goes in circles – on a comprehensive, broadly contextual objectivity. He is a psychologist who forever winds himself into everything and out again, and who is not solid enough to deserve the tough designation of a rigorous relativist. (Bloch, 1918, pp. 246–7; trans. Maus, 1959, pp. 194–5)

So, while admitting that Simmel's analyses are dazzling, Bloch laments that Simmel is empty, never reveals where he stands, and is also inarticulate with regard to his methodology which, on top of it all, is entirely circular. Yet, after listing all these weaknesses, Bloch concludes that Simmel has nevertheless 'given to thought nuances and a heightened temperature which [...] can indeed be of great service to philosophy, which owes much to Simmel's subtlety' (Bloch, 1918, p. 246; trans. Maus, 1959, p. 195).

A similar kind of ambivalence towards Simmel was expressed by Max Weber. Weber regretted the fact that no comprehensive, critical commentary had been published on Simmel's work, and so he began writing such a piece himself in 1908. However, the text was never finished and published. Around the time he embarked on the project Simmel was applying for a position at Heidelberg where Weber was based, and Weber did not want to publish anything that might work to Simmel's disadvantage (Levine, 1971, p. xlv). Of Weber's text there remains a short fragment preserved at the Max Weber Institute, and it was translated into English by Donald N. Levine in 1972. Weber begins the draft by depicting his relation to Simmel's work in highly ambivalent terms:

In evaluating the work of Georg Simmel, one's responses prove to be highly contradictory. On the one hand, one is bound to react to Simmel's works from a point of view that is overwhelmingly antagonistic. In particular, crucial aspects of his methodology are unacceptable. His substantive results must with unusual frequency be regarded with reservations, and not seldom they must be rejected outright. In addition, his mode of exposition strikes one at times as strange, and often it is at the very least uncongenial. On the other hand, one finds oneself absolutely compelled to affirm that this mode of exposition is simply brilliant and, what is more important, attains results that are intrinsic to it and not to be attained by any imitator. Indeed, nearly every one of his works abounds in important new theoretical ideas and the most subtle observations. Almost every one of them belongs to these books in which not only the valid findings, but even the false ones, contain a wealth of stimulation for one's own further thought, in comparison with which the majority of even the most estimable accomplishments of other scholars often appear to exude a peculiar odor of scantiness and poverty. (Weber, 1972, p. 158)

So, while Weber clearly seemed to appreciate Simmel for his brilliance and as a stimulator who offered refined, artistically stylized original ideas, he did not think particularly highly of Simmel's sociology, to say the very least, downright refuting its methodology and rejecting many of its substantive results. Weber criticized, especially, Simmel's extensive use of analogies. As he writes: 'Simmel draws examples from the most diverse provinces of knowledge to illustrate a sociological matter, and indeed frequently in the form of an "analogy"'. Weber considers the basic principles of this 'analogical procedure' as dubious (Weber, 1972, p. 160). Additionally, he also laments Simmel's concept of 'form' for being extremely vague and also notes in a critical tone that the concept of *Wechselwirkung* 'has a good deal of ambiguity in it'. According to Weber, the idea of reciprocal influence is much too broad and general. He argues that within physical reality, for example, 'an influence that is not somehow "reciprocal" in the strictest sense of the word and as a *general* phenomenon is scarcely conceivable' (p. 162). Thereby, Weber thinks that Simmel stretches the notion of *Wechselwirkung* all too far. In Simmel's sociology, Weber writes:

> one will find this concept of 'interaction' extended so far that only with the greatest artificiality will one be able to conceptualize a pure 'one-way' influence, i.e., an instance of one man [sic] being influenced by another where this is *not* some element of 'interaction' (p. 163).

However, despite his criticism of Simmel, Weber also found Simmel's texts highly stimulating and was himself greatly influenced by them, though he did not always acknowledge his debt openly. It has been speculated that some of Weber's most fundamental methodological ideas and substantial insights in *The Protestantic Ethic and the Spirit of Capitalism* have been inspired by Simmel's writings (e.g. Levine 1971, p. xlv). For example, scholars have stressed the significance of Simmel's *Philosophy of Money* for Weber's theory of occidental rationalism and for his studies in cultural history and the sociology of religion (e.g. Lichtblau, 1991). Lukács had already observed that Weber's contributions to the sociology of culture were possible only on the foundation created by Simmel (Lukács, [1918] 1993, p. 175; 1991, p. 149). What is more, Weber took Simmel's treatment of interpretation and ideal-typical concept formation in *Die Probleme der Geschichtsphilosophie* as a model and heuristic frame of reference for his enterprise of 'interpretive sociology' (*Verstehende Soziologie*) (see e.g. Tenbruck, 1958, p. 604ff; Schnabel, 1974, pp. 104ff; Bevers, 1985, pp. 125ff; Lichtblau, 1991, p. 36). Weber thought that in the book Simmel had worked out 'by far the most logically developed approaches to a theory of "interpretation"' (Weber, 1985, p. 92). Finally, Weber's famous notion of ideal types bears affinities with Simmel's pure types of forms.

Nevertheless, Simmel's sociology of forms and Weber's programme of interpretive sociology differ in many respects from each other. First, whereas Weber works out a theory of action and order, Simmel bases his sociology on the notion of *Wechselwirkung*. In his interpretative sociology Weber emphasizes the subjectively intended meaning, and thereby he founds his own approach on the meaning subjects give to their actions: 'Behind the action is the person', Weber suggests (1985, p. 496). Simmel's sociology of forms stands in striking contrast to such a perspective. Unlike Weber, Simmel does not subscribe to methodological individualism. Instead of beginning from individual subjects and the meanings they provide to their actions, Simmel insists, as we have seen, that sociology should focus on the forms of *Wechselwirkung*, interrelations, between subjects. For Simmel, these forms are irreducible to the individual members involved in the *Wechselwirkung* or to the meanings that they give to their (inter)action. As Simmel states in *Die Probleme der Geschichtsphilosophie*: 'For the fabric of social life it is particularly true: no weaver knows what he [sic] is weaving' ([1905] GSG 9, p. 252). In *Wechselwirkung*, it is the relation that is fundamental, not what is related.[6] Consequently, as Weber read Simmel's work from the perspective of interpretive sociology, he ultimately read it by using criteria that are largely inappropriate to it (Lichtblau, 1991, p. 39). For Simmel, the strivings, intentions, and motivations of individuals must always be understood within the framework of social forms. A relation of power, for example, as was already noted in Chapter 3, may not be intended by the person who is in the position of the superordinate, nor is the obedience of the subjected towards one's master and towards rules and regulations necessarily an explicit aim of his/her action, but they are operative in the interrelation (Tenbruck, 1959, p. 73). In Simmel's take on sociology, the interpretation of subjective meanings only paves the way for the analysis of social forms.

Second, while there are similarities between Simmel's idea of pure types of forms and Weber's idea of ideal types, there are also crucial differences between the two notions. With ideal types, Weber does not seek universally valid knowledge of social phenomena, but he is interested in the role and meaning of phenomena in their concrete historical settings instead. Whereas Weber uses ideal types above all as means of historical research, to study, for example, the rationalization process of Western culture, Simmel's types, by contrast, are more general and abstract by character – or universal, even. They do not vary from one culture to another or through history. On the contrary, Simmel contends that according to their pure and ideal meaning the typical forms of social relationships are valid irrespective of whether they are realized once or a thousand times. Accordingly, Weber was of the view that Simmel remained a philosopher also in his sociology. Weber regarded Simmel not as a specialist dealing with empirical questions of fact, but for him 'Simmel's ultimate *interests* are directed to metaphysical problems, to the "*meaning*" of life', and 'these interests are so very noticeable [even] in his treatment of technical substantive questions', as Weber writes in the draft of his commentary on Simmel (Weber, 1972, p. 161). Unlike Simmel, Weber was not interested in identifying universally valid forms, but in investigating concrete historical institutions and institutional constellations.

Third, while Weber worked by starting from a precise method, Simmel's work is much more elusive and shifting. And, because he read Simmel from his own perspective with emphasis on method, Weber also failed to fully notice the crucial differences between Simmel's various works and the particularities of each text.

Let it also be noted that Simmel and Weber's intellectual friendship was in many respects fairly asymmetric. While Weber refers to Simmel both directly and indirectly in various of his texts and also embarked on writing the aforementioned commentary on him, Simmel never refers to Weber's work explicitly in any of his texts. This is not to say that Simmel would have acted out of disrespect for Weber. On the contrary, their mutual friend Sophie Rickert ([1948] 1993, p. 212; trans. Scaff, 1991, p. 127) reports Simmel once telling her about Weber: 'Yes, yes, what should one say about him? ... There is no other way to put it: he was simply a genius.' This estimation is loaded with all the more meaning given the place that the notion of 'genius' holds in Simmel's thought. The Webers were also regular guests at the salon Simmel hosted at his house, and he dedicated his book *Goethe*, which he regarded as one of his most significant works, to Marianne Weber. In addition, Simmel addressed one of his last letters before his death to Max and Marianne Weber. Simmel ends the letter, dated 15 September 1918, by asking the Webers to 'be warmly thanked for all the friendship and love you have given me. As long as I breathe I will regard you as a great gift to my life and as long as I live I will also respond to you' (GSG 23, p. 1024). The Webers, however, did not seem to think as warmly of Simmel. Max Weber was a relatively cold and reserved person, who addressed very few people by their first name, and Simmel did not belong to this limited circle of close friends. In addition, while Marianne Weber was publicly grateful for the dedication expressed by Simmel in *Goethe*, privately she confessed that 'Simmel always likes to please'. Max Weber also never fully expressed just how much Simmel had taught him about philosophy and about Kant, Nietzsche, Schopenhauer, and Goethe, nor did he have a particularly high regard of Simmel as a founding figure of sociology, as I have already mentioned.[7]

In German sociology, Simmel's influence was perhaps the greatest on Theodor Litt (1880–1962), Alfred Vierkandt (1867–1953), and Leopold von Wiese (1876–1969). Interestingly, what they had in common is that all of them took up Simmel's focus on relations. In *Individuum und Gemeinschaft* (1926), Litt, who was a social philosopher, philosopher of culture, and pedagogist, made substantial use of Simmel's notion of the triad when developing his theory of social relations and structures. Vierkandt and von Wiese, for their part, drew especially on Simmel's sociology of forms. Vierkandt, who was a sociologist, ethnographer, social psychologist, social philosopher, and philosopher of history, gave primacy to 'relation' (*Beziehung*) as the grounding category of sociological thinking. He held that the study of society has to do above all with relations. By drawing explicitly from Simmel, Vierkandt defined society 'as a group, whose individuals stand in relations of interaction [*Wechselwirkungen*] to one another' and suggests that what is essential in society is 'the sheer form, the sheer fact of a relationship itself' (Vierkandt, 1916, pp. 217–18). Ultimately, Vierkandt laid his social theory on a foundation of certain 'protoforms' and established forms of social relations. Von Wiese was a sociologist and economist who received the first chair in sociology in Germany in 1919 and was also the president of the German Sociological Association between years 1946 and 1955. Already in his review of Simmel's *Soziologie* from the year 1910 von Wiese acknowledged the great contribution of Simmel's sociology: 'I am ready to consider his way as correct, and to see in his sociology a significant advance over all past attempts' (von Wiese, [1910] 1965, p. 55). Later, in his *System der allgemeinem Soziologie* ([1924/29] 1933), von Wiese made the effort to develop a general sociology, which to a great extent built on Simmel's ideas.[8] In the first place, like Simmel, von Wiese saw sociology as an independent discipline distinct from neighbouring social sciences, such as anthropology and social politics. As he writes in an article demarcating the field of social sciences in Germany: 'sociology [...] must, I said to myself, must [...] develop a field in the knowledge of social processes by which it is clearly distinct from the territories of the other neighboring sciences'. Von Wiese acknowledged that 'Simmel had, in an intelligent way, already broadened the understanding for the particularization of social subjects'. However, at the same time he also felt that Simmel had not demarcated the terrain particular to sociology in a manner that was systematic enough (von Wiese, 1951, p. 3). Secondly, von Wiese also defined that terrain in alignment with Simmel. For him, the true object of sociology should be the relationships between human beings, and sociology should, according to him, become the focal point around which the other social sciences, appearing as 'special fields of social action, that is to say, human interaction', could gather (von Wiese, 1951, pp. 2, 3). In the book *System der allgemeinem Soziologie* von Wiese aimed to classify a vast number of forms of these relationships – 650 in total – according to a few basic variables (Levine, 1971, p. xlvii).

As regards the influence that Simmel exerted in and on the German intellectual culture during the first decades of the 20th century, it is telling that he was a key source of information and inspiration for intellectuals both of the radical left and radical right. For example, Marxist philosopher Lukács (1885–1971) and National Socialist sociologist Hans Freyer (1887–1969) were both students of Simmel.[9] Lukács was highly influenced by Simmel in his early work, which combines Simmelian and Marxist elements, yet later he grew more critical towards Simmel. Simmel's sociology and philosophy are the soil from which many of the key concepts of Lukács's early work and its methodological orientation grow. It is especially Lukács's work on art and drama that Simmel's thought underpins. As Lukács admitted later in his life in an interview, 'the philosophy of my own work on drama is, truth be told, Simmel's philosophy' (Lukács, 1986, p. 48; trans. Vandenberghe, 2009, p. 135). The influence of Simmel's sociology is unmistakable, for example, in Lukács's insistence on the concept of *form* (Vandenberghe, 2009, p. 135). Lukács thinks that previously there hardly existed any *sociology* of literature, a sociology which would focus on what is 'social' in literature. For him, the failure of previous sociology of art is that it focuses on the contents of art and hastens to draw connections between them and economic relations. In contrast to this, Lukács emphasizes that the sociology of literature should study form, for 'form is what is truly social in literature' (Lukács, 1972, p. 71). And he suggests that the sociology of literature needs to 'reduce the historical-temporal elements of life, as well as the content of art forms, to a formal type and then to study the interaction between forms of life and forms of art' (Lukács, 1914, p. 303). All of this bears a strikingly Simmelian imprint.

For Lukács, drama is above all a prism through which to study the modern bourgeois. And his understanding of modern bourgeois life draws substantially from Simmel. Lukács relies especially on Simmel's ideas of alienation and reification (*Verdinglichung*) that the latter develops in *The Philosophy of Money*. As we have noted earlier, according to Simmel the cultural products created in the interactions of individuals tend to gain a life and dynamism of their own, and thus it is difficult for the individuals to assimilate them and use them to fulfil their own needs. Lukács takes up this tragic vision of culture in his essay 'Metaphysics of Tragedy', published in the book *Soul and Form* ([1910] 2010, p. 162):

> Tragedy is the becoming-real of the concrete, essential nature of man [sic]. [...] The deepest longing of human existence is the metaphysical root of tragedy: the longing of man [sic] for selfhood, the longing to transform the narrow peak of his [sic] existence into a wide plain with the path of his [sic] life winding across it, and his [sic] meaning into a daily reality. The tragic experience, dramatic tragedy, is the most perfect, the only perfect fulfilment of this longing.

Much in the manner of Simmel, Lukács also contrasts the real life of the individual to that which is general and abstract. He writes:

> Tragedy gives a firm and sure answer to the most delicate question of platonism: the question whether individual things can have idea or essence. Tragedy's answer puts the question the other way around: only that which is individual, only something whose individuality is carried to the uttermost limit, is adequate to its idea – i.e. is really existent. That which is general, that which encompasses all things yet has not a colour or form of its own, is too weak in its universality, too empty in its unity, ever to become real.[10]

Freyer, in turn, is a good example of how several of Simmel's students transformed what they received from him to their own uses. Today, Freyer is almost completely unknown among English-speaking social scientists, and he is somewhat forgotten among the younger generation of German scholars and students as well. Yet Freyer was one of the leading neo-Hegelians of his day, and he was also one of the first sociology professors in Germany, appointed at the University of Leipzig in 1924. Later, Freyer was also elected as the president of the German Sociological Association in 1933. He was an important educator, who taught many of the most influential West German sociologists and historians of the 1950s and 1960s (Muller, 1987, p. 3).

Freyer cultivated an extremist right wing strand of social thought. He believed that the solution to the problem of the loss of shared purpose and higher meaning in modernity would be found in a fully integrated society guaranteed by the state. Religious faith had lost its appeal and strength for many of Freyer's generation, and philosophical doctrines, too, were unable to provide a sense of purpose, and so Freyer found his faith in the state. He was also one of the most established German intellectuals to lend his support to Nazism, though he became disillusioned by it later. Freyer was thus both a social scientist and a political ideologist. The two roles were not at all separated from each other, but according to Jerry Z. Muller '[i]t was Freyer's radical conservative sensibilities that led him to his interest in sociology' (Muller, 1987, p. 22).[11]

In his writings, Freyer expresses dissatisfaction with capitalist society, and in Simmel it was especially the pessimistic aspects of Simmel's diagnoses of modern culture that appealed to him the most. Another key theme that Freyer took great interest in was that of 'life' (*Leben*). The cultural context of the young Freyer was the 'youth movement', *Jugendbewegung*, which sought a shared collective purpose and meaning which the younger generation felt that their educated middle class elders failed to provide (Muller, 1987, p. 4). Simmel's notion of life as restless, unstoppable flow 'fit perfectly with the self-image of the *Jugendbewegung* as a dynamic, youthful force restrained and straining against the ossified social and cultural institutions of Wilhelmine Germany' (p. 49). Freyer was also attracted to Simmel's essay 'Das individuelle Gesetz' ('The Individual Law'), published in 1913 and later incorporated into the book *The View of Life* (orig. *Lebensanschauung*). The essay proposes a solution to the problem of moral relativism which preoccupied Freyer to a great extent in his early writings (p. 49).

Simmel was an important interlocutor also for Karl Mannheim (1893–1947), a pioneer of the sociology of knowledge. Mannheim was Hungarian-born like Lukács, who was also Mannheim's mentor. In 1914, Mannheim travelled to Berlin to study with Simmel, and it was Lukács who advised him to do so, although at that point he had already come to the conclusion that he himself had nothing to learn from Simmel anymore. Simmel's influence is present, for example, in *Ideology and Utopia*, where Mannheim's account of the 'intellectual' is inspired by the Simmelian notion of the stranger (Kettler, 2012, p. 280). In addition, Mannheim engaged with Simmel's work explicitly by writing pieces on it. In 1917, Mannheim wrote a review of Simmel's wartime writings, and the next year, following Simmel's death, he published a piece 'Georg Simmel as Philosopher'. The review of Simmel's war writings discusses both Simmel's analysis of the crisis of culture that in Simmel's view had led to the war and his thoughts of the possibilities that the war might bring. According to Simmel, the pre-war culture was characterized by objectification, alienation, and the preponderance of means over ends. Though he did not think that the war could really solve the crisis, he nevertheless was convinced that the war opened up new possibilities, such as the idea of humanity gaining a new form in a forthcoming 'man' who would arise from the war. For Mannheim, this is the only thing that brings consolation and hope in Simmel's war writings that he otherwise finds utterly pessimistic (Kettler, 2012, p. 281). The text 'Georg Simmel as Philosopher', in turn, is a mixture of an obituary tribute and a philosophical, critical assessment of Simmel's work. While Mannheim appreciates Simmel as a profound philosopher who possessed the Socratic virtue of wonder, he laments that Simmel's studies lack truth, for in them the personality of the author overshadows rather than lights up the subject matter. The text marks Mannheim's departure and distancing from Simmel for a long time afterwards. It was only in his later work that he came to re-appreciate Simmel's philosophical themes which he had judged in a negative manner in 'Georg Simmel as Philosopher' (Kettler, 2012, p. 283).

Herman Schmalenbach (1885–1950), too, who later became professor of philosophy in Göttingen and Basel, was a student of Simmel. Schmalenbach is renowned especially for refining the sociological categories of *Gemeinschaft* and 'league' or 'alliance' (*Bund*) (Lüschen & Stone, 1977). In 1919, following Simmel's death, Schmalenbach also wrote an appraising obituary of his former teacher, which was published in *Sozialistische Monatshefte*. As for other contemporaries in Germany influenced by Simmel, it is crucial to mention Martin Buber (1878–1956), who was once a student of Simmel's. There are significant resonances between Simmel's conception of the dyadic relation between the I and the you and the dialogical philosophy of Buber. Buber's theorizing on the I–you relation in his book *Ich und Du* (1923), which is without doubt among the essential works and key sources of 20th-century dialogicalism, bears parallels and resemblance to Simmel's ideas and formulations, but Buber mentions Simmel not even once in the book. This is quite telling of Simmel's position also more generally. As he himself had predicted, his students took from him what they had found useful, and the uses to which these ideas were put did not necessarily acknowledge their indebtedness to the original source. Simmel's ideas became less and less known by his name.

Influence on continental philosophy: the case of Simmel and Heidegger

Even though Simmel's impact was the most profound in sociology, his work opened a significant path in 20th-century continental philosophy, too. Several features and elements of his stance were shared with major philosophical currents, such as phenomenology, existentialism, and vitalism. And the issue actually goes beyond sheer parallels and common features, as Simmel also exerted influence on certain key figures of continental thought, such as some members of the Frankfurt school, Karl Jaspers (1883–1969), and Martin Heidegger (1889–1976). Of the representatives of the Frankfurt school, it was Walter Benjamin (1892–1940) who was most influenced by Simmel. Benjamin took up some aspects of Simmel's work in his *Arcades Project* and its analyses of modernity as well as in his work on tragic drama, and his notion of the 'origin' (*Ursprung*), too, bears a debt to Simmel (Frisby, 2006, p. 56). Even Theodor Adorno, despite his severe criticism towards Simmel, gave him credit as the master of the essay form and, as was noted earlier, for turning the attention of philosophical enquiry into concrete objects (Adorno, 1984, pp. 9, 558). As for Jaspers, his concepts of 'self-being' (*Selbstsein*) and 'authenticity' (*Echtheit*) have been traced back to Simmel (Landmann & Susman, 1957, p. vi).[12] But it is Heidegger's relation to Simmel's work that is most fascinating, because Heidegger's thought has largely set the agenda for subsequent continental thought. In this section, I will therefore examine in more detail the parallels between Simmel and Heidegger and traces of possible influence.

When Heidegger's *Being and Time* (orig. *Sein und Zeit*) came out in 1927, the book was an immediate sensation. In 1969, Hannah Arendt wrote of the work that it had exerted an 'extraordinarily lasting influence, which very few writings of this century can match' (in Arendt & Heidegger, 2004, p. 149).[13] In the book, Heidegger treats posing the question of 'being' as the primary task of philosophy. According to him, human beings differ from all other beings in that what is at stake in their being is being itself. Thus for him the being of human beings, which Heidegger addresses with the term *Dasein*, meaning literally 'being-there', also discloses all other modes of being. Heidegger insists that *Dasein*'s being is both spatial and temporal; spatial insofar as *Dasein is* by being-in-the-world, and temporal insofar as its being is finite, being-towards-death.

Interestingly, in *Being and Time* Heidegger makes reference to Simmel a couple of times, in particular when discussing *Dasein*'s being-towards-death. For example, in §49, Heidegger writes in a note: 'Recently, G. Simmel has also explicitly included the phenomenon of death in his characterization of "life", though admittedly without clearly separating the biological-ontic and the ontological existential problematics' (Heidegger, 1962, pp. 494–5 n. vi). However, Simmel had already figured in Heidegger's earlier writings. In *Grundprobleme der Phänomenologie* ([1919/20] 2010, p. 9; *The Basic Problems of Phenomenology*), Heidegger refers to the contribution of Simmel's *View of Life* by acknowledging that 'Simmel [has] created access to a new way of looking at the living spirit and its productions'. However, Heidegger criticizes Simmel's thought for being 'very formalistic', which has only got worse in the hands of all the 'busy small "Simmels"' who turn his ideas to sheer 'witticist conceptual play' and empty formalism (p. 9). In Simmel's own thought, by contrast, Heidegger finds something original and of value. For him, Simmel's last works are close to 'genuine intuition' and present a 'valuable ferment of philosophical problematic' (p. 10). In addition, when discussing life's self-sufficiency Heidegger refers in §7 to Simmel's observation of the bounded nature (*Grenzcharakter*) of life.

However, Simmel's presence in Heidegger's thought goes much deeper than what the passing references manifest. Simmel's life-philosophy, in particular the book *The View of Life*, had a deep impact on Heidegger. The influence has been reported among others by Hans Georg Gadamer. In *Truth and Method*, Gadamer notes:

> As early as 1923, Heidegger spoke to me with admiration of the late writings of Georg Simmel. This was not just a general acknowledgment of Simmel as a philosophical personality. The specific stimulus that Heidegger had received from his work will be apparent to anyone who today reads, in the first of the four 'Metaphysical Chapters' gathered together under the title *Lebensanschauung*, what the dying Simmel conceived as his philosophical task. (Gadamer, [1975] 2004, p. 264 n. 138)

But we do not have to rely here on Gadamer's assessment alone, for we also have Heidegger's own testimony of the matter at hand (though one mediated, again, by Gadamer). In his *Erinnerung* (1986/7, p. 24), Gadamer recounts Heidegger once confessing to him: 'Simmel's "Vier metaphysische Kapitel" were of fundamental significance for my introduction to philosophy.'

In *Being and Time*, Heidegger goes through great pains to keep his existential-ontological analytic of *Dasein* at a safe distance from any analysis of sheer life. This holds as much for biology and psychology as for anthropology, but it is especially in opposition to life-philosophy that Heidegger delineates his existential analytics.[14] Life-philosophy poses the question of 'life' as its grounding problem, and for Heidegger this designates the forgetting of the question of 'being' (*Sein*), which he himself regards as fundamental. Heidegger does give life-philosophy credit among other things for the fact that in it, at least in its 'serious and scientifically-minded' versions (he seems to have in mind here especially Dilthey), 'there lies an unexpressed tendency towards an understanding of Dasein's Being'. However, for him the principal flaw of life-philosophy is that it never comes to treat life as *a mode of being* in ontological terms (Heidegger, 1962, §10 p. 72). Even at its best it is only on the way towards an existential analytic; the existential analytical intention is not articulate enough in it.

Nevertheless, despite Heidegger's persistent efforts to keep his project at distance from life-philosophy, Simmel's insights are to a great extent immanent in his existential analytics, so much so that Simmel's life-philosophy even seems to belong to the soil from which Heidegger's analysis of time and especially *Dasein*'s being-towards-end grows. I will settle for making three concise points:[15]

First, like Simmel, Heidegger (1962, §49 p. 290) perceives death as a 'phenomenon of life', as a boundary of life still part of life. Neither of the two philosophers think of death as a violent interruption of life that would befall to it as if from outside. Simmel abjures this kind of idea by introducing a conceptual distinction between 'dying' (*Sterben*) and 'being killed' (*Getötetwerden*) (Simmel, [1918] GSG 16, p. 300). Whereas in being killed death remains something exterior and alien to life, something accidental that falls upon it from outside, in dying, by contrast, death as that which ultimately abolishes life belongs originally and inwardly to the very nature and being of life. Dying is therefore primordial to being killed, for a living being can be killed only on the condition that it is possible for it to die ([1918] GSG 16, p. 300). Hence, for Simmel, death is immanent in life. In a manner similar to Simmel, Heidegger rejects the idea of *Dasein*'s death as something advening from the outside and, as already hinted, it is to this end that he makes the distinction into 'dying' (*Sterben*) and 'perishing' (*Verenden*), the latter of which he equates with physiological death (Heidegger, 1962, §47 p. 284; §49 p. 291). According to Heidegger, dying is not external to the life of *Dasein* but immanent in it. The care of *Dasein*, its everyday concern of others and things in its environment, and its own mode of existence, is always fundamentally connected to the threat of death. On page 289 in section §48 of *Being and Time* he writes that:

> just as Dasein *is* already its 'not-yet', and is its 'not-yet' constantly as long as it is, it *is* already its end too. The 'ending' which we have in view when we speak of death, does not signify Dasein's Being-at-an-end [*Zu-Ende-Sein*], but a *Being-towards-the-end* [*Sein zum Ende*] of this entity. Death is a way to be, which Dasein takes over as soon as it is. 'As soon as man comes to life, he is at once old enough to die.'

Heidegger thus concludes that death belongs to the existence of *Dasein* as its ownmost possibility: with proper-being-towards-death, *Dasein* stands before itself in its 'ownmost potentiality-for-Being' (Heidegger, 1962, §50 p. 294). Proper being-towards-the-end creates an anxious moment of resolution in which *Dasein* does not anymore flee into everyday averageness of *das Man*, but rather nullifies its routinized being-in-the-world by confronting the nothingness of death. For Heidegger, dying is *Dasein*'s absolutely ownmost, independent and non-relational possibility that does not depend on the everyday power of others.

Herein lies the second striking similarity between Simmel and Heidegger besides the aforementioned idea of the immanence of death in life. While Heidegger regards dying as something proper to *Dasein*, Simmel sees dying as a defining factor of the life of the individual: it is only individuals who are capable of dying. For Simmel, non-individual beings may be killed, have their thread of life suddenly and accidentally cut off; but in their case, death is not yet an internal possibility of life (Simmel, [1918] GSG 16, pp. 300, 328, 330). According to Simmel only the life of the individual is accompanied by immanent death in each and every moment.

On this account, death is thus the foundation of my ownmost, independent and non-relational individuality and, as such, also the ownmost, independent and non-relational *possibility* of *my* existence, Heidegger thinks. Indeed, analogous to Simmel ([1918] GSG 16, p. 328), who insists that only the individual dies 'fully' (*vollständig*), Heidegger (1962, §48 p. 288) contends that it is only *Dasein* who 'ends fully' (*vollendet*).

The third parallel between Simmel and Heidegger I would like to draw attention to pertains to the interconnectedness of life/*Dasein* and time. If one acknowledges that time is the essence of *Dasein*, in temporal terms *Dasein* even becomes equivalent to life. In *Der Begriff der Zeit* (1989, p. 19; *The Concept of Time*), Heidegger writes that 'Dasein, conceived in its most extreme possibility of Being, *is time itself*, not *in* time'. In *The View of Life* ([1918] GSG 16, p. 221; 2010, p. 8), Simmel had noted in a manner not dissimilar to this: 'Time is real only for life alone. [...] Time is the – perhaps abstract – form in our consciousness of that which is life itself, as experienced in inexpressible, immediate concreteness.' The identification of life/*Dasein* with time is afforded for both Simmel and Heidegger by the *self-transcendence* that both see as being characteristic of life/*Dasein*. According to Simmel, life ceaselessly reaches out beyond its old forms and creates new ones. Constant striving beyond itself belongs to the character of life's mode of being (Simmel [1918] GSG 16, p. 221). As Simmel puts it in *Rembrandt* ([1916] GSG 15, p. 385; 2005, p. 57), 'life is that which at all points wants to go beyond itself, reaching out beyond itself'.

To sum up, in spite of Heidegger's efforts to separate his existential-ontological analysis of *Dasein* from the ontic question of the life of entities, he never fully managed to escape the question of life. When seen from the life-philosophical perspective, life appears as nothing more or less than the necessary ground for the ontological analysis of *Dasein*. However, even though Heidegger could not keep the question of life at the distance he desired, in *Being and Time* he yet managed to discuss death as an ontological question concerning how the world unfolds for *Dasein*. Existential-ontological analysis of death thus does not refer to death as an ontic question concerning the end of the life of beings, including human beings, but rather as an ontological question concerning the possibility for the openness of being and its unfolding (Pyyhtinen & Joronen, forthcoming). In fact, the proper definition of *Dasein* refers precisely to the kind of being for whom its own way of being is a question. Nevertheless, since death is also a phenomenon of *life*, the existential interpretation of death is intrinsically connected to life and life-philosophy.

However, what remains on the Simmelian side beyond the affinities between the two thinkers is a kind of animal vitality – a life embodied in the living organism without fully coinciding with it. Though Simmel's life-philosophy is mainly concerned with the world-relation of humans, rather than confirming human exceptionality, it places humans on a par with all living organisms. In *Rembrandt* ([1916] GSG 15, p. 401; 2005, p. 71), Simmel concedes: 'Death is a quality of organic existence.' That is, unlike an inorganic piece of matter, which finds its limits determined from the outside, the limits of an organic body are not only spatial but also temporal: the form of the organic body is limited from within, by the fact that it is finite (Simmel, [1918] GSG 16 p. 297; 2010, p. 63). A death that is immanent in life is appropriate to anything that is living, and thus it is also indifferent to any conceptual barriers erected between living beings.[16] The human individual, too, is dying precisely as a living *organism*, as some-body that is alive.

Early reception in France and the broken collaboration with Durkheim

Although Simmel's influence was the greatest in Germany, he was also known abroad. In France, Simmel was introduced to the social scientists above all by Célestin Bouglé, who was a student of Durkheim's and a member of the journal *Anneé sociologie* founded by Durkheim. After the Franco-Prussian War in 1870–1, it was common for French students and young scholars to go to Germany to study. This applied not only to France, but the German university institution had prestige even more widely. For instance the US and Japan were sending many students to Germany each year to absorb and bring back German thought and education. Durkheim, too, visited Germany in the academic year 1885–6. He went to Berlin, but this was before Simmel received his position as a *Privatdozent*, an unpaid lecturer, at the University of Berlin, and at that point Simmel had not yet gained much recognition, either (Fitzi, 2002, pp. 20–1). It was rather the younger scholars of the next generation who began their studies in the 1890s who attended Simmel's lectures and learned from him, Bouglé among them.

The year 1894 marks the beginning of Simmel's early reception in France. That year were published the first French translations of his writings, the texts 'La differentiation sociale' in *Revue international sociologie* and 'Le problem de la sociologie' in *Revue de la métaphysique*. The first was translated by René Worms, who had established the Institut International de Sociologie a year earlier in Paris. Simmel was also in correspondence with Worms. Their relation was seriously damaged, however, by the fact that Simmel was very unhappy with Worm's translation, which contained several errors and to some extent Worms also changed the content without consulting Simmel before publication. Therefore Simmel did not want to publish in *Revue* anymore. Even though he still published the piece 'Influence du nombre des unites sociales sur les caractéres des sociétés' in Worms's *Annales de l'institut international de sociologie* the following year, in 1895, Simmel was so dissatisfied with the poor quality of work that Worms had done with 'La differentiation sociale' that he did not want to give his essay 'Das Problem der Sociologie' to Worms for translation, but sought other contacts instead.[17] The essay came out in September 1894 as translated by Bouglé, and Simmel was quite happy with the quality (see his letter to Bouglé dated 31 May 1894: GSG 22, pp. 124–5). In 1894, Bouglé also published two texts, *Notes d'un étudiant français* and 'Les sciences sociales en Allemagne: G. Simmel', which were the first French texts discussing Simmel's sociology.

Bouglé regards Simmel's sociology as very different from that of Durkheim and allies it with that of Tarde: 'Whichever way you look at it, Simmel's thought moves away from that of Durkheim and approaches that of Tarde.' (Bouglé, 1965, p. 63) The extensive similarities Bouglé sees in Simmel's and Tarde's methods are ultimately based on the fact that for both 'the analysis of mental interaction is the essence of sociology' (p. 62). Nevertheless, despite opposing Simmel's sociology to that of Durkheim, Bouglé also acted as a key mediator between the two thinkers, when Durkheim invited Simmel to participate in the founding of *L'Année de sociologique*. Fitzi (2002, p. 35) suggests that the invitation was motivated by their shared striving to establish sociology as an autonomous science. In addition, Simmel was already an 'advising editor' of *The American Journal of Sociology*, and it would certainly not have been of any harm to the *Année* to have on board a scholar who enjoyed some international recognition and had contacts to the US. However, the collaboration between Simmel and Durkheim did not last for long. It was already starting to break during the preparations of the first volume of the journal. Durkheim had asked Simmel to contribute to *L'Année* with a piece on the self-preservation of society that he would himself translate together with Bouglé. Durkheim originally suggested that the text be around 50 pages in total length, but the draft Simmel eventually submitted was approximately three times longer. Durkheim ended up shortening the piece considerably by excluding some passages, and he also changed the title without consulting Simmel. Whereas the German text came out in 1898 titled 'Die Selbsterhaltung der socialen Gruppe. Soziologische Studie' ('The Self-preservation of Social Groups. A Sociological Study'), the title of the French translation published the same year read 'Comment les formes sociales se maintiennent' ('How social forms are maintained') (Fitzi, 2002, pp. 36–7).

However, in the last instance, the conflict resulting from their diverging views about the piece published in *L'Année de sociologique* was not what broke the collaboration. Durkheim's and Simmel's conceptions of sociology as well as of its method and epistemological foundation simply lie so far from each other that a fruitful collaboration was not possible. Their relation continued in more hostile terms a couple of years later. For example, Durkheim responded to *The Philosophy of Money* with an utterly negative and critical tone. While he found the first analytical part of the book 'by far the clearer', in his view the examinations in the second synthetic part:

> defy analysis; too many different issues are examined in them, and it is not always easy to make out the thread that binds them into a unified whole. It is true that the work contains a number of ingenious ideas, pungent views, curious or even at

times surprising comparisons, and a certain number of historical and ethnographic facts, unfortunately imprecise and unwarranted as reported. The reading of the book, though laborious, is interesting and in places suggestive. But the objective value of the views that are proposed to us is not commensurate with their ingenuity. (Durkheim, 1980, p. 97)

However, the two authors were in conflict even prior to that. In 1899, an Italian translation of Simmel's 1894 essay 'Das Problem der Sociologie', 'Il problema della sociologica', was published in the journal *La riforma sociale*. For the publication of the translation Simmel had revised the piece considerably.[18] A year later, in 1900, Durkheim responded to Simmel's essay with the article 'La sociologia e il suo domino scientifico' that he published in another Italian journal, *Rivista italiana di sociologia*. In the text, Durkheim criticizes Simmel's work explicitly. While he admits that Simmel has made a significant contribution in attempting to secure sociology a firm foothold as a scientific field, Durkheim laments that the foundation Simmel lays out to sociology is merely subjective, expressing the thinker's individual worldview, instead of giving sociology an objective epistemological basis.

What is more, Durkheim accused Simmel of psychologism. In Durkheim's view, social facts are independent of the individual psyche (Durkheim 1982, pp. 54–7). In *The Rules of Sociological Method* (1982, p. 52), Durkheim suggests that social facts consist of 'certain manners of acting, thinking and feeling external to the individual, which are invested with a coercive power by virtue of which they exercise power over him' [sic]. Their fundamental characteristics for Durkheim are in other words exteriority and coerciveness. And thus he formulates the following rule: 'The determining cause of a social fact should be sought among antecedent the social facts and not among the states of individual consciousness.' (p. 134) Thereby, in Durkheim's view, sociology deals with collective representations which are independent of the psychological processes of individuals. This is also why Durkheim objected to Simmel's idea that the preconditions of society would be found in individual consciousness. He insisted that collective representations cannot be explained by individual psychology.

Durkheim also refuted Simmel's distinction into form and content – or 'container' (*contenant*) and 'content' (*contenu*), as he misinterpreted it. According to him, the distinction is not justified. Accordingly, Simmel and Durkheim had a very different idea of what it means to do sociological research. Whereas Simmel regards the forms of interrelations that constitute society as the object of sociology, for Durkheim sociology is about observing social facts scientifically. The distinction between form and content does not help to identify collective phenomena or collective representations.

The negative reception by Durkheim and his school around the turn of the century was significantly contrasted by the publication of *Mélanges de philosophie relativiste* (1912), a collection of Simmel's essays in French translation, and the renewed interest in Simmel that it gave rise to. Bergson had an active role in the process of its publication, as it was he who initiated it and he also recruited the translator Alix Guillain to the task. Bergson regarded it as important to make Simmel known as a philosopher in France, though later in his war writings he denied having had anything to do with the translation (Fitzi, 2002, pp. 238–9). *Mélanges* appeared a year later than the German collection *Philosophische Kultur*, which had been published in 1911. Interestingly, both of the volumes focus on philosophical culture, as is clearly announced by the title of the German book and the subtitle *Contributions à la culture philosophique* of *Mélanges*. However, it is crucial to observe that *Mélanges* has a quite different emphasis compared to *Philosophische Kultur*. Unlike the latter, it is explicitly ordered under the keyword 'relativism'. Fitzi notes that while in Germany the notion of 'relativism' bore negative connotations, in France it was not associated with epistemological or ethical scepticism. On the contrary, the expression *philosophie relativiste* had a very positive meaning (Fitzi, 2002, pp. 243–4).

So, interestingly, the renewed French interest in Simmel already appreciated his relational mode of thought. In contrast to the earlier reception around the turn of the century, Simmel was now read above all as a relativist philosopher. Alfred Mamelet's *Le Relativisme Philosophique chez Georg Simmel* (1914) exemplifies this well. Originally the study had appeared as four individual essays in issues of *Revue de la métaphysique* between years 1912 to 1913, but Mamelet subsequently collected the papers together into the monograph. In the book, Mamelet interprets relativism within the framework of Kant's transcendental philosophy, and thereby he also sees Simmel's relativism as growing from Kant's work (Fitzi, 2002, p. 247). Although the book focuses on Simmel as a philosopher, Mamelet touches on Simmel's sociology, too, and links it with his relativist philosophy.[19] As he writes: 'The sociology of Simmel is very clearly governed and directed by his relativist point of view, in particular by the notion of the complementarity and reciprocity of action' (Mamelet, 1965, p. 73). Mamelet sees that Simmel's sociological relativism is 'from the outset, clearly opposed to contemporary French sociology' (p. 64). He contrasts Simmel's conception of sociology above all to that of Durkheim. For Mamelet, Simmel's sociology has the advantage over Durkheimian sociology that, first, it is not only 'much wider in scope' but, second, it also pays attention to the processes on which social formations are based. As Mamelet remarks, Simmel's sociology does 'not limit itself, as does Durkheim's sociology, to the study of social macrocosms which are objectified, large-scale, synthetic, secondary, and detached from the human interactions from which they derive', but it 'show[s] us the microcosmic structures of society and help[s] us to grasp the detail of the processes of which large-scale institutions [...] are the result' (pp. 65–6).

Due to its open-ended relation to the world, Mamelet sees relativism as a usable heuristic means. Nevertheless, *Le Relativisme Philosophique chez Georg Simmel* criticizes Simmel's 'relativism' or relational mode of thought – and all transcendental philosophy in general – especially for being unable to grasp the metaphysical unity of the world. Mamelet insists that only a philosophical system can achieve this. For him, relativism remains too tightly within the domain of science to build a metaphysics (Fitzi, 2002, pp. 248–9). Mamelet's placement of Simmel's relational approach under Kant's transcendental philosophy is without doubt dubious, for Simmel's relationalism is in no way reducible to it, and Simmel's mature work, especially his life-philosophy, is in fact highly critical of it. Further, it can also be argued against Mamelet that Simmel's philosophical relationalism is primarily concerned with supplementing scientific knowledge by offering an overarching view of the totality of the world. All these problems notwithstanding, Mamelet's study is significant and interesting in that it stands as a testimony of how already some of Simmel's contemporaries engaged themselves in his 'relativism' or relationalism. What is more, it also exemplifies that in France the word 'relativism' was not understood in a negative sense, associated with subjectivism and scepticism (p. 249), but it was conceived in a manner truer to Simmel, as referring to how relations are constitutive of reality.

Early North American reception

Simmel's sociology also had a following very early in the United States, and this was much wider than, for example, in France, where Simmel remained within relatively limited circles and was never accepted as a key author and only rarely used as a theoretical resource. Donald N. Levine, Ellwood B. Carter, and Eleanor Miller Groman (1976a, p. 813) suggest that in American sociology 'Simmel stands in the unusual position of being the only European scholar who has had a palpable influence on sociology in the United States throughout the course of the 20th century'. The influence is all the more remarkable considering the fact that American sociology has been a characteristically 'homegrown product' (p. 813). In their paper, published in two parts in *The American Journal of Sociology* in 1976, Levine and his colleagues identify three different phases in the transmission of Simmel's ideas into American sociology. It began with an initial wave of translations which took place between 1890 and 1930. Around that time, the assimilation of Simmel's work was strongly associated especially with the University of Chicago. During the second phase, in 1930–55, the engagement with Simmel's thought became more widely dispersed and also collections of his writings were published as English translations. Finally, the authors identify the third period, running from 1955 to 1975, as a period of more systematic and critical scrutiny, during which Simmel's writings were mined in search of new theoretical ideas and hypotheses.

In this section, I will focus on the early reception of Simmel's work in the United States; I will cover its subsequent rediscovery and transmission later in Chapter 9. The initial transmission of Simmel's thought was largely due to student mobility. Simmel's ideas were brought into North American sociology by people who had visited Germany during their studies and been in direct contact with him. Levine and others remark that 'nearly every translation of Simmel into English and nearly every major presentation of Simmel through university instruction had been the work of Americans who had been in Germany, immigrants from central Europe, or students of either or both of these two small groups' (Levine et al., 1976a, p. 820).

During the last quarter of the 19th century, several young students from the United States travelled abroad, mostly to Germany, to escape the great intellectual insecurity of their home country and seek proper education. Most of them went to Leipzig and Berlin, which were the two centres of education in Germany at the time. As for the University of Berlin, it had been successful in appointing a galaxy of leading German academics, such as Wilhelm Dilthey, Hermann von Helmholtz, Gustav Schmoller, and Johann Gustav Droysen.

Among the many Americans who had spent some of their student days in Germany was Albion W. Small (1854–1926), who later became the first sociology professor in the United States. Small also founded the first department of sociology in the United States at the University of Chicago in 1892. He himself had not studied with Simmel, for he had stayed in Berlin already in 1879–1880, before Simmel started teaching courses at the university, but the two men met later and also were in correspondence. Small was a key figure in the early North American Simmel reception by insistently promoting Simmel's work. Though he was not really a follower of Simmel, he nevertheless had high appreciation of Simmel and his efforts to define the sociological domain. Small held the task of primordial value. As he wrote to a colleague in 1908, 'the main business of my life is to show that there is a definitely definable field for the division of social science to which we are applying the name Sociology' (cited in Levine et al., 1976a, p. 816). While Small criticized Simmel's conception of sociology for being too narrow, he nonetheless regarded the study of social forms as 'an important *part*' of sociology (Levine, 1971, p. xlviii) and felt that in their investigation Simmel was 'without a rival'.

Small's contribution to the American reception of Simmel took place especially via the journal *American Journal of Sociology* (*AJS*) that was founded by him in 1895. Small also invited Simmel to join the editorial board as an 'advising editor'.[20] Under Small's editorship and mostly using his translations the journal published all in all nine essays by Simmel between years 1896 and 1910:

(1) 'Superiority and Subordination as a Subject-Matter of Sociology' (vol. 2, in 1896–7);
(2) 'The Persistence of Social Groups' (vols 3–4, in 1897–8);
(3) 'A Chapter in the Philosophy of Value' (vol. 5, in 1898–9);
(4) 'The Number of Members as Determining the Sociological Form of the Group' (vol. 8, in 1902–3);
(5) 'The Sociology of Conflict' (vol. 9, in 1903–4);

(6) 'A Contribution to the Sociology of Religion' (vol. 11, in 1905);
(7) 'The Sociology of Secrecy and Secret Societies' (vol. 11, in 1906);
(8) 'The Problem of Sociology' (vol. 15, in 1909); and
(9) 'How is Society Possible?' (vol. 16, in 1910).

It is noteworthy that this list of translations includes none of Simmel's early sociological writings influenced by Spencerian perspectives, but they focus on what is typically considered as his middle, sociological, period, and display his sociology of forms accordingly. Small was a fierce critic of Spencer's sociology and its idea of natural selection, as he felt it leads to 'societary fatalism'. The efforts to counter the Spencerian approach are explicit especially in the early issues of *AJS*, and besides appreciating Simmel's attempt to provide sociology a firm methodological foundation, Small also regarded Simmel's work as helpful in this endeavour of dethroning Spencer (Levine, 1971, p. xlviii; Jaworski, 1997, p. 9).

However, to be precise, *AJS* was not the first journal to introduce Simmel to an American audience. Extensive and favourable reviews of Simmel's books had already come out in *The Philosophical Review* ever since its first volume in 1892 and, prior to the translations published in *AJS*, translations of Simmel's texts had appeared in two American journals: 'Moral Deficiencies as Determining Intellectual Functions' came out in *International Journal of Ethics* in 1893, and 'The Problem of Sociology' was originally published in *Annals of the American Academy of Political and Social Science* in 1895 (hence preceding its publication in *AJS* by 14 years). Nevertheless, *AJS* was the first academic journal to have a systematic programme of translating Simmel's writings. The leitmotif of the programme was very clear, as all of the *AJS* translations lay out the methodological foundation of sociology as an independent discipline.

Despite Small's important efforts, Simmel would probably have remained a marginal figure in American sociology were it not for Robert E. Park (1864–1944), who was Small's successor at the Department of Sociology in Chicago. While translations are without doubt important in making accessible the ideas of an author writing in a foreign language, they do not yet guarantee that those ideas are actually taken up and used by scholars. Unlike Small, Park also studied with Simmel. During the winter semester of 1899–1900, Park took Simmel's courses in sociology, ethics, and 19th-century philosophy (Jaworski, 1997, p. 15).

Park had a key role in the development of what has later come to be known as the Chicago School of sociology. Park has become famous especially for his work on human ecology, race, ethnic relations, minority groups, social movements, and social disorganization, all of which he studied by conducting ethnographic fieldwork in Chicago. Indeed, Park considered the city as an exemplary site for sociological investigation, a kind of 'laboratory or clinic' to study 'human nature and social processes', as he suggests in his seminal essay

'The City' (1915, p. 612). Park contributed significantly to the development of urban sociology by broadening its field and formulating some guiding principles, and the perspective on the city developed by Park and other members of the Chicago School gained a privileged and paradigmatic position in subsequent urban sociology.

Much like Simmel, Park thought that the city is intimately intertwined with the 'vital processes of the people who compose it' and has consequences for the social interaction of the people inhabiting it. However, curiously Park does not mention Simmel at all in his 1915 essay. Of the members of the Chicago School it was in particular Park's student Louis Wirth who brought to attention Simmel's significance for the sociological analysis of the city and urban way of life. Wirth (1925, p. 219) famously hailed Simmel's metropolis essay as 'the most important single article on the city from a sociological standpoint'. He also drew on it later in his important paper 'Urbanism as a Way of Life' (1938). In the paper Wirth sets out to identify the characteristic elements of urbanism, which mark it as a distinctive mode of collective life. He felt that the city cannot be defined with the help of any single criterion, but instead proposed a definition that emphasizes several features: size, density, permanence, and heterogeneity. As Wirth formulates it himself: 'For sociological purposes a city may be defined as a relatively large, dense, and permanent settlement of socially heterogeneous individuals' (Wirth, 1938, p. 8). The definition has subsequently become classic in urban studies. Simmel had already paid attention to the size, density, and heterogeneity of metropolises. And the paper does bear great resemblance to Simmel, for example when Wirth addresses the great amount of social contacts that an urban inhabitant has and yet knows personally only a small proportion of the people s/he interacts with. In the following passage Wirth clearly seems to have Simmel in mind when he refers to the 'students of the mental life of cities':

> the segmentalization of human relationships [...] has sometimes been seized upon by students of the mental life of cities as an explanation for the 'schizoid' character of urban personality. This is not to say that the urban inhabitants have fewer acquaintances than rural inhabitants, for the reverse may actually be true; it means rather that in relation to the number of people whom they see and with whom they rub elbows in the course of daily life, they know a smaller proportion and of those they have less intensive knowledge. (Wirth, 1938, p. 12)

Coming back to Park, even though Simmel is not mentioned in his 1915 essay on the city, he does cite Simmel elsewhere and is greatly indebted to him. Later Park acknowledged that it was from Simmel that he received his only 'formal instruction in sociology' (Hughes, 1964, p. 18). From Simmel, Park received the fundamental point of view for his sociological studies. The key concept of Park's sociology, 'interaction', is an extension and rendering into English of Simmel's notion of *Wechselwirkung*.

Park appears to have explicitly received from Simmel the following ideas (Levine, 1971, p. lii):

(1) sociology should examine the ideal types of forms of interaction abstracted from their contents;
(2) when describing forms one should also attend to their emergence (what Park called 'natural histories') and also be alert to the tensions between stabilized form and spontaneous process;
(3) the idea of social distance, and its use in investigating social types, such as the stranger (Park: 'marginal man');
(4) the idea of circular interaction;
(5) the idea of conflict, and 'the oscillation between conflict and accommodation; the relation between out-group hostilities and in-group morale; the way in which group antagonisms provide a basis for stabilizing social structure.'

Hence, Park took up several of the key aspects of Simmel's thought, among them the relational emphasis on interaction as well the focus on form. Nevertheless, Park did not simply emulate Simmel but, as with so many students of Simmel, he transformed what he had received to his own uses. For example, as Levine argues, Park 'altered Simmel's definition of what constitutes a social fact, and he shifted the main referent of interaction from that of *trans*action to that of *concerted* action' (Levine, 1971, p. lii). This rendering shows the influence of both William G. Sumner (1840–1910) and Durkheim who emphasized moral regulation as the most significant aspect of social life (p. lii). Simmel's understanding of *Wechselwirkung*, by contrast, is pre-normative or morally neutral. For him, norms themselves are based on *Wechselwirkung* and present one of its side effects. Unlike Simmel, for whom sociology is the science of forms of association (*Vergesellschaftung*), Park conceived of sociology as 'the science of collective behavior', with its focus on the processes of communication through which collectivities attain consensus about values and goals. Levine (1971) has proposed that this shift has three methodological implications. First, whereas for Simmel sociology should study the 'empirical referents of analytically abstracted types of social interaction', Park insisted that the empirical focus of sociology should be on 'the types of concrete collectivities' (p. liii). Second, Levine suggests that Park's understanding of sociology as the science of collective behaviour shifts sociology's 'explanatory focus' to how the collectivities based on shared values and goals 'come into being, persist, and change' (p. liii). However, I think Levine gets it wrong when he portrays Simmel's sociology as focused on 'the structural implications of a particular kind of form' (p. liii). As I have argued above (in Chapter 3), Simmel is greatly preoccupied with the dynamics of social life as well as with the interplay of life and form, and the coming into being, development, and cessation of relations hold a central place in his sociology. Third, and finally, Levine aptly observes that

Park and Simmel ultimately had a substantially different notion of sociality. Whereas Simmel regarded all social phenomena as being based on dualisms, contrasts, or tensions, Park identified sociality with consensus (he relegated competition and conflict to the sphere of the 'presocial' or 'subsocial') (p. liii).

In sum, while Park, unlike Small, was a follower of Simmel, he did not continue the latter's programme of sociology. For example, while Park insisted, in a manner owing much to Simmel, that collectives are not substantive entities but products of interaction, he arrived at a very different notion of the social than Simmel. As Park equated social order with moral order, he came to regard conflict as a source of disruption, whereas for Simmel conflict may also serve to stabilize social order (Levine et al., 1976a, p. 826).

It was above all the reader *Introduction to the Science of Sociology*, which Park published with his younger colleague Ernest W. Burgess in 1921, that came to form his most significant contribution to the transmission of Simmel's thought to American sociology. The book, based on materials collected from various sources, has as its goal to 'bring into the perspective of a single volume the whole wide range of social organization and human life which is the subject-matter of a science of society' (Park & Burgess, [1921] 1969, p. v). The collection includes texts from a long list of both European and North American authors, the former group including, for example, Tönnies, Sombart, Durkheim, and Simmel, and the latter Sumner, Small, William James, and Park himself. What is noteworthy in the book is the large amount of texts included from Simmel. Whereas the reader presents not a single text from Marx, Weber, or Freud, for example, and only two from Durkheim, there are all in all ten excerpts from Simmel selected to the volume, which is more than from any other author. Some of the texts were newly translated just for the volume, and others were excerpted from the translations by Small originally published in *AJS*. The ten selections include excerpts from *Soziologie* and *Philosophie des Geldes* as well as from individual essays:

(1) 'The Sociological Significance of the "Stranger"';
(2) 'Social Interaction as the Definition of the Group in Time and Space';
(3) 'Sociology of the Senses: Visual Interaction';
(4) 'Money and Freedom';
(5) 'Conflict as a Type of Social Interaction';
(6) 'Types of Conflict Situations';
(7) 'The Reciprocal Character of Subordination and Superordination';
(8) 'Three Types of Subordination and Superordination';
(9) 'War and Peace as Types of Conflict and Communication';
(10) 'Compromise and Accommodation'.

The first of the texts, the one on the stranger, has had great influence on American sociology. Levine and his co-authors acknowledge its stimulus to two significant research traditions: the social psychology of the stranger on the one hand, and the measurement of social distance on the other (Levine et al., 1976a, p. 829). Park himself published the influential essay 'Human Migration and the Marginal Man' in 1928, where he coined the notion of 'marginal man' intended as equivalent to Simmel's concept of the stranger. The concepts have indeed been regarded as synonymous in much scholarship (e.g. Hughes, 1949; Boskoff, 1969; Rose, 1977), even though they have crucial differences, as for example Everett V. Stonequiest (1937; see also Levine et al., 1976a, pp. 830–1) has pointed out. However, there have also been published studies which have been more faithful to Simmel's original conceptualization of the stranger. While some of them have analysed the properties of communities of strangers, others have extended Simmel's ideas regarding the stranger to other individual types which bear formal resemblance to it (Levine et al., 1976a, pp. 833–5).

While the transmission of Simmel's thought in the United States heavily relied in the beginning on a relatively small circle of scholars who had been in immediate contact with him and who taught Simmel to their students, the book *Introduction to the Science of Sociology* exposed whole generations of students to his ideas, as 'Park and Burgess' became in American universities the canonized introduction to sociology in the 1920s and 1930s. Nevertheless, interest in Simmel's work remained relatively scarce in the 1930s and 1940s, and systematic commentaries of his sociology, not to mention of his philosophy, were lacking almost completely.

Nicholas Spykman's *The Social Theory of Georg Simmel* ([1925] 2004) makes perhaps the only exception. The book was the first monograph ever to appear on Simmel's social theory in English. Spykman's book is divided into three parts. The first discusses Simmel's contributions to the methodology of the social sciences in general and of sociology in particular. The second part focuses on Simmel's practical applications of his sociology by discussing some of the specific forms of association examined by him (subordination and superordination, conflict, and struggle). In the second part Spykman also examines Simmel's treatment of the quantitative determination of social forms, the spatial aspects of social relations, social conservation, social differentiation, and the relationship between the individual and the group. Finally, the third part of the book covers Simmel's social metaphysics. And it is by focusing on *The Philosophy of Money* that Spykman illustrates it, thus disregarding the life-philosophy of Simmel's mature work. The section centres on the relation of money to individual liberty and to the style of modern life.

What is particularly noteworthy in Spykman's book is that, against the, to some extent still nowadays common, judgement of Simmel's work as fragmentary, Spykman already stressed the functional unity of Simmel's writings. According to him, Simmel's essays on the most diverse subjects are bound together by a common mode of thought or method of approach, namely relationalism. However, its virtues notwithstanding, as Frisby (2004b) remarks in his informative introduction to the book, Spykman's treatment of Simmel's social theory remains compartmentalized and somewhat circumscribed, thereby failing to do justice to the breadth of Simmel's work. Levine and his co-authors are even harsher in their criticism, calling Spykman's exposition 'uninspired' (Levine et al., 1976a, p. 817) and 'a dry skeleton that gave no hint of the luminosity of Simmel's mind or the trenchancy of his sociological perceptions' (p. 818).

Oblivion

This chapter has sketched the early reception of Simmel's work and his influence on his contemporaries. In Germany he was one of the most renowned thinkers of his day, an immensely popular lecturer and a prolific, bestselling author, with active relations with other prominent figures of the turn-of-the-century intellectual culture. And he earned recognition not only in Germany, but overseas as well. As we have seen with regard to American sociology, in the first decades of the 20th century Simmel's attempt to define sociology was regarded as seminal, along with his writings on the stranger and the metropolis. What is more, Simmel's writings were also distributed widely in translations. By the 1910s no other European sociologist had more pieces translated into English than Simmel. As was mentioned above, the English translations, 13 in all, also reached a broad audience in North America. Their wide dissemination was guaranteed by the fact that the majority of them were published in *The American Journal of Sociology*, as translations by Small, the founder and first ever editor-in-chief of the journal.[21]

But Simmel's influence was not confined within Europe and the United States, but it extended for example as far as Japan. Masamicha Shimmei (1959, p. 206) reports that as a name Simmel was known in Japanese sociology as early as 1898, when N. Kishimoto published a book on sociology where Simmel was mentioned. While around this time, however, almost no one knew anything about his sociology, in the 1920s and 1930s Simmel's influence reached its peak in Japan. Then his impact exceeded even the one that he had in the United States (p. 214). Shimmei depicts that 'Japanese scholars were ready to welcome [Simmel's sociology] wholeheartedly, and it soon became a sort of cult among them' (p. 202). In addition, a large number of Simmel's texts appeared as Japanese translations. For example, *Philosophie des Geldes* was translated into Japanese in 1923, and the Japanese translation of *Grundfragen der Soziologie*, which appeared in 1926, was the first translation of the book anywhere. Further, a great many of Simmel's philosophical books, such as *Die Probleme des Geschichtsphilosophie*, *Schopenhauer und Nietzsche*, *Philosophische Kultur*, *Rembrandt*, *Kant und Goethe*, and *Lebensanschauung*, were available as Japanese translations very early on, long before they were translated into English (though according to Shimmei Simmel's influence on Japanese philosophy remained much weaker in comparison to sociology) (pp. 202–3).

Yet Simmel's influence on Japanese thought did not last. While German sociologists were still important in Japanese sociology in the late 1950s when Shimmei wrote his piece, Simmel was no longer regarded as a significant figure, but he had been replaced by such authors as Freyer, Mannheim, and Alfred Weber (pp. 212–13).

Simmel's influence waned in North American sociology, too. The aforementioned flood of English translations dried up almost entirely. Levine and his co-authors note that 'almost no new translations of Simmel's work were published in the United States for nearly three decades after the Park and Burgess volume' which came out in 1921 (Levine et al., 1976a, p. 817). Interest in his work survived but throughout the 1930s and 1940s it remained limited. In 1925, Small expressed that the people deliberately promoting Simmel's work for example by systematically publishing translations of his writings in *AJS* had had high hopes:

> We fondly hoped that not only sociologists but social scientists in general in all English-speaking countries would respond [to the translations], if not to the extent of adopting Simmel's theories, [then] at least to the extent of general admission that science without a recognized methodology is unthinkable.

However, now Small felt that the efforts of making Simmel's work widely appreciated and renowned had mostly been in vain, as he had got the impression that 'the Americans who have given indubitable evidence of having considered Simmel thoroughly might be counted on the fingers of one hand' (Small, 1925, p. 84). Spykman's book, too, remained largely without lasting influence. Very soon it changed from something 'very much in vogue' to 'completely forgotten', as Everett Hughes has described its fate (cited in Jaworski, 1997, p. 127 n. 10).

In Germany, too, Simmel went from an acknowledged and influential author to near oblivion. Rammstedt reports that in the years 1933–45 no new editions of Simmel's works or monographs on his work were published (Rammstedt, 2012, p. 305).[22] Considering Simmel's fame, his relative oblivion only two or three decades after his death is all the more curious. He was still at the height of his success when he was approaching the end of his life,[23] and immediately after his death the interest in his work grew even greater than it ever was in his lifetime.[24] So, how, we must ask, is it possible that one of the most renowned philosophical and sociological authors of his time was forgotten almost completely so soon, with hardly any traces of his legacy remaining visible?

The reasons for the cultural decline of Simmel's work are partly similar and partly different in Germany and the United States. Even though the national disciplinary traditions were connected to an exceptional degree in that many of the pioneering representatives of American sociology had studied in Germany and also had looked for a theoretical foundation and legitimation from German sociology when seeking to establish the discipline in the United States, the two traditions are also largely separate. Overall, as Peter Baehr (2002) aptly reminds, national traditions in sociology 'have never been synchronized, and we cannot assume that an exemplary figure in one country, at one time, can be generalized to other countries and other periods'.

In American sociology, Simmel's oblivion coincided with and relates to the development and predominance of empirical, quantitative sociology valuing scientific methods and data; due to this, interest in philosophical and theoretical works from European literature waned significantly. There was a small minority of scholars who drew theoretical inspiration from Simmel, but for most he was definitely not a figure to whom to turn in search of empirical hypotheses or methodological tools. In Germany, a significant reason for Simmel's neglect must have been anti-Semitism. When the National Socialist party seized power, all 'Jewish elements' were expelled almost immediately. In May 1933, for example, a student mob burned Simmel's books, and his writings were banned (Rammstedt, 2012, p. 305).

But anti-Semitism is certainly not the only factor. Another reason for his oblivion in Germany must be the fact that Simmel had not established any school. His 'influence remained an influence on the general atmosphere' (Troeltsch, 1922, p. 594; cited in Maus, 1959, p. 196). He had no disciples who would have taken up his work and continued it after him. While he was appreciated for his talent and even used as a theoretical resource, there really were no true 'Simmelians'. For example, after their initial enthusiasm, authors like Lukács and Mannheim departed ways with him and even neglected him. The same happened with von Wiese. When he shifted from the sociology of forms to the 'relationship doctrine' (*Beziehungslehre*) in the 1920s, he no longer mentioned Simmel's name in association with his theoretical programme. Simmel's presence in other words became anonymous. Heinz-Jürgen Dahme (1990, p. 18) writes that later von Wiese even downright denied the obvious influence that Simmel had had on his theorizing. What is more, some authors, like most of the members of the Frankfurt School, viewed Simmel mostly negatively from the very start. Adorno, for example, advised Benjamin not to read Simmel (Dahme, 1990, p. 18).

Yet another reason for Simmel's passing into oblivion is practical: a significant part of his vast oeuvre was poorly accessible for a long time. This holds for his writings in German, and even more so for English translations. Until late 1970s, only one of Simmel's books had been made available in English. Most of the translations consist either of selected shorter essays or of excerpts of his larger works. Accordingly, the somewhat one-sided and selective reception that Simmel's work has had in the Anglophone world, as well as its persistent image as unsystematic, essayistic, impressionistic, and fragmentary, is largely due to the scarce availability of his works in translation. But not even the German original texts have been easy to find. A large number of Simmel's writings have originally appeared as essays and articles in newspapers, art magazines, and literary monthlies and were not incorporated into any of his monographs. Further, a part of Simmel's literary remains has gone missing. A suitcase containing a number of Simmel's unpublished manuscripts were stolen from Kantorowicz in 1921 during a train journey, and the rest were lost during Hitler's regime. Simmel's son Hans had sent his father's literary remains, containing, for example, Simmel's diary, personal copies of his books with notes in the margins, and the letters sent to him, to the United States, where Hans had managed to emigrate with his four children after escaping the Dachau concentration camp, but the Gestapo got hold of the delivery and it was never shipped overseas (Landmann, [1958] 1993, p. 14). What happened to it afterwards remains unknown.

Because of the scarce availability of Simmel's writings, it was recognized early on by his admirers in Germany that a collected edition of his works would be needed. As Schmalenbach wrote in his obituary of Simmel in 1919: 'If a collected edition of Simmel's works is to be produced soon, it must be sure to preserve his legacy for many years to come.' (Schmalenbach, 1919, p. 288; trans. Harrington in Rammstedt 2012, p. 302) However, the several attempts to produce such a collection initiated in the decades following his death all failed. For example, Simmel's wife Gertrud tried to have three volumes of Simmel's collected essays published in the early 1920s, but no publisher offered to publish them, probably at least partly due to rising inflation. In 1948, Schmalenbach's student Michael Landmann breathed new life into the idea of a collected works, but he did not succeed in the endeavour. It was only decades later, after the persistent work by Otthein Rammstedt, that the collected works gradually started to become a reality, with the first two books in the series, volumes GSG 2 and GSG 3, published in 1989.

Notes

1 In 1959, Heinz Maus wrote that in Germany 'Durkheim seems to have attracted attention only recently', mainly 'through American sociology' (Maus, 1959, p. 198 n. 33).
2 The words were uttered in *Handwörterbuch der Staatswissenschaften* (cited in Maus, 1959, p. 186), which at the time was the standard handbook in the social sciences in Germany. The book appeared originally in six volumes (and two additional volumes) between 1890 and 1897. The edition cited by Maus must be the revised third one, which came out in 1909–11.
3 This was the 'Soziologie der Geselligkeit' ('The Sociology of Sociability') talk mentioned earlier in Chapters 3 and 6.
4 Simmel was also committed to creating 'a south-west German corner of philosophical culture' that, as he suggested in a letter to Rickert, would ultimately enable one to 'enlarge the concept of "philosophical culture"' (GSG 23, p. 284; trans. Frisby, 1997, p. 4).
5 For example, on 27 January 1900 Simmel wrote to his friend Rickert: 'I have ca. 315 hearers in my 3 private collegia. It is wonderful to see the kind of interest that

these people take in the most difficult and deepest questions' (GSG 22, p. 346). However, even though the number of listeners that he drew to his lectures seemed to please him, Simmel nevertheless felt that he was lecturing primarily to himself, not to his audience (see GSG 22, p. 305). This is confirmed, for instance, by Ludwig reporting how Simmel did not seek contact with his audience; the questions that he took up during his lectures he posed to himself, not to the audience (Ludwig, [1914] 1993, p. 155). Salomon, too, remarks that, 'He really did not address the audience in the reciprocal give and take of a good teacher; he was talking in a monologue' (in Jaworski, 1997, p. 93). What is more, as Simmel felt that with his words he was addressing above all himself, in a letter to Rickert he, for example, expressed how he would have liked his audience to be as homogeneous as possible and dressed in colourless pieces of clothing. And Simmel identified this heterogeneity especially with foreigners and women. Contrary to how Simmel is usually praised as a liberal cosmopolitan and for welcoming women to his lectures, in the letter he upsettingly expresses to Rickert that 'I cannot say that I'm particularly happy about the large percentage of female listeners: for me they disturb the unity of the auditorium.' (GSG 22, p. 305)

6 In *The Genealogy of Morals* (2003, p. 26), Nietzsche proposes that 'there is no "being" behind doing, working, becoming; "the doer" is a mere appen[d]age to the action. The action is everything.' Simmel would probably have had it that we can say the same – *mutatis mutandis* – about *Wechselwirkung*.

7 For more on the relation of Simmel and Weber, see e.g. Scaff (1987) and Lichtblau (1991). More recently, the affinities, differences, and tensions between Simmel and Weber were treated in a series of dialogues performed at the 'Weber/Simmel Antagonisms' conference organized in December 2015 in Edinburgh by the British Sociological Association's Max Weber Group together with the Sociology department of Edinburgh University. With Carlos Frade as Weber and myself as Simmel I performed in one of them exploring Simmel's and Weber's philosophical and political stances. Some of the dialogues of the conference, including ours (see Frade & Pyyhtinen, 2017), have been published in a Special Issue of the *Journal of Classical Sociology*.

8 The book appeared in 1932 in English with the title *Systematic Sociology* as an 'adapted' and 'amplified' version by Howard P. Becker (1899–1960), who had met von Wiese during his visiting fellowship in 1920s in Cologne, where the latter had been professor at the Handelshochschule Köln since 1915.

9 This was not, however, the only thing that was common to Lukács and Freyer. Besides being Simmel's students, both were also neo-Hegelians and influenced by neo-romanticism and by the critique of capitalist society formulated by the young Marx (Muller, 1987, p. 14).

10 For more on Simmel's influence on Lukács, see, for example, Wessely (1990) and Vandenberghe (2009).

11 For the intimate relations of German sociology and Nazism in the 1930s and 1940s, see Rammstedt (1986).

12 For a comparison of Simmel and Jaspers, see Tennen (1976).

13 Heidegger had gained a reputation even before he had published practically anything. As Arendt, among other things once also a student of his, reports: 'the name [Heidegger] made its way through all of Germany like the rumor of a secret king' (in Arendt & Heidegger, 2004, p. 149).

14 Interestingly, in Heidegger's early work, by contrast, the presence and influence of life-philosophy is much more clear and overt. For example, in *Grundprobleme der Phänomenologie* (*Basic Problems of Phenomenology*), life appears as the fundamental problem of phenomenology. Heidegger posits life as the 'domain of origin' (*Ursprungsgebiet*) (Heidegger, [1919/20] 2010, p. 25) and defines phenomenology as the 'primordial science' of 'life in and for itself' (p. 1). Michael Großheim (1991) has documented in detail the presence and influence of life-philosophy in general and that of Simmel in particular in Heidegger's early work, and also how Heidegger gradually began to grow apart from life-philosophy and, respectively, from Simmel, so that, by the time of the publication of *Being and Time* the distance had developed into a downright separation and rejection.

15 For a more detailed discussion, see e.g. Großheim (1991); Krell (1992, pp. 92–4); Gawoll (1993, pp. 147–50); Jalbert (2003, pp. 271–4); Pyyhtinen (2012); Pyyhtinen & Joronen (forthcoming).

16 This should also make it clear why Simmel's conception of the individuation of life does not have much to do with the heroic individuality of Goethe, Michelangelo, or Rembrandt, for example, who appear in Simmel's texts as privileged examples of qualitative individuality or the individual law.

17 The piece 'Influence du nombre des unites sociales sur les caractéres des sociétés' was originally translated by Worms, but Simmel was so unhappy with the quality of work that he contacted Bouglé to ask whether the latter could consider retranslating it. In a letter to Bouglé from 27 January 1895, Simmel complains that when he received the first draft of the translation from Worms he realized after reading the first page that it was impossible to correct it, since not a single sentence corresponded with his original text. He had therefore sent the translation back to Worms and told him that he would withdraw the piece unless the translation was redone entirely. And he suggested to Worms that Bouglé could do the translation, without mentioning the translator in the final publication, if Bouglé wanted that (see Simmel, GSG 22, pp. 142–3).

18 See Simmel's letter to Bouglé, 13 Dec 1899 (GSG 22, p. 342). With regard to Simmel's early reception in Italy, according to Claudia Portioli (2012) it is striking that it began with the translation of his philosophical texts, with the exception of the translation 'Il problema della sociologica', accompanied by a translation of 'Zur Soziologie der Armut' in 1906. Thus, in contrast to his reception elsewhere, notably in Germany and the United States, in Italy Simmel was initially appreciated above all as a philosopher.

19 The section discussing Simmel's sociology has also been published in English translation under the title 'Sociological Relativism' in the collection *Georg Simmel* (1965) edited by Lewis A. Coser.

20 See Simmel's letter to Bouglé 22 June 1895 (GSG 22, pp. 149–50). It is not known, however, how active a role Simmel had in the journal.

21 In Britain, by contrast, Simmel remained unknown for quite some time. When his translator, Small, visited the library of the London School of Economics some years after the volumes of *AJS* containing Simmel's translators had come out he was shocked to find out that the leaves were still uncut (Frisby, 2004b, p. xv). The lack of interest in Simmel, as Jaworski (1997, p. 14) assumes by drawing on Paul Kennedy (1980), was perhaps 'due in part to cultural snobbery, in part to

Anglo-American distaste for abstract reasoning, and in part to growing anti-German sentiment before and after World War I'.

22 Simmel himself preferred some of his books, such as *Einleitung in die Moralwissenschaft* ('Introduction to Moral Science') of 1892/3 and *Der Krieg und die geistigen Entscheidungen* ('The War and Spiritual Decisions') of 1917 'not to be reissued' (Rammstedt, 2012, p. 310 n. 7), as he considered them as 'theoretically obsolete or as no longer relevant' (p. 303).

23 Even though he was not sure 'what the younger generations can and want to take from me', Simmel himself was very self-conscious of the fact that 'they would rather turn to me than to any other living philosopher' (GSG 23, p. 946; trans. Austin Harrington in Rammstedt, 2012, p. 303).

24 For example, when a selection of Simmel's aphorisms edited by Gertrud Kantorowicz was published posthumously in the journal *Logos* in 1919, the aphorisms created so much public interest that the publisher J. C. B. Mohr wanted to publish Simmel's entire journal as a book. However, the endeavour did not succeed, as the publisher did not receive permission from Kantorowicz (Karlsruhen & Rammstedt, 2004, pp. 496–7).

9

Renewed Interest: Post-War Reception

This chapter examines how interest in Simmel's work revived after World War II in North America and Germany. American sociologists took up and used many themes from Simmel. He influenced several scholars, among them Robert Merton, Lewis A. Coser, Theodore Abel, and Erving Goffman. What is striking about the German reception, in turn, is not only that by the late 1940s Simmel had fallen into nearly complete oblivion, but also that when he was rediscovered in the 1950s, it was partly from across the Atlantic that he was re-imported as a classic of urban studies, role theory, conflict theory, and analyses of small groups (Rammstedt, 1994, p. 112; Köhnke, 1996, p. 14 n. 7). However, the efforts of scholars like Michael Landmann and Kurt Gassen were crucial, as well, in building the German Simmel tradition. The volume *Buch des Dankes an Georg Simmel* (Gassen & Landmann, [1958] 1993; 'Festschrift for Georg Simmel'), edited by them, became the bedrock upon which subsequent German scholarship was largely built. The survey of the two traditions in this chapter is by no means exhaustive. It will only provide examples of how Simmel's work was received, distributed, and appropriated after World War II, and portray the diversity between and within the North American and the German Simmel tradition. The chapter will also highlight how Simmel has been received in a strikingly partial and uneven manner especially in the Anglophone world: an appreciation of the full scope of his work has been missing. What is more, only some of the subsequent uses of Simmel by American sociologists take up the relational mode of thought that is the cornerstone of his legacy.

I will start by examining how Simmel was received by Talcott Parsons. Parsons was familiar with Simmel's work and regarded Simmel as relevant for his own theoretical aspirations. However, the fact that Parsons left Simmel out of the group of European authors discussed in and canonized by his hugely influential 1937 book *The Structure of Social Action* seemed decisive for Simmel's fate: it made Simmel appear as an author of second rank, not to be reckoned with. After looking at Parsons's reception of and engagement with Simmel, I will show how things changed between the 1950s and 1970s when interest in Simmel became greater than ever before in American sociology. From there I will move on to Simmel's reception in Germany, where his work underwent a real renaissance in the 1970s and 1980s. While Simmel had already been appreciated as an eminent predecessor prior to that, now he was also being read in a manner that stressed his actuality and proximity to contemporary social thought.

Canonizing the European classics with the exception of Simmel: the case of Talcott Parsons

As mentioned earlier, in the 1930s and 1940s interest in Simmel remained limited in the United States. Up until the early 1950s, Simmel was perceived by many American sociologists as a 'talented but archaic figure who could readily be dispensed with in any properly scientific view of the discipline' (Levine et al., 1976a, p. 820). This neglect of Simmel owes much to the authoritative 1937 book *The Structure of Social Action* (hereafter *Structure*) by Talcott Parsons (1902–79). Parsons's views took shape through a critical engagement with the work of a group of European authors, as its lengthy subtitle *A Study in Social Theory with Special Reference to a Group of Recent European Writers* indicates. In the book, the giants on whose shoulders Parsons places himself are Alfred Marshall, Vilfredo Pareto, Émile Durkheim, and Max Weber. He suggests that the four authors converged on a unified theory of action somewhat similar to the one that he develops and argues for in his book; he perceives his own theory as a synthesis and refined version of the theories of these thinkers.

The selection of the work of the four authors as representing classical developments of social theory left out a number of other significant authors, among them Simmel. Interestingly, however, Parsons was familiar with the work of Simmel. Originally, Parsons had even written a chapter on Simmel for *Structure*, but he ended up omitting it from the final manuscript. In the paperback edition Parsons included the following famous note in which he openly admits his neglect of Simmel:

> Along with the American social psychologists notably Cooley, Mead, and W. I. Thomas, the most important single figure neglected in the *Structure of Social Action*, and to an important degree in my subsequent writings, is probably Simmel. It may be of interest that I actually drafted a chapter on Simmel for the *Structure of Social Action*, but partly for reasons of space finally decided not to include it. (Parsons, [1937] 1968, p. xiv)

Levine (1985, pp. 122–3) has suggested that the lack of space is just an excuse, and that the real reason behind leaving out the section on Simmel is that Simmel did not fit the convergence thesis of *Structure*. In fact, Levine bases this view on Parsons's 'direct testimony'. In a letter to Jeffrey Alexander from 1979, Parsons admits that the 'decision not to include the Simmel chapter had various motives [...] The space problem was by no means the whole problem in relation to Simmel. *It is true that Simmel's program did not fit my convergence thesis*' (Levine, 1985, p. 123; citing Parsons, 1979, p. 1; emphasis Levine's).

On the face of it, Levine's argument seems sound and justified. However, the matter may be more complex. As Gary D. Jaworski (1997, p. 53) has argued, 'the nonconvergence argument is inconsistent with what Parsons in fact wrote about Simmel'. By examining Parsons's writings and outlines for *Structure*, Jaworski is able to make a convincing case of how Parsons had not changed his mind about Simmel, but 'had a very clear and consistent view of the relevance of Simmel's sociology to his theoretical pursuits'. First of all, Parsons appreciated Simmel's general strategy for defining the scope of sociology. Parsons objected to the view of sociology as a broad encyclopaedic science without principles peculiar to itself and with no subject matter of its own. In contrast to this, like Simmel, Parsons thought that only a specific viewpoint would give sociology 'a subject matter essentially its own and not shared by any other systematic theoretical discipline' (Parsons, 1934, p. 529). What is more, in *Structure*, Parsons explicitly acknowledges Simmel's contribution in this. As he expresses it himself, Parsons thinks that:

> Simmel's [*Sociology*] was perhaps the first serious attempt to gain a basis for sociology, as, in this sense, a special science. His formula is unacceptable for reasons that cannot be gone into here. But it was founded on a sound insight, and the view just stated may be regarded as a restatement of its sound elements in more acceptable terms. (Parsons, [1937] 1968, pp. 772–3)

So, while Parsons rejected Simmel's view of the scope of sociology, he nevertheless accepted his basic insight that sociology needs a specific subject matter of its own. Instead of just rejecting Simmel on the basis that he was 'wrong', Parsons's relation to Simmel is thus much more subtle. He in fact thought that Simmel's writings made a significant contribution to sociology. As he writes in the withdrawn section on Simmel in the manuscript of *Structure*:

> I also do not think it is a useful procedure to define sociology as a 'science of social forms.' But that does not prevent recognizing that Simmel had very important insights into the facts and made a very genuine contribution [...] The critic, it seems to me, should first attempt to find out what it is, especially in relation to the empirical facts Simmel was concerned with. Then he [sic] should attempt to find out how the author arrived at the propositions the critic regards as objectionable. Only after having done this and having restated the author's empirical insights in more acceptable terms is he [sic] entitled to 'criticize.' The progress of science consists in the continual amendment and restatement of conceptual schemes, not in deciding they are 'right' or 'wrong.' (Parsons, [1936] 1971, p. 80)

Parsons refused Simmel's definition of sociology as a science of social forms, because he ultimately regarded it as unable to explain social order, which for him was the basic task of sociological theory. Parsons himself tried to accomplish this with his voluntaristic theory of action, which in his view had the strength of explaining social order without disregarding the subjective element of social action. For Parsons, the problem of the possibility of social order came down to the question of coordination: how is it that the actors who are free to choose nevertheless act in the manner that they are oriented towards common ends? Parsons's theory of action focuses on the 'unit act', which consists of four action elements: first, the actor; second, an end towards which action is oriented and means to reach it; third, the situation where the action occurs; and, fourth, the norms and values that guide and rule action. According to Parsons ([1937] 1968), it is on values and norms that the coordination of ends is based. And he criticized Simmel's approach of focusing on social forms precisely because he considered that 'Simmel's conceptual scheme entirely fails to provide [values and norms]' (Parsons, [1936] 2001, p. 77).

However, it is important to note that while in his view unable to explain social cohesion, social forms were for Parsons not entirely devoid of value. Quite the contrary, he thought that 'form concepts are indispensable tools for sociological research' (p. 15). For Parsons, they had two uses in particular. First, they are significant for directing attention to social structure and differentiating between various structural types (p. 15). Second, Parsons was aware that his voluntaristic theory of action was to a certain extent limited, and he felt that Simmel's focus on forms of relationships could potentially present an important corrective to it. As he writes in the withdrawn section on Simmel:

> On the whole the action schema states social facts in a form which tends to minimize structural elements. Hence the relationship schema, which throws them directly into the center of attention, is a highly important descriptive corrective. [...] Simmel has performed a signal service in bringing these things so forcibly to our attention. (pp. 15–16)

While Parsons's identification of Simmelian social form with social structure presents a severe substantialist misunderstanding of Simmel, it is nevertheless important that Parsons saw Simmel's 'relationship schema' as a corrective to his own theory of action. However, it is not so much by paying attention to 'structural elements' that it accomplishes this but by extending the focus beyond the isolated individual actor to the dynamic relational field. In the article 'The Place of Ultimate Values in Sociological Theory', published in 1935, Parsons himself is indicating towards this direction without, however, mentioning Simmel by name this time: 'The "extensive" view of social life which looks upon it as a web of relationships between individuals may have something to teach us not revealed by the study of the action elements alone' (Parsons, 1935, p. 310).

So, it is clear that Parsons considered Simmel as a relevant figure for his own theoretical strivings, and it is interesting that Parsons acknowledged Simmel's relational approach, his 'relationship schema', too. Nevertheless, the fact that he excluded Simmel from the group of authors on whose theories he based his voluntaristic theory of action in *Structure* was in itself enough to decide Simmel's fate: Simmel was subsequently deemed irrelevant for a long time and not included in the canon of the classical founders of sociology.

Diffusion of Simmel's ideas in North American sociology between the 1950s and 1970s

Whereas the canon of classical sociologists that Parsons built with his *Structure* ([1937] 1968) doomed Simmel to insignificance in American sociology for about two decades, in the late 1950s and immediately thereafter the interest in Simmel's work bloomed and became bigger than ever.[1] For example, in 1958 *The American Journal of Sociology* published a special issue titled 'Émile Durkheim – Georg Simmel, 1858–1958' to honour the centennial of Durkheim and Simmel, who, as the editor Peter H. Rossi (1958, p. 579) suggests, 'Each in his own way has contributed so much to the development of social science that it would be ungrateful not to mark the occasion of the one-hundredth anniversary of their births without some special tribute'. For Rossi, the 'greatness' of Simmel and Durkheim lies, first, in the fact that 'each played an important part in his own time in giving life and body to our discipline in its earliest days'; and, second, in their continuing relevance: 'their works today continue to stand as inspiring models of scientific endeavor, providing sharp insights into scientific problems still under consideration' (p. 579). A year later, in a paper published in the *American Sociological Review*, Theodore Abel (1959, p. 474) celebrated Simmel 'as the founder of modern sociology', arguing:

> What Simmel initiated has become the tradition from which the present body of sociological knowledge has grown. Whatever other features they may possess, all contributions that are sociologically relevant embody the approach and viewpoint which Simmel was the first to make explicit.

In a similar manner, Robert Nisbet (1959, p. 480) declared that 'of all the pioneers, Simmel is the most relevant at the present time'. So, by the late 1950s much had indeed changed since the 1930s and 1940s, when Parsons's influential *Structure* seemed to have doomed Simmel into insignificance for good, and even in the mid-1950s Simmel was still 'widely regarded as an archaic amateur', as Levine (1981, p. 61) recollects. It was in particular the volumes *The Sociology of Georg Simmel* (1950) and *Georg Simmel, 1858–1918* (1959), edited by Kurt H. Wolff, that played a highly significant part in the revival of the interest in Simmel. Wolff, a sociologist and publisher, was a German immigrant who had moved to New York in the preceding decade. He was by far not the only German immigrant in the United States who was familiar with and had developed an interest in Simmel. For example Alfred Schutz and Albert Salomon at the New School of Social Research in New York, which was a haven for many European scholars escaping the horrors of Nazism, made the New School an important centre for the diffusion of Simmel's thought in American sociology, and Reinhard Bendix, Lewis A. Coser, Hans Gerth, Gustav Ichheiser, and Kurt Lewin, for example, were contributing to the new wave of interest elsewhere in the country (Levine et al. 1976a, p. 819).

An important figure behind the volume *The Sociology of Georg Simmel* and in the post-World War II American Simmel tradition in general is Everett C. Hughes (1897–1983). A student of Small and Park, Hughes was a 'living link' to the origin of the American Simmel reception. He identified himself as a 'Simmel man' and, following his teachers, kept alive the Simmel tradition at Chicago. As senior American Simmel scholar, he was also a man whose opinions mattered. When Hughes was contacted by Jeremiah Kaplan, the co-founder of The Free Press, about the publisher's plans for translating Simmel, he recommended Wolff for the job (Jaworski, 1997, p. 22).[2] Hughes himself translated the piece 'The Sociology of Sociability' (Simmel, 1949) and he also wrote a foreword to the volume *Conflict and the Web of Group Affiliations* (1955) also published by The Free Press and translated by Wolff and Reinhard Bendix.

It was primarily Hughes's lectures and seminars that initially got for instance Erving Goffman (1922–1982) to develop an interest in Simmel. Goffman, portrayed as 'the most influential American sociologist of the twentieth century' (Fine & Manning, 2003, p. 34), is known especially for his dramaturgical sociology, frame analysis, and work on the presentation of self, everyday life, total institutions, and stigmas. Goffman's references to Simmel's works suggest that he was familiar with the then available English translations. Goffman cites Simmel especially in his early work: most citations appear by 1956, that is, in his doctoral dissertation and writings belonging to his postdoctoral phase, after which references to Simmel become significantly less frequent, to fall off completely in later publications (Smith, 1989, pp. 210–12). Goffman built especially on Simmel's ideas regarding interpersonal knowledge but re-casted them to the domain of face-to-face interaction (pp. 217–20). Simmel contends that in interaction one necessarily knows something but not everything of the person one interacts with. Goffman (1953, pp. 300–1) uses this to support his own idea that orderly interaction necessitates an initial identification of the other. When discussing impression management and how individuals try to preserve their private spheres, Goffman also cites Simmel's observation that we know more about the others than they voluntarily reveal about themselves (p. 81). Beyond explicit citations there are also fascinating congruencies between Simmel and Goffman in how they see the fact that we play a certain role in affairs of everyday life not as hypocrisy or deceit, but we necessarily assume different roles in various situations (see Smith, 1989, pp. 221–3).

The aforementioned volume *The Sociology of Georg Simmel*, which was the first book-length English translation of Simmel's texts, did an important favour to the American reception of Simmel by introducing to the American readership a substantial amount of material that had not been previously translated into English. The importance of the book simply cannot be exaggerated. Levine and his co-authors state that the volume 'was more than any single factor responsible for the revival of American students' interest in Simmel in the postwar years' (Levine et al. 1976a, p. 819). It covers most parts of *Sociology* as well as the book *Grundfragen der Soziologie* ('Basic Problems of Sociology'). Wolff also wrote a lengthy and helpful introduction to it, in which he both introduces Simmel's work and discusses the availability of his writings. The volume *Georg Simmel, 1958–1918*, which was also edited by Wolff, contains a selection of Simmel's own writings – including 'The Adventure', 'The Ruin', 'The Handle', 'The Problem of Sociology', and 'How is society possible?' – but the material consists mostly of chapters on Simmel by well-versed scholars, such as Tenbruck, Levine, and Rudolph H. Weingartner. The volume also contains the English translation of Gertrud Kantorowicz's preface to Simmel's *Fragmente und Aufsätze aus dem Nachlaß und Veröffentlichungen der letzten Jahre* ('Fragments, Posthumous Essays, and Publications of His Last Years'), which was published posthumously in 1923 and edited by her.

While the fact that Simmel was left out from Parsons's *Structure* seemed to have sealed his fate as an archaic figure of the second rank, in the early 1930s Parsons taught at Harvard an influential course on social theory dealing with the work of Simmel, Durkheim, Weber, and Leonard Hobhouse.[3] For example Robert K. Merton situates the origin of his interest in Simmel in that course, along with Park and Burgess's book *Introduction to the Science of Sociology* (Levine et al., 1976a, p. 819). In an autobiographical sketch, Merton mentions Simmel among his most important influences: 'Beyond [the] teachers with whom I studied directly, I learned most from two sociologists: Emile Durkheim, above all others, and Georg Simmel, who could teach me only through the powerful works they left behind' (in Ritzer, 2011, p. 254). Merton refers to Simmel in his influential book *Social Theory and Social Structure* (1949), but it is perhaps above all through his teaching that he contributed to the diffusion of Simmel's thought in American sociology. In Columbia University, as Levine and his co-authors note, Merton paid 'concentrated attention to Simmel in his basic courses on the history of sociological theory and analysis of social structure' (Levine et al., 1976a, p. 819).

Merton's interest in Simmel was passed on to several of his students at Columbia, who later became important figures in advancing the popularity of Simmel's theories in American sociology. One of them is Lewis A. Coser, who completed his doctoral dissertation, *Toward a Sociology of Social Conflict*, in

1956 under Merton's supervision. The thesis was subsequently published as a book in the same year with the title *The Functions of Social Conflict* (1956). In it, Coser draws substantially from Simmel's discussion of conflict in Chapter 4 of *Sociology*, though he tries to refine Simmel's original thoughts and render them into more clearly formulated propositions. Even though Coser's use of Simmel does not exhaust the breadth and richness of the latter's analyses of conflict, and the way Coser translates Simmel's ideas into the terminology of functional analysis severely distorts some of his insights, he nevertheless made a highly significant contribution both to the sociology of conflict and to the recovery and modernization of American Simmel scholarship (Levine et al., 1976b, p. 1124). As Joseph Himes (1966, p. 2) suggests, Coser's work on conflict not only 'led to the revival of sociological attention to the study of social conflict', but also thereby 'injected the very considerable contributions of the German sociologist Georg Simmel into the stream of American sociological thought'. What is more, with the volume *Georg Simmel* (1965) which he edited and with his book *Masters of Sociological Thought* (1977) Coser contributed significantly to the canonization of Simmel as a classical sociologist.

In addition to social conflict, another key theme of American sociology that stemmed from Simmel after the 1950s was exchange. At that time, most of the key representatives of the so-called social exchange theory related to Simmel's ideas, one way or another. Interestingly, this connection also shows clear traces of a grasp of the relational mode of thought so crucial to Simmel's overall approach. In his article 'The Norm of Reciprocity' (1960), Alvin Gouldner insists on the significance of the duty to reciprocate in social relationships: for Gouldner, the norm of reciprocity is both a 'starting mechanism' for social relations and also serves a stabilizing function (p. 176). In the paper, Gouldner sets as his aim to both clarify the concept of reciprocity and argue for its centrality – according to him, the notion is 'tacitly involved in but formally neglected by modern functional theory' (p. 162). In both of these tasks Simmel figures as a key source for Gouldner. Gouldner praises Simmel for having 'emphasi[zed] the importance of reciprocity [...] for all societies' (p. 162). In addition, Gouldner mentions Simmel – along with, for instance, George Homans and Bronislaw Malinowski – as one of the authors who have paid attention to how the reciprocity norm stipulates the rough equivalence of what has been received and the repayment (p. 171).

Besides Gouldner, Peter M. Blau, too, belonged to the pioneers of social exchange theory influenced by Simmel. Like Coser, Blau was Merton's student. Blau's book *Exchange and Power in Social Life* (1964) is largely built on Simmel's thoughts on exchange and the role of gratitude in human relations. In the book Blau also explicitly refers to Simmel several times. To pick yet another example, Barry Schwartz, too, draws extensively from Simmel and cites him frequently in his article on the social psychology of the gift (Schwartz, 1967). Schwartz, for example, refers to Simmel's attention to form and content in sociological analysis (p. 1), acknowledges his insight into how gratitude binds people (pp. 8–9), and emphasizes Simmel's important observation regarding how gift-exchanging dyads are characterized by a power imbalance (p. 9).

Simmel's discussion of the dyad and the triad, too, was very influential within the study of small groups and group dynamics in American sociology, social psychology, and to some extent in anthropology alike. For example, in their paper 'Sociological Analysis of the Dyad' (1942), Howard Becker and Ruth Hill Useem set as their task to 'outline a frame of reference for the study of the dyad' (p. 13) and identify the general characteristics of the dyad. The authors reference Simmel's work, too: not only the text 'The Number of Members as Determining the Sociological Form of the Group' published 1902 in *AJS*, but also the piece 'The Sociology of Secrecy'. In the article 'A Study of Interaction and Consensus in Different Sized Groups' (1952, p. 261) based on his doctoral dissertation presented at the University of Chicago, Paul A. Hare notes the increasing interest in the study of small groups among sociologists and psychologists, and he maintains that among the earlier scholars who have addressed the topic 'the best remembered' are Charles Cooley and Simmel. Furthermore, Hare acknowledges that '[t]he most extensive discussion of the importance of the size of the group in sociological literature is given by Simmel who provides numerous historical accounts of the importance of group size in social life'. And he continues by stating that although many of Simmel's remarks are not directly related to the problem examined by himself in the article, for they deal either with very small groups or very large groups, Simmel nevertheless 'does provide the basic premise which underlies this research: that size is a significant determining factor in group interaction' (Hare, 1952, p. 261). Theodore Caplow (1956), for his part, argues for Simmel's relevance for the analysis of the triad. Caplow explores coalitions in triads in cases where the formation of coalitions depends on the initial distribution of power in the triad, and he draws substantially on Simmel's 'powerful but unsystematic analysis', as Caplow describes it (p. 489). In his article in the aforementioned *AJS* Special Issue on Durkheim and Simmel, Theodore Mills (1958) reformulates some of Simmel's ideas concerning small group dynamics as hypotheses and notes experimental procedures for testing them. Finally, in her article 'Two's Company, Three's a Crowd' (1970) published in *American Anthropologist* and relying chiefly on Simmel, Susan S. Bean discusses the social implications of the dyad and the triad. Interestingly, Bean pays special attention to distance absent in the dyad but inherent in the triad.

Besides urbanism, the stranger, social distance, interpersonal knowledge, and the analysis of small groups, another key Simmelian theme in American sociology has been fashion. Simmel's essay 'Fashion' appeared originally in the journal *International Quarterly* in 1904, a year before it came out in German, and the text was reprinted in *The American Journal of Sociology* in 1957.

It has exerted wide influence. For example Herbert Blumer (1900–87), who is known in particular as a representative of symbolic interactionism, refers to Simmel in his celebrated article 'Fashion: From Class Differentiation to Collective Selection' (1969). In the paper, Blumer invites sociologists to take fashion seriously. He mentions Simmel among the very few scholars who have previously paid solemn attention to the topic. Blumer acknowledges that Simmel's 'analysis, without question, has set the character of what little solid sociological thought is to be found on the topic' (Blumer, 1969, p. 277). According to Blumer:

> There are several features of Simmel's analysis which are admittedly of high merit. One of them was to point out that fashion requires a certain type of society in which to take place. Another was to highlight the importance of prestige in the operation of fashion. And another, of particular significance, was to stress that the essence of fashion lies in a process of change – a process that is natural and indigenous and not unusual and aberrant. (p. 278)

Nevertheless, despite being so far 'the best in the published literature', for Blumer Simmel's analysis has shortcomings. It failed not only 'to catch the character of fashion as a social happening', but also to provide an apt account of the modern fashion mechanism. As Blumer puts it, Simmel's essay on fashion 'is quite well suited to fashion in dress in the seventeenth, eighteenth, and nineteenth century Europe with its particular class structure', but it is not able to depict the operation of the modern fashion mechanism, which according to Blumer is increasingly independent of the class structure (p. 278). In modern fashion, Blumer argues, collective selection replaces class differentiation:

> *The fashion mechanism appears not in response to a need of class differentiation and class emulation but in response to a wish to be in fashion, to lie abreast of what has good standing, to express new tastes which are emerging in a changing world.* These are the changes that seem to be called for in Simmel's formulation. They are fundamental changes. They shift fashion *from* the fields of *class differentiation to* the area of *collective selection* and center its mechanism in the process of such selection. (p. 282)

Blumer's criticism is to some extent misplaced. First, the accusation that Simmel fails to grasp the character of fashion as a social happening is mistaken and presents a more or less erroneous substantialist reading of Simmel. The basic motif of Simmel's analysis of fashion is to examine it as a social form of interaction, not as class differentiation. The connection to class structure is only an empirical observation; at the time Simmel wrote the 1904 piece, fashions were indeed mostly class-based. Second, apparently Blumer was familiar only with the English piece 'Fashion' published in 1904, not with the slightly reworked and enlarged German essay 'Die Mode' published in 1911 in the volume *Philosophische Kultur*, for in the latter Simmel points explicitly towards the growing independence of the mechanism of fashion from class structure. What is more, theoretically the form of fashion as a contrast between differentiation and conformity is not dependent on class hierarchy, but operates self-sufficiently: the form of fashion is constituted by the interplay of imitation and individual differentiation. What is more, the main problem with Blumer's conception of fashion, as Jukka Gronow (1997, pp. 94–5) has argued, is that it cannot provide a satisfying explanation for the constant change of fashion; once collective taste converges, there is no given reason to breach the consensus. Blumer could have been able to give a better account of the dynamism of fashion had he played closer attention to Simmel's analysis. According to Simmel, fashion, as we have seen in Chapter 4, changes as soon as it becomes widely accepted, for at that point it can no longer produce individual differentiation.

In Levine and his co-authors' extensive review of Simmel's influence on American sociology Blumer's contribution is mentioned only very briefly in a footnote (see Levine et al., 1976b, p. 1128 n. 4). But even more curious is that Kaspar D. Naegele (1923–65), who is much more important for the American Simmel reception than Blumer, is completely absent. Naegele was a native German born in Stuttgart. He emigrated to North America as a teenager with his family, because his mother was Jewish (though according to some reports his parents and brothers arrived there in 1939, and Naegele himself a year later, around 1940, having been sent to England before that). In North America, Naegele was 'one of the most passionate and comprehensive readers of Simmel in the period after World War II' (Kemple, 2013b, p. 5). Simmel's grandson Arnold Simmel reports in a letter to Jaworski that, 'finding [Simmel] congenial to his way of thinking', Naegele 'threw himself into reading Simmel – with energy, concentration, understanding and learning' (Jaworski, 1997, p. 131 n. 1).

Interestingly, Naegele was a student of Parsons's, and he also set out to connect Simmel's thought and Parsonian functionalism. The attempt, however, turned out unsuccessful. Yet there are several texts by Simmel incorporated into the volume *Theories of Society* (1961) edited by Parsons, Edward Shils, Naegele, and Jesse R. Pitts – with most of them suggested by Naegele. More than any other American scholar until then, Naegele stressed in his reading of Simmel the use of paradoxes as Simmel's basic formula. Simmel, Naegele suggests, 'seeks to formulate facts through stating contradictions' (Naegele, 1958, p. 584). In addition, what is most remarkable is that already in his early papers Naegele stressed aspects of Simmel's thought, such as his life-philosophy, that the most recent scholarship has only now begun to realize and appreciate, though largely independently of Naegele, without acknowledging his precedence. First, for Naegele Simmel was much more than just the sociologist of social forms. He suggested that 'it is Simmel as *lebensphilosoph* that social sciences might well reevaluate'. What appealed to Naegele in Simmel's life-philosophy was especially its tragic view of life. Like Simmel,

Naegele thought that 'in order to live we must produce the very things that destroy us. That is our tragedy.' Second, in late 1940s Naegele already emphasized Simmel's contributions to the study of everyday life, which is something that was becoming more widely appreciated only in the 1980s and 1990s. In a 1948 paper 'Jewish Contributions to Social Theory: A Suggestion for Further Research' that Naegele wrote when he was still a student he maintains that Simmel 'invariably points out the subtleties to daily occurrences', and thus 'evolved a highly suggestive sociology of everyday life and gave it the framework of a tragic view of life' (Naegele, 1948, p. 16; cited by Jaworski, 1997, p. 62).

While in the late 1940s the time was obviously not right for Naegele's efforts to link Simmel's and Parsons's work, a decade later the idea of bringing them together seemed much more acceptable. In connecting Simmel's work to current trends in sociology, Abel goes in his aforementioned 1959 piece as far as to suggest: 'It is clear, for example, that Simmel would have given full support to the "structural functional" approach' (Abel, 1959, p. 477). The analytical connections between Simmel and Parsons were explored by others as well. In 1957, Donald N. Levine (1931–2015) defended his doctoral dissertation *Simmel and Parsons: Two Approaches to the Study of Society*. In it, Levine examines Simmel's sociology as an important supplement to Parsons's work. Like Goffman, Levine was inspired by Hughes, but his first encounter with Simmel's work nevertheless assumably happened during 1952–3 when he was an exchange student at the Goethe University of Frankfurt in Germany. As Lawrence Scaff recollects Levine telling him about this encounter:

> He went to Germany against his parents' wishes, who thought it was too soon after the war (the family was Jewish). The father in the family who hosted him had hidden his copies of Simmel's work during the Nazi era, and because of Don's sociological interests, the father dusted off the old volumes and introduced him to Simmel's work. Don was fascinated and his life-long engagement with Simmel had begun. (Scaff, 2015)

Later Levine became a key figure of the American Simmel tradition. The volume *Georg Simmel on Individuality and Social Forms* (1971) that he edited has become a crucial source for the American Simmel scholarship. When it was published, it not only substantially broadened up the scope of Simmel's work available as English translations, but also helped to constitute Simmel's reputation among a broader academic audience. In his lengthy introduction to the volume, Levine presents a well-informed interpretation of Simmel's work and also discusses his influence on contemporaries in Germany as well as his impact on American sociology. Importantly, Levine challenges the then dominant preconception of Simmel's work as unsystematic and fragmentary, arguing: 'Whether he is examining a social process or a developmental pattern, a world, a culture or a philosophical system, a historic individual or a personality type, the logic of Simmel's inquiry is the same' (Levine, 1971, p. xxxi). Levine identifies four principles[4] that underlie all of Simmel's analyses:

(1) *Form:* 'The world consists of innumerable contents which are given determinate identity, structure, and meaning through the impositions of forms which man [sic] has created in the course of his [sic] experience' (p. xxxii)
(2) *Reciprocity:* 'No thing or event has a fixed meaning; the meaning only emerges through interactions with other things or events' (p. xxxiii)
(3) *Distance:* 'The properties of forms and the meanings of things are a function of the relative distances between individuals and other individuals or things' (p. xxxiv)
(4) *Dualism:* 'The world can best be understood in terms of conflicts and contrasts between opposed categories.' (p. xxxv)

The principles identified by Levine are very much in line with the key elements of Simmel's method that I outlined in Chapter 2. What is more, the principles clearly indicate that Levine also acknowledges Simmel's relational approach. While in his work on Simmel Levine has been focused mostly on Simmel's sociology, he has made a significant contribution to the potential dissemination of Simmel's philosophy, too, by translating the book *Lebensanschauung* into English with John A. Y. Andrews; the translation came out in 2010 bearing the title *The View of Life*, and it also includes translations of Simmel's aphorisms from his journal as well as notes concerning metaphysics from an unpublished file kept safe by the Simmel family after his decease.

The translation *The View of Life* no longer allows Anglophone readers to disregard Simmel's life-philosophy. For it is true that Simmel has been appreciated in American scholarship above all as a sociologist, largely sidelining his philosophy which has indeed had only very little impact on the American philosophical tradition. Naegele's appreciation of Simmel's life-philosophy is one exception. Another is Rudolph Weingartner's book *Experience and Culture* (1960), which is to this day the only monograph on Simmel's philosophy written in English. In the book, Weingartner's aim is to reconstruct Simmel's philosophical position. The work is not, however, just a historical reconstruction trying to situate Simmel in relation to historical antecedents, but Weingartner is far more interested in the key ideas and internal organization of Simmel's work. He remarks that the exposition is synthetic in nature, as Simmel himself nowhere defined and reflected on his philosophical position in as explicit terms and in so many words. For Weingartner, Simmel's philosophy is primarily organized around the concepts of life and experience with an interest in concrete and particular cultural phenomena. While putting forth an informed and informative reading of Simmel's philosophy, at times Weingartner nevertheless exaggerates its systematic character, describing Simmel's thought in too rigid terms, even as a system of some kind.

All in all, despite Simmel's work was given a strong foothold in American sociology through the various translations and the themes emanating from him, in the late 1970s a 'thorough, critical study of Simmel's sociology' still awaited 'to be undertaken' (Levine et al., 1976a, p. 822). What is more, in their review of Simmel's influence on American sociology Levine and his co-authors disappointedly remark that even though Simmel's ideas have been widely used by American sociologists 'they have patently misrepresented what Simmel was saying', by either carelessly selecting some of his ideas while ignoring their context and other ideas germane to their statements or deviating from Simmel's position without knowing (pp. 822, 824). An overall understanding of the whole of his work has been missing, and the reception that he has had is thereby characterized by selectivity, partiality, and unevenness. Yet another thing which needs to be mentioned is the, in many places anonymous, nature of Simmel's posthumous legacy. One could perhaps say that his influence has been marked as much by invisibility and absence as by visibility and presence.

German Simmel renaissance

Unlike in North America, where interest in Simmel's work remained limited yet alive before its upsurge in the 1950s, by the late 1940s Simmel had lost all of his previous fame in Germany. In 1948, when reopening the issue of a collected works that had failed to make headway, Michael Landmann observed that in Germany Simmel had fallen into oblivion in just three decades after his death (Landmann, 1949, p. 204). For example, as was mentioned in the previous chapter, between 1933 and 1945 in Germany there appeared no new editions of Simmel's writings and no monographs on his thought (Rammstedt, 2012, p. 305). Dahme suggests that immediately after World War II Landmann was perhaps the only one in Germany working seriously on Simmel (Dahme, 1990, pp. 18–19).

Simmel's oblivion in German scholarship seemed so complete that in 1959 Günther Busch surmised it presented 'an exemplary case of a forgetting that seems irreparable' (cited in Lichtblau, 1997, p. 142). However, as it later turned out, Simmel's reputation was not beyond reparation. In the 1970s and 1980s there in fact took place what several scholars have called a real Simmel 'renaissance' in Germany. Interest in his work had already begun to revive in the late 1950s. The volume *Buch des Dankes an Georg Simme* ('Festschrift for Georg Simmel') edited by Kurt Gassen and Landmann was published in 1958, on the centenary of Simmel's birth. The book was an important early attempt to revitalize Simmel's intellectual legacy. It includes, for example, Landmann's outline of Simmel's intellectual biography, a bibliography by Gassen, and a collection of Simmel's letters to contemporaries like Edmund Husserl, Heinrich Rickert, as well as Max and Marianne Weber. The volume also contains a hefty assortment of recollections of Simmel by friends and former students. Landmann was involved in the production of other significant volumes on Simmel as well. A year earlier, in 1957, he had edited together with Margarete Susman a collection of Simmel's philosophical essays on religion, art, and society under the title *Brücke und Tur* ('Bridge and Door'), and in 1968 published yet another collection of Simmel's philosophical essays, titled '*Das Individuelle Gestetz*' ('The Individual Law'), also edited by Landmann. In 1968, also, the fifth edition of *Soziologie* saw daylight.

Another important edited volume contributing to the revival of Simmel's legacy in Germany was *Ästhetik und Soziologie um die Jahrhundertwende* (1976; 'Aesthetics of Sociology Around the Turn of the Century') edited by Hannes Böhringer and Karlfried Gründer. The volume displays and takes up various sociological themes and aspects of Simmel's work.

In the 1970s more and more monographs on Simmel's sociology also began to appear. Heribert J. Becher's *Georg Simmel – Die Grundlagen seiner Soziologie* (1971; 'Georg Simmel – The Foundations of his Sociology') lays out an influential interpretation of *Wechselwirkung* as the key notion of Simmel's work, and Peter-Ernst Schnabel's *Die Soziologische Gesamtkonzeption Georg Simmels. Ein wissenschaftshistorische und wissenschaftstheoretische Untersuchung* (1974; 'Georg Simmel's Overall Conception of Sociology. A Historical and Theoretical Treatise of Scientific Inquiry') seeks to rehabilitate Simmel as a sociologist tackling fundamental questions of scientific inquiry. In the book, Schnabel provides an analysis of previous Simmel scholarship to the end of, on the one hand, demonstrating the limitations and consequences of the fairly uncritical conception of history that according to him has plagued much Simmel reception and, on the other, transcending these limitations and thereby giving Simmel scholarship a new impetus. In the book *Einheit und Zwiespalt. Zum hegelianisierenden Denken in der Philosophie und Soziologie Georg Simmels* (1978; 'Unity and Opposition. On the Hegelianized Aspects of Georg Simmel's Philosophy and Sociology') Petra Christian, for her part, looks into the influence of Hegel on Simmel in connection with the revival of interest in Hegel in Germany during the first decades of the 20th century. In her interpretation, Christian lays special emphasis on the notions of 'life' (*Leben*) and *Wechselwirkung*. She argues for the interconnectedness of Simmel's sociology and metaphysics, apparent for instance in how the notion of *Wechselwirkung*, serving initially as a sociological concept, grows in his work into a broad metaphysical principle that concerns the whole of reality. In the book, Christian also interestingly traces the pre-Simmelian history of the concept of *Wechselwirkung*, as a path leading from Kant to Hegel and via Schleiermacher and Dilthey eventually to Simmel. What is also fascinating in her take on Simmel is the way she sees the content and form of Simmel's own thought as one: she argues that both language and thinking are for Simmel something 'living'.

Heinz-Jürgen Dahme's comprehensive two-volume study *Soziologie als Exakte Wissenschaft. Georg Simmels Ansatz und seine Bedeutung in der gegenwärtige Soziologie* (1981; 'Sociology as an Exact Science. Georg Simmel's Contribution and his Significance in Contemporary Sociology') is yet another important monograph on Simmel in the German context. Dahme examines, on the one hand, the reception and contemporary relevance of Simmel's work and, on the other, the foundation that it provides for sociology. As its title also hints, Dahme suggests that in his work Simmel develops a much more systematic conception of sociology than is usually thought: Simmel sought to define and legitimize sociology as an exact science.

In the 1980s, new studies investigating the key principles and ideas of Simmel's work continued to appear. For example, in her book *Georg Simmels Konzeption von Gesellschaft. Ein Beitrag zum Verhältnis von Soziologie, Äesthetik und Politik* (1982; 'Georg Simmel's Conception of Society. A Contribution to the Relation of Sociology, Aesthetics, and Politics'), Sibylle Hübner-Funk sets out to explicate Simmel's notion of society. She suggests that Simmel's worldview is marked by delicate relations between sociology, aesthetics, and politics, and argues that it is only by looking through his theory of society that those relations become perceptible. Hübner-Funk stresses the presence and significance of aesthetics in Simmel's sociology. She argues that, considering that Simmel's contributions to modern sociology have remarkable potential, their aesthetics components are not outdated but stand in an intimate relationship with the methodology of building sociological theory, especially with the interactionist strand. Further, Antonius M. Bevers (1985) has made the effort to reconstruct the methodological and theoretical unity of Simmel's work. In his book, Bevers argues that Simmel's epistemology, sociology, and life-philosophy conflate in two themes that run throughout his oeuvre: the distinction between form and content and the principle of *Wechselwirkung*, reciprocal effect.

In addition to the historical reconstructions and exegetic interpretations, in the 1980s Simmel's work was also increasingly used in German scholarship as a source of theoretical ideas. Scholars emphasized, for instance, his contributions to theorizing society, to social differentiation, and to philosophy of culture, but it was above all as a sociologist of modernity that he was appreciated and presented. The volume *Georg Simmel und die Moderne. Neue Interpetationen und Materialien* (1984; 'Georg Simmel and the Modern. New Interpretations and Materials') edited by Heinz-Jürgen Dahme and Otthein Rammstedt presents most fascinating attempts by eminent experts at addressing Simmel's relevance. Most of the contributions were originally presented as talks in the first Georg Simmel Colloqium organized in 1982 in Bielefeld, with the actuality of Simmel (*'Die Aktualität Georg Simmels'*) as its general theme. The volume starts with David Frisby's chapter '*Georg Simmel's Theorie der Moderne*' ('Georg Simmel's Theory of Modernity'). Other contributors explicitly emphasizing Simmel's actuality are Coser, with a chapter on Simmel's writings on gender and the masculinity of modern culture, Birgitta Nedelmann presenting Simmel in her chapter as a significant forerunner of sociological process analysis, and Bruno Accarino discussing Simmel's contributions to the study of trust. However, most of the other chapters in the volume are characterized by more exegetic aspirations. For example, Landmann explores Simmel's relation to the poet Stefan George, Hübner-Funk discusses the aesthetic constitution of societal knowledge in Simmel's *Philosophy of Money*, Dahme looks at the demarcation problem of philosophy and science in Simmel's work, Klaus Lichtblau examines the relation between Simmel's sociology and philosophy through his reception of Nietzsche, and Levine reports how Simmel was received in an ambivalent and negative manner by Durkheim, Weber, Park, and Parsons.

Of eminent recent and contemporary German social theorists, Simmel influenced above all the system theorist Niklas Luhmann (1927–98). Luhmann acted as a significant mediator in making social scientists of today aware of Simmel's work on trust (Möllering, 2001, p. 408). What is more, Simmel's ideas also influenced Luhmann's own conception of the nature of trust. In *Trust and Power* (1979, p. 26), Luhmann subscribes to Simmel's notion of trust as a mixture of knowing and not-knowing: 'Trust always extrapolates from the available evidence; it is, as Simmel pointed out, a blending of knowledge and ignorance.' Further, a bit later in the book Luhmann also draws on Simmel when emphasizing the renewal of trust as significantly solidifying relations: 'Simmel very rightly points out that it is the continual problem of always having to renew trust which becomes a strong binding force' (p. 47).[5] Luhmann also belonged to the group of scholars headed by Rammstedt who in the 1980s tried to secure funding for the project of editing the *Georg Simmel Gesamtausgabe*, a systematic collected works of Simmel in German, and he also belonged to the provisional editorial board of the series (see Rammstedt, 2012).

Whereas Luhmann openly acknowledges his debt to Simmel, it is curious how Jürgen Habermas (b. 1929), another highly influential German sociologist and philosopher, cites Simmel hardly at all, for example in his analyses of modernity. There are only two references to Simmel, for instance, in the two-volume *The Theory of Communication* published in 1981, and in the essay 'Modernity – An Unfinished Project' of the same year Habermas does not cite Simmel even once (Frisby, 1985, p. 49). However, Habermas has written a postscript to the reprinted version of Simmel's *Philosophische Kultur* published in 1986. In the text, Habermas (1996, p. 403) states that 'Simmel as a critic of culture is in a peculiar way both near to, and far away from, us'. For Habermas it is above all Simmel's neo-Kantian concept of culture that makes him distant from us. He belongs to a different epoch than we do, to the one of Kant, Hegel, Schiller, and Goethe though being already overshadowed by Schopenhauer and Nietzsche (p. 407). However, what in Habermas's eyes makes Simmel near to us – and at the same time distant from his contemporaries – is his sensitivity for 'the spirit of the age'. Accordingly, Habermas reads Simmel as 'a philosophical diagnostician of the times with a social-scientific bent rather than a philosopher or sociologist solidly placed in the academic profession' (p. 405).

To sum up, in the German tradition scholars have been very much preoccupied with presenting Simmel's ideas faithfully, placing them in the whole of his work, reconstructing them historically in their context, and investigating the conceptual preconditions of his thought. Thereby, in the German reception the breadth of Simmel's work has been acknowledged and appreciated to a much greater extent than has been the case in the American (or Anglophone) tradition. Several Germanophone authors have also stressed Simmel's relational mode of thinking, with, for example, Becher, Christian, and Bevers, among others, having placed special emphasis on the notion of *Wechselwirkung*. However, especially beginning from the 1980s, Simmel has been read not only as a classic, but his *actuality*, too, has been emphasized: he has not been treated solely as an eminent figure from the past but as someone who in a peculiar manner also stands close to us.

Conclusion

In this chapter, I have looked at the resurgence of the interest in Simmel in North America and Germany after World War II. The two traditions are strikingly different. Whereas the North American tradition has, from the outset, characteristically centred on the operationability of Simmel's theses and on his theory fragments of particular bits and pieces of social reality irrespective of their connection to the whole of Simmel's work, the German reception is characterized by a more philological and historicist approach, with its focus on situating Simmel's work within the context of the time it was written rather than on the usability of his theses (Schnabel, 1974).

Besides providing an important model of defining the subject matter of sociology, in American sociology, as we saw, Simmel has influenced several substantive fields of research, from, for example, urban studies and the studies of small groups to studies of interpersonal knowledge, social exchange theory, theories of conflict, and fashion studies. There are also various centres through which Simmel's work has been disseminated. While the earliest reception around the turn of the 20th century was strongly associated with the University of Chicago, by the 1950s there were many more centres, with, for example, Parsons teaching Simmel to his students at Harvard, Merton at Columbia University, Schutz and Salomon at the New School for Social Research in New York City, and Naegele working at the University of British Columbia.

If in North America the University of Chicago has been more important than any other place in the transmission of Simmel's thought especially from the turn of the century to the interwar period, in the German Simmel reception after World War II Bielefeld has been the main hub of matters Simmelian.

Not only was the Simmel archive based there, but so was the journal *Simmel Studies* (formerly called *Simmel Newsletter*). The mastermind and key operative behind both was Otthein Rammstedt, who also initiated in the 1980s the editing process of *Georg Simmel Gesamtausgabe*, Simmel's collected works in German, and acted as the general editor of the series. Before Rammstedt, the chief Simmel authority in Germany was Landmann. If the 1950 volume *The Sociology of Georg Simmel* edited by Kurt H. Wolff was perhaps more than any other factor responsible for the revival of the interest in Simmel among students in North America, in Germany the volume *Buch des Dankes an Georg Simme*, published on the centenary of Simmel's birth in 1958 and edited by Gassen and Landmann, more or less marks the launch of the renewed German interest in Simmel.

The inventory provided here admittedly offers a fairly limited image of Simmel's influence and reception in that while the North American and German strands have internationally been the two grand traditions of interpreting Simmel's work, it leaves out its reception, dissemination, and appropriation in South America, for instance, where Simmel's ideas have found a remarkably fertile ground. Simmel has had a long reception history for example in Argentina (see Maioli, 2010) and Brazil (see Waizbort, 2008), and he has a noteworthy following in Columbia and Mexico as well. There is also a very active Latin American research network, *Red Simmel*, focusing on his work.[6] Unfortunately, the Anglophone audience knows almost nothing of the vast Latin American Simmel scholarship and of Simmel's influence on Latin American sociology, as most of the texts on Simmel by Latin American scholars have been published in either Spanish or Portuguese. Still today a lot of work remains to be done in bringing these different traditions together.

Notes

1. Interestingly, the opposite happened with Simmel's influence on Japanese thought that was briefly discussed in the previous chapter: Simmel's influence reached its peak during the 1920s and 1930s, but thereafter lost its power. Shimmei (1959, p. 215) remarks that what is curious in this loss of interest in Simmel is that the Japanese sociologists did not recover it when German thought was replaced by the American sociology as the 'supreme model', even though at the time Simmel's presence had become very strong in North America.
2. In the acknowledgements section, Wolff (1950) acknowledges Hughes – along with Parsons, which indicates that the latter had indeed interest in matters Simmelian – 'for general consultation'.
3. Hobhouse (1864–1929) was a British political theorist and sociologist.
4. Levine's text was italicized in the original.
5. In his doctoral dissertation, Janne Jalava (2006) has examined Simmel and Parsons as two key influences of Luhmann's theory of trust.
6. See www.redsimmel.org

10

Resonance with Contemporary Discussions and Debates

Today, after having remained for a long time at the margins of the sociological canon, Simmel's position among the classical founders of sociology and his actuality are no longer denied. On the contrary, Simmel's work has undergone not one but in fact a number of repeated renaissances. In his lifetime and right after his death, Simmel's work was first given a new life in North American sociology. The early American reception appreciated Simmel, among other things, for defining the sociological domain and as a classic of urban sociology. Later he was rediscovered after World War II, when American sociologists read him, for example, as a classic of small groups, role theory, and conflict theory. The rediscovery was given momentum especially by the publication of *The Sociology of Georg Simmel* (1950), which, as was already mentioned, was the first book-length volume containing translations of Simmel and which significantly promoted the dissemination of Simmel's texts and ideas. Around that time, in the 1950s, interest in Simmel began to increase in Germany as well, partly due to American influence, though on the whole the German reception has been very different from the American one. Later, in the 1980s and 1990s, Simmel was internationally revived especially as a cultural theorist and a theorist of modernity. Finally, most recently, the new wave of scholarship has rediscovered Simmel as a life-philosopher and refined aesthete. In this concluding chapter I will discuss how the actuality of Simmel's work has been addressed in contemporary discussions and debates and also sum up how his concepts and ideas might provide us resistance against the limiting dominant systems and modes of sociological thought and perhaps current social conditions as well.

Simmel's actuality

Nowadays Simmel is appreciated both as an important figure in the history of sociology and as an inspiring source of a numerous ideas, concepts, and hypotheses for current research. It depends on the manner of approaching him which aspect is stressed more and gains prominence. A historical and systematic investigation into the premises of Simmel's thought lays greater emphasis on the historical context within which he wrote his texts and tries to understand him in his own terms and as his ideas appeared to his contemporaries. But if it is his actuality that is emphasized, scholars are far less interested in the historical context of Simmel's work than in our commonality with him. In this strain of thought Simmel is not solely remembered and revered as an important figure of the past for his contributions to the development of the discipline, but his ideas are seen as still relevant to us sociologically (or philosophically) and they are used in order to better understand the contemporary world we ourselves are living in.

Simmel's actuality has been – and is still today – asserted in roughly three ways. First, by utilizing in a more or less selective manner Simmel's ideas and formulations concerning specific themes. Second, besides being a treasure chest of ideas and observations about particular phenomena, Simmel's work has also been appreciated for defining the subject matter of sociology. According to Simmel, as I have repeatedly stressed, sociology should focus on a specifically demarcated problem area: it should study what amounts to society in various socio-historical phenomena, that is, investigate society as such, without further additions. Third, the actuality of Simmel's work has also been emphasized by using it as a source of general theoretical orientations. This mode of incorporation has to do with the analytical perspective provided by Simmel. To me, as I have argued, his legacy consists especially of his relational and processual mode of thought. Simmel has made a significant contribution to laying out a relational foundation for sociology (Cantó-Milà, 2005; 2016; Pyyhtinen 2010; 2016),[1] and his manner of investigating social reality by studying relations is in congruence with many of the programmatic calls for relational sociology that have been voiced in the last couple of decades (see e.g. Emirbayer, 1997; Crossley, 2011; Donati, 2011; Dépelteau & Powell, 2013; Powell & Dépelteau, 2013). Indeed, the relational and processual emphases central to contemporary thought – and often assumed as much more recent developments – are already forcefully and vividly present in Simmel's work. In my book *Simmel and 'the Social'* (2010) I pointed towards affinities of certain recent theoretical approaches, such as actor-network theory (ANT), with aspects of Simmel's thought in theme and approach. Setting aside their differences Simmel and ANT, notably the work of Bruno Latour, have in common, for example, the fact that they question the self-evident durability and stability of social formations; that they focus on relations and associations; and that they place emphasis on the event and the dynamic, unstable nature of connections. Both Simmel and ANT attend to how durable and stable structures are made in and through fragile and precarious links.

As appreciation of Simmel's work has been growing, new aspects of it have been discovered, and so today Simmel comes forth as a much more versatile thinker compared to the partial and uneven reception that he has had in the past. For example the North American reception between the 1950s and 1970s, as we have seen, stressed Simmel's relevance for particular themes such as urbanism, small groups, conflict, and exchange and focused on fetishized individual texts disconnected from the whole of his oeuvre. In the Anglophone world, the more recent appreciation of Simmel as a multifaceted thinker owes much to the contributions of the British sociologist David Frisby (1944–2010) and the American scholar Donald N. Levine (1931–2015). It was Frisby (1985) who famously portrayed Simmel as the 'first theorist of modernity', and both his writings and translations present Simmel's omnivorous analytical taste for a wide range of themes and phenomena, from money to the metropolis, culture, aesthetics, individuality, the Alpine journey, the ruin, the problem of style, and trade exhibitions. Accordingly, recent scholarship has emphasized Simmel's relevance for the study of a remarkably rich variety of themes, such as money, value, taste, and consumption;[2] aesthetics;[3] neoliberalism;[4] gender;[5] subjectivity;[6] space;[7] time;[8] limits;[9] gratitude;[10] secrecy and mendacity;[11] information;[12] competition and structural holes,[13] distance;[14] objects and material culture;[15] nature;[16] film;[17] and trust.[18]

In spite of the remarkable diversity of themes, many contemporary scholars agree with Levine (1985; 2012) in taking issue with the famous idea of Simmel as a sociological *flâneur* (Frisby, 1985) or *bricoleur* (Weinstein & Weinstein, 1991), whose ideas would never add up to a whole. Instead, it is a fairly widely accepted view among Simmel scholars today that Simmel's writings actually do make up a connected body of work (e.g. Dahme, 1981; Bevers, 1985; Léger, 1989; Staubmann, 1998; Darmon & Frade, 2012; Schermer & Jary, 2013). He is definitely not a system builder, but his writings evince a system of some sort, if the notion is understood in a thermodynamic sense, as one based on movement, variation, and change instead of stability, invariance, and permanence, as I suggested in Chapter 2. Simmel's work manifests the living process of thought.

Besides discovering Simmel's relevance for a wealth of specific themes, the latest Simmel scholarship has, indeed, also stressed the coherence of Simmel's overall approach. While Simmel rejects the idea that philosophical thoughts would 'necessarily converge at one ultimate point', for such an idea presents for him nothing but a 'monistic prejudice that contradicts [...] the essence of philosophy' ([1916] GSG 15, p. 310; 2005, p. 3), practically all of Simmel's pieces are nonetheless driven by a common leitmotif: by the aspiration to come to grips with the totality of being. Simmel sees this as a fundamental feature of philosophy. Instead of merely trying to carefully establish particular facts, philosophical thought ultimately concerns for him the whole of life – the totality of being is a living element in its operation. However, at the same time Simmel is fully aware that the totality is unattainable as such, in itself, already in principle. Simmel's own take on coming to grips with the totality is in accordance with his relational mode of thinking: he puts forth a pervasively relational view of the totality, a kind of relational pantheism. He suggests that one can only grasp the totality by starting from a fragment and then spread out from it in all directions along the lines of a network.[19] He does not thus reduce the multiplicity of phenomena to a single concept of their unity, but rather tries to demonstrate how each fragment, through interconnectedness, expresses the totality of being from its own perspective. The core of Simmel's philosophical concerns is laid out right before our eyes in the essay 'Soziologische Aesthetik' ('Sociological Aesthetics'), if we simply substitute 'philosophical investigation' for 'aesthetic observation'. After implementing the change, the passage reads:

> For us, the essence of [philosophical investigation] and interpretation lies in the fact that the typical is to be found in what is unique, the law-like in what is fortuitous, the essence and significance of things in the superficial and transitory. ([1896] GSG 5, p. 198)

Every point carries the possibility of expressing philosophical significance, and from every point radiates the entire sense of the unity of the world (cf. [1896] GSG 5, pp. 198–9). The true challenge for philosophy is thus to be able to master the totality without losing the multiple.

Related to the broader appreciation of the scope of Simmel's work, the new wave of Simmel scholarship has also stressed the philosophical or 'trans-sociological' (Harrington & Kemple 2012, p. 8) aspects of his work and the confluence of his sociological and philosophical concerns (Pyyhtinen 2010; Goodstein 2016; 2017), arguing that we cannot understand Simmel's sociology properly unless we take into consideration his philosophy as well. It has been customary in the secondary literature to treat Simmel's life-philosophy as separate from his sociological project. For example, as was noted above, Friedrich Tenbruck notes that the book *Sociology* was published at the time when 'sociological study was already left far behind him [i.e. Simmel] and he had definitely turned his attention to philosophical and aesthetic questions' (Tenbruck, 1958; trans. Frisby, 1981, p. 24). Further, in a more recent text Kauko Pietilä (2011) maintains that the critical condition of the outbreak of World War I made Simmel turn his back on his sociological programme. However, in contrast to this line of interpretation, Gregor Fitzi (2002; 2016), for instance, asserts that Simmel's mature work presents in fact an extension of the sociological ideas developed in his early and mid-career. Fitzi suggests that in his post-1908 writings Simmel seeks to extend the sociological a priorities from the societal domain to the domain of culture, art, politics, law, and religion, for example. Fitzi (2016) addresses this link by employing the notion of 'life-sociology', and he identifies the dynamics of social life and social forms as its primary concern.[20] In her book *Georg Simmel and the Disciplinary Imaginary* Elizabeth Goodstein (2017) ties Simmel's shifting disciplinary location between sociology and philosophy in an interesting manner to the disciplinary imaginary, suggesting that the preoccupation with Simmel's work and its reception allows us to come to grips with our own inter-disciplinary culture today. According to Goodstein, in considering Simmel solely as a sociologist, sociologists risk forgetting how their discipline is rooted in philosophy, and, in neglecting Simmel philosophy easily ignores what was lost when it became a discipline among others.

An important factor in enriching the image of Simmel and widening the scope of the reception of his work has without doubt been the publication of the *Georg Simmel Gesamtausgabe* (GSG) series of Simmel's collected works for which Otthein Rammsted acted as the general editor. Initiated in 1989, the 24 volumes were finally completed in 2016. The series has made available several of Simmel's writings that were previously scattered and hard to find. The volumes of the GSG series have become standard sources in the most recent Simmel scholarship, and the series has also inspired and informed new insights and interpretations in the secondary literature (with several leading Simmel scholars involved in the editing process as editors of individual GSG volumes).

Recently, the availability of English translations has improved, too. For a long time, most of the translations comprised either selected essays or excerpts of his larger works. Until the late 1970s, *Fundamental Problems of Sociology* (orig. *Grundfragen der Soziologie* [1917]), which was published as part of the volume *The Sociology of Georg Simmel* (1950), edited by Kurt H. Wolff, was the only book by Simmel available in English. It took nearly 30 years until it was followed by others. *The Problems of the Philosophy of History* came out in 1977, and *The Philosophy of Money* the next year, in 1978 (latest edition in 2011). After that, only five others have seen daylight: *Schopenhauer and Nietzsche* (1991b), *Rembrandt* (2005), *Kant and Goethe* (2007), *Sociology* (2009), and *The View of Life* (2010). A number of Simmel's essays, too, have appeared in the past few decades as English translations. The volume *On Women, Sexuality, and Love* (1984), edited by Guy Oakes, contains four of Simmel's essays on gender issues. In 1997 appeared two volumes of Simmel translations: the collection *Simmel on Culture* (1997) edited by David Frisby and Mike Featherstone comprises a great variety of Simmel's writings on culture, and *Essays on Religion* (1997b), edited and translated by Horst Jürgen Helle, makes Simmel's ideas on religion available to Anglophone readership for the first time.

New English translations of Simmel's essays have also appeared in journals, with many of them published in *Theory, Culture & Society*. Simmel's work has held a central place in the journal, from its first volumes in the 1980s to the present. Several of the themes discussed by Simmel, as Featherstone puts it in his introduction to the journal's first Simmel special issue in 1991, 'centrally encapsulate the range of issues we have sought to develop in the journal' (Featherstone, 1991, p. 12). The 1991 special issue focused especially on Simmel's writings on culture, aesthetics, and individuality, and presented English translations of four texts by Simmel: 'Money in Modern Culture', 'The Problem of Style', 'The Alpine Journey', and 'The Berlin Trade Exhibition', with all of them to be later included in the 1997 volume *Simmel on Culture* edited by Frisby and Featherstone. The journal's 2007 special issue 'Simmel: On Aesthetics, Ethics and Metaphysics' edited by Thomas Kemple broadened the scope of translations of Simmel's writings, making for example Simmel's essays on metaphysics available for the first time to an Anglophone readership. The translations not only extend the corpus of Simmel's texts available in English but, if they are read through Simmel's sociology, give us a new, broader and richer understanding of alternative social theory and what it could look like (Kemple, 2007).

Lines of flight

Notwithstanding Simmel's canonization as a classical sociologist, to some extent he also forms part of a 'counter history' of sociology, offering us ways to escape the canonized history of the discipline and restructure the sociological imagination. Indeed, attempts to canonize Simmel, as Goodstein (2017) argues, risk effacing the anomalous aspects of his thought. There is something in Simmel that resists assimilation and provides a shock. Thus, by assimilating his work as part of the recognized canon of sociological and cultural theory we may lose what is untypical, strange, and transgressive in and about his work.

In *A Thousand Plateaus* (1987), the French philosophers Gilles Deleuze and Félix Guattari employ the notion of the 'line of flight', by which they refer to practices, actions, relations, and processes which designate transformation and the ability to change: lines of flight unsettle, rupture, elude, and dissolve established forms and stable configurations. I find in Simmel's work, too, several lines of flight providing resistance not only against the dominant systems and modes of sociological thought but also current social conditions, and some of them have been mapped in this book. Three of them, in particular, are of utmost importance. One is the *relational* view of reality that Simmel's sociology and philosophy presents, and that I have identified as the cornerstone of his contribution or legacy. Simmel's work counters the substantialist reifying assumptions still very much prevalent in sociological modes of thinking and speaking today and shows that the notion of an enduring substance is mistaken. There are no natural unities, but each entity is an achievement, produced in and through relations. There is also no substance to entities other than their relations or, more exactly, their event, their actualization in relations. Relations are one with the essence or substance of a thing. Instead of beginning from static, self-closed entities in a state of rest, Simmel turns attention to their emergence, movement, and stabilization, as well as cessation in and through relations of interdependence. The approach has also political potential in that it may allow people to realize themselves as active participants in the making of history and society.

Second, another line of flight provided by Simmel's work is his attention to *the small* and the seemingly insignificant. Murray S. Davis (1997, p. 377) has proposed that Simmel's (as well as Goffman's) sociology is 'professionally dangerous', as it 'discredits official views of sociology' by suggesting that the small and the minuscule have primacy over the large social formations emphasized by other pioneers of sociological thought, such as Marx, Durkheim, and Weber. Simmel's work shows that all structures, however mighty, result from relations and processes. What is more, instead of just disclosing the sociological significance of the small, Simmel practises 'synecdochal' thinking (from the Gr. συνεκδοχή, *synekdoche*, literally 'simultaneous understanding') in that he tries to get hold of the large by the small, see the whole through the parts. The small thus appear to him as backdoor entrances to tackle more general issues. Importantly, Simmel does not turn to the minuscule and the concrete to 'apply' a theory to it or to illustrate a more general point, but, as was noted above, he uses the minuscule object as a passage to access the whole of things and life, as a prism through which to gaze on totality. The lesson to be learnt here is that we should not fear getting our hands dirty with the seemingly small, superficial, banal, and insignificant, for they allow us to grasp and access such phenomena as the economy, value, society, and life, for example, that otherwise would remain hopelessly vague and abstract.

Simmel's synecdochal thinking relates to the third anomalous element of his work that gives us an escape from the dominant forms of sociological thought, namely his *style*. Besides the synecdoche trope, Simmel's prolific use of analogies, his way of dividing things into form and content, and his manner of thinking via contrasts, dualities, and oppositions – and reconciling thirds – can be taken as examples here. Matters of style such as these are not superfluous and simply about decoration; style has an important function, as it goes to the very heart of thinking and the world. Style has formative power. Ideas do not exist apart from their expressions and manifestations, and even though 'incorporeal' and having a different structure than the world,[21] concepts connect to what their use brings into existence – and thus they are 'incarnated or effectuated in bodies', as Deleuze and Guattari (1994, p. 21) put it.[22] Style is never reducible to the thinking person. Instead of being just 'personal', style may not only resonate with how others experience the world but also invent new ways of thinking and acting, and thereby be suggestive of 'a possibility of life, of a mode of existence' (Deleuze, 1995, p. 100).

The idea of the possibilities or potentials of life connects to the reasons behind engaging with Simmel's work. The return to Simmel has been made in this book not as a form of reverential commentary for the sake of sanctifying him as an object of worship and praise, but in order to revitalize his project in relation to transformations of society and life and the parallel developmental trajectories of scholarship. In its liminality, Simmel's work is situated at once both within and outside established modes of thought, thus not only marking

Resonance with Contemporary Discussions and Debates **187**

the borderline between inside and outside but also opening up the possibility at any moment of stepping out of our limitation into greater freedom. At best it stimulates the sociological imagination and increases our sensibilities, produces a break with the given, and thus potentially offers new possibilities for thinking, acting, and being.

Notes

1 See also Chapter 3.
2 Dodd (1994; 2014; 2016); Zelizer (1994); Gronow (1997); Sassatelli (2000); Cantó-Milá (2005).
3 de la Fuente (2007).
4 Kemple (2016).
5 Oakes (1984); Dahme (1988); Kandal (1988); van Vucht Tjissen (1991); Leck (2000); Witz (2001).
6 Darmon & Frade (2012); Lee & Silver (2012).
7 Lechner (1991); Frisby (1992; 2001); Ziemann (2000); Löw (2001); Schroer (2006).
8 Scaff (2005).
9 Kemple (2007).
10 Cantó-Milà (2012)
11 Welty (1996); Barbour (2012).
12 Lash (2005).
13 Burt (1993)
14 Cantó-Milá (2016)
15 Miller (1987); Appadurai (1988); Pyyhtinen (2010); de la Fuente (2016a and b).
16 Gross (2000; 2001); Giacomoni (2006).
17 Fritsch (2009).
18 Luhmann (1979); Accarino (1984); Möllering (2001); Jalava (2006).
19 In *Hauptprobleme der Philosophie*, Simmel phrases the relation of the fragment and the totality into a paradox: 'The world has been given to us as a sum of fragments, and philosophy strives to set a totality in the place of the fragment; it succeeds in this insofar as it is able to set a fragment in the place of the totality.' ([1910] GSG 14, p. 32)
20 Scott Lash (2005), too, has stressed the connection between Simmel's sociology and life-philosophy by introducing the notion of *Lebenssoziologie*. But whereas Lash develops it to the end of constructing a Simmelian 'vitalism' and making it sociological, with the notion of life-sociology Fitzi attends to Simmel's treatment of the continuous developmental tensions of complex societies.
21 Simmel himself briefly touches on this in *Sociology*. He writes: 'No scientific discipline can describe or formulate the richness of real existing events [*Vorgänge*] or the qualitative determinations of some thing exhaustively. When we therefore employ concepts which crystallize that immensity in themselves and, in a sense, make it tractable, the whole is not represented in the concepts as if in parts made of essentially identical matter. On the contrary, concepts have a different inner structure,

different epistemological, psychological, and metaphysical sense than a whole consisted of the things underlying it. Concepts project this whole on a new level; they do not express the extensive nature of the world with the same albeit minor extensity, but in a form which is already in principle different. The syntheses of those forms do not form a miniature image of the totality of immediate phenomena, but are autonomous formations made of the materials of the forms.' ([1908] GSG 11, pp. 606–7)

22 By drawing on Ian Hacking (2002), this idea could be termed 'dynamic nominalism'.

References

Simmel's works cited

English translations

Simmel, Georg (1949) Sociology of Sociability. Trans. Everett C. Hughes. *The American Journal of Sociology*, 55(3): 254–61.
Simmel, Georg (1950) *The Sociology of Georg Simmel*. Trans. and ed. Kurt H. Wolff. New York: The Free Press.
Simmel, Georg (1955) *Conflict & The Web of Group Affiliations*. Trans. Kurt H. Wolff & Reinhard Bendix. New York: The Free Press.
Simmel, Georg ([1904] 1957) Fashion. *The American Journal of Sociology*, 62(6): 541–58.
Simmel, Georg (1965) The Poor. Trans. Claire Jacobsen. *Social Problems* 13(2): 118–40.
Simmel, Georg (1971) *Georg Simmel on Individuality and Social Forms. Selected Writings*. Ed. Donald N. Levine. Chicago and London: The University of Chicago Press.
Simmel, Georg (1977) *The Problems of the Philosophy of History. An Epistemological Essay*. Trans. and ed. Guy Oakes. New York: The Free Press.
Simmel, Georg (1991a) Money in Modern Culture. Trans. Mark Ritter & Sam Whimster. *Theory, Culture & Society*, 8(3): 17–31.
Simmel, Georg (1991b) *Schopenhauer and Nietzsche*. Trans. Helmut Loiskandl, Deena Weinstein & Michael Weinstein. Urbana and Chicago: University of Illinois Press.
Simmel, Georg (1997a) *Simmel on Culture: Selected Writings*. Ed. David Frisby & Mike Featherstone. London, Thousand Oaks and New Delhi: Sage.
Simmel, Georg (1997b) *Essays on Religion*. Ed. and trans. H. Jünger in collaboration with L. Nieder. New Haven and London: Yale University Press.
Simmel, Georg (2004) *The Philosophy of Money*. Third enlarged edition, trans. David Frisby & Tom Bottomore. London and New York: Routledge.
Simmel, Georg (2005) *Rembrandt. An Essay in the Philosophy of Art*. Trans. Alan Scott & Helmut Staubmann. New York and London: Routledge.
Simmel, Georg (2007) Kant and Goethe. On the History of the Modern Weltanschauung. Trans. Josef Bleicher. *Theory, Culture & Society*, 24(6): 159–91.
Simmel, Georg (2010) *The View of Life. Four Metaphysical Essays with Journal Aphorisms*. Trans. John A. Y. Andrews & Donald N. Levine. Chicago: University of Chicago Press.
Simmel, Georg (2012) The Fragmentary Character of Life. Trans. Austin Harrington. *Theory, Culture & Society*, 29(7–8): 237–48.

Other works cited

Abel, Theodore (1929) *Systematic Sociology in Germany*. New York: Columbia University Press.
Abel, Theodore (1959) The Contribution of Georg Simmel: A Reappraisal. *American Sociological Review*, 24(4): 473–9.
Accarino, Bruno (1984) Vertrauen und Versprechen. Kredit, Öffentlichkeit und individuelle Entscheidung bei Simmel, pp. 116–46 in Heinz-Jürgen Dahme & Otthein Rammstedt (eds) *Georg Simmel und die Moderne. Neue Interpretationen und Materialien*. Frankfurt am Main: Suhrkamp.
Adorno, Theodor W. (1984) *Noten zur Literatur. Gesammelthe Schriften 11*. Frankfurt am Main: Suhrkamp.
Agamben, Giorgio (1998) *Homo Sacer. Sovereign Power and Bare Life*. Trans. Daniel Heller-Roazen. Stanford: Stanford University Press.
Appadurai, Arjun (1988) Introduction: Commodities and the Politics of Value, pp. 3–63 in Arjun Appadurai (ed.) *The Social Life of Things. Commodities in Cultural Perspective*. Cambridge: Cambridge University Press.
Arendt, Hannah & Heidegger, Martin (2004) *Letters 1925–1975*. Ed. Ursula Ludz, trans. Andrew Shields. Orlando: Harcourt.
Backhaus, Gary (1998) Georg Simmel as an Eidetic Social Scientist. *Sociological Theory*, 16(3): 260–81.
Backhaus, Gary (2003a) Simmel's Philosophy of History and Its Relation to Phenomenology: Introduction. *Human Studies*, 26(2): 203–8.
Backhaus, Gary (2003b) Husserlian Affinities in Simmel's Later Philosophy of History: The 1918 Essay. *Human Studies*, 26(2): 223–58.
Baehr, Peter (2001) The 'Iron Cage' and the 'Shell as Hard as Steel': Parsons, Weber, and the Stahlhartes Gehäuase Metaphor in the Protestant Ethic and the Spirit of Capitalism. *History and Theory*, 40(2): 153–69.
Baehr, Peter (2002) *Founders, Classics, and Canons: Modern Disputes over the Origins and Appraisal of Sociology's Heritage*. New Brunswick, NJ: Transaction Publishers.
Barbour, Charles (2012) The Maker of Lies: Simmel, Mendacity and the Economy of Faith. *Theory, Culture & Society (Annual Review)*, 19(4): 218–36.
Baudelaire, Charles ([1863] 1964) *The Painter of Modern Life and Other Essays*. Trans. and ed. Jonathan Mayne. London: Phaidon Press.
Bean, Susan S. (1970) Two's Company, Three's a Crowd. *American Anthropologist*, 72(3): 562–4.
Becher, Heribert J. (1971) *Georg Simmel – Die Grundlagen seiner Soziologie*. Stuttgart: Enke.
Becker, Howard & Useem, Ruth Hill (1948) Sociological Analysis of the Dyad. *American Sociological Review*, 7(1): 13–26.
Benjamin, Walter ([1940] 2003) On Some Motifs of Baudelaire. In Walter Benjamin, *Selected Writings. Volume 4: 1938–1940*. Trans. Edmund Jephcott & others, eds Howard Eiland & Michael W. Jennings. Cambridge Mass. & London: The Belknap Press of Harvard University Press.
Bennett, Jane (2010) *Vibrant Matter: A Political Ecology of Things*. Durham: Duke University Press.

Bergson, Henri (1999) *An Introduction to Metaphysics*. Trans. T. E. Hulme. Indianapolis: Hackett.
Berlin, Isaiah (1953) *The Hedgehog and the Fox: An Essay on Tolstoy's View of History*. London: Weidenfeld & Nicolson.
Bevers, Antonius M. (1985) *Dynamik der Formen bei Georg Simmel. Eine Studie über die methodische und theoretische Einheit eines Gesamtwerkes*. Berlin: Duncker & Humblot.
Blau, Peter M. (1964) *Exchange and Power in Social Life*. New York: Wiley.
Bleicher, Josef (2007) From Kant to Goethe: Georg Simmel on the way to Leben. *Theory, Culture & Society*, 24(6): 139–58.
Bloch, Ernst (1918) *Geist der Utopie*. München: Duncker & Humblot.
Blumer, Herbert (1969) Fashion: From Class Differentiation to Collective Selection. *The Sociological Quarterly*, 10(3): 275–91.
Boskoff, Alvin (1969) *Theory in American Sociology: Major Sources and Applications*. New York: Crowell.
Bouglé, Célestin (1965) The Sociology of Georg Simmel, pp. 58–63 in Lewis A. Coser (ed.) *Georg Simmel*. Englewood Cliffs: Prentice-Hall.
Bourdieu, Pierre (1990) *In Other Words: Essays toward a Reflexive Sociology*. Trans. Matthew Adamson. Cambridge: Polity Press.
Buber, Martin ([1951] 1993) Erinnerungen an Simmel, pp. 222–3 in Kurt Gassen & Michael Landmann (eds) *Buch des Dankes an Georg Simmel. Briefe, Erinnerungen, Bibliographie. Zu seinem 100. Geburtstag am 1. März 1958*. 2. Aufl. Berlin: Duncker & Humblot.
Burt, Ronald (1993) The Social Structure of Competition, pp. 57–91 in Richard Swedberg (ed.) *Explorations in Economic Sociology*. New York: Russell Sage Foundation.
Böhringer, Hannes & Gründer, Karlfried (eds) (1976) *Ästhetik und Soziologie um die Jahrhundertwende: Georg Simmel*. Frankfurt am Main: Vittorio Klostermann.
Callon, Michel (1998) Introduction: The Embeddedness of Economic Markets in Economics, pp. 1–57 in Michel Callon (ed.) *The Laws of the Markets*. Oxford and Maiden: Blackwell/The Sociological Review.
Campbell, Colin (1987) *The Romantic Ethic and the Spirit of Modern Consumerism*. Oxford: Basil Blackwell.
Cantó-Milà, Natàlia (2005) *A Sociological Theory of Value: Georg Simmel's Sociological Relationism*. Bielefeld: Transcript.
Cantó-Milà, Natàlia (2012) Gratitude – Invisibly Webbing Society Together. *Journal of Classical Sociology*, 13(1): 8–19.
Cantó-Milà, Natàlia (2016) On the Special Relation between Proximity and Distance in Simmel's Forms of Association and Beyond, pp. 81–100 in Thomas Kemple & Olli Pyyhtinen (eds) *The Anthem Companion to Georg Simmel*. London and New York: Anthem Press.
Caplow, Theodore (1956) A Theory of Coalitions in the Triad. *American Sociological Review*, 21(4): 489–93.
Christian, Petra (1978) *Einheit und Zwiespalt. Zum hegelianisierenden Denken in der Philosophie und Soziologie Georg Simmels*. Berlin: Duncker & Humblot.
Coser, Lewis A. (1956) *The Functions of Social Conflict*. New York: The Free Press.
Coser, Lewis A. (1965) Georg Simmel, pp. 1–26 in Lewis A. Coser (ed.) *Georg Simmel*. Englewood Cliffs: Prentice-Hall.

Coser, Lewis A. (1977) *Masters of Sociological Thought. Ideas in Historical and Social Context*. New York: Harcourt Brace Jovanovich.

Crossley, Nick (2011) *Towards Relational Sociology*. London and New York: Routledge.

Dahme, Heinz-Jürgen (1981) *Soziologie als Exakte Wissenschaft. Georg Simmels Ansatz und seine Bedeutung in der gegenwärtige Soziologie. I & II Simmel's Soziologie in Grundriß*. Stuttgart: Enke.

Dahme, Heinz-Jürgen (1988) On Georg Simmel's Sociology of the Sexes. *International Journal of Politics, Culture, and Society*, 1(3): 412–30.

Dahme, Heinz-Jürgen (1990) On the Current Rediscovery of Georg Simmel's Sociology – A European Point of View, pp. 13–37 in Michael Kaern, Bernard Phillips & Robert S. Cohen (eds) *Georg Simmel and Contemporary Sociology*. Dordrecht: Kluwert.

Dahme, Heinz-Jürgen & Rammstedt, Otthein (1984) *Georg Simmel und die Moderne. Neue Interpetationen und Materialien*. Frankfurt am Main: Suhrkamp.

Dahme, Heinz-Jürgen & Rammstedt, Otthein (1986) Einleitung. In Heinz-Jürgen Dahme & Otthein Rammstedt (eds) *Georg Simmel – Schriften zur Soziologie. Eine Auswahl*. Frankfurt am Main: Suhrkamp.

Darmon, Isabelle & Frade, Carlos (2012) Beneath and Beyond the Fragments: The Charms of Simmel's Philosophical Path for Contemporary Subjectivities. *Theory, Culture & Society*, 29(7–8): 197–217.

Davis, Murray S. (1997) Georg Simmel and Erving Goffman: Legitimators of the Sociological Investigation of Human Experience. *Qualitative Sociology*, 20(3): 369–88.

de la Fuente, Eduardo (2007) On the Promise of a Sociological Aesthetics: From Georg Simmel to Michel Maffesoli. *Distinktion*, 15: 91–110.

de la Fuente, Eduardo (2016a) Frames, Handles and Landscapes: Simmel and the Aesthetic Ecology of Things. In Thomas Kemple & Olli Pyyhtinen (eds) *The Anthem Companion to Georg Simmel*. London and New York: Anthem Press.

de la Fuente, Eduardo (2016b) A Qualitative Theory of Culture: Georg Simmel and Cultural Sociology. In David Inglis & Anna-Mari Almila (eds) *The SAGE Handbook of Cultural Sociology*. London: Sage.

Deleuze, Gilles (1991) *Bergsonism*. Trans. Hugh Tomlinson and Barbara Habberjam. New York: Zone Books.

Deleuze, Gilles (1995) *Negotiations. 1972–1990*. New York: Columbia University Press.

Deleuze, Gilles & Guattari, Félix (1987) *A Thousand Plateaus. Capitalism and Schizophrenia*. Trans. Brian Massumi. Minneapolis and London: University of Minnesota Press.

Deleuze, Gilles & Guattari, Félix (1994) *What Is Philosophy?* Trans. Hugh Tomlinson & Graham Burchell. New York: Columbia University Press.

Dépelteau, François & Powell, Christopher (eds) (2013) *Applying Relational Sociology: Relations, Networks, & Society*. New York: Palgrave Macmillan.

Derrida, Jacques (1995) *The Gift of Death*. Translated by David Wills. Chicago and London: Chicago University Press.

Dodd, Nigel (1994) *The Sociology of Money. Economics, Reason and Contemporary Society*. Cambridge: Polity Press.

Dodd, Nigel (2014) *The Social Life of Money*. Princeton, NJ: Princeton University Press.

Dodd, Nigel (2016) Vires in Numeris: Taking Simmel to Mt Gox, pp. 121–40 in Thomas Kemple & Olli Pyyhtinen (eds) *The Anthem Companion to Georg Simmel*. London and New York: Anthem Press.

Donati, Pierpaolo (2011) *Relational Sociology: A New Paradigm for the Social Sciences*. London & New York: Routledge.

Duncan, Hugh Dalziel (1959) Simmel's Image of Society, pp. 100–18 in Kurt H. Wolff (ed.) *Georg Simmel, 1858–1918. A Collection of Essays, with Translations and a Bibliography*. Ohio: Ohio State University Press.

Durkheim, Émile (1964) Sociology and Its Scientific Field. In Kurt H. Wolff (ed.) *Essays on Sociology & Philosophy*, pp. 354–75. New York: Harper & Row.

Durkheim, Émile (1980) Georg Simmel, Philosophie des Geldes. in Y. Nandan (ed.) *Emile Durkheim: Contributions to L'Année Sociologique*, New York and London: Free Press.

Durkheim, Émile (1982) *The Rules of Sociological Method*. Trans. W.D. Halls. New York: Free Press.

Elias, Norbert (1978) *What Is Sociology?* Trans. Stephen Mennell & Grace Morrissey. London: Hutchinson & Company.

Emibayer, Mustafa (1997) Manifesto for a Relational Sociology. *The American Journal of Sociology*, 103(2): 281–317.

Emirbayer, Mustafa (2013) Relational Sociology as Fighting Words, pp. 209–11 in Christopher Powell & François Dépelteau (eds) *Conceptualizing Relational Sociology: Ontological and Theoretical Issues*. New York: Palgrave Macmillan.

Featherstone, Mike (1991) Georg Simmel: An Introduction. *Theory, Culture & Society*, 8(3): 1–16.

Fechter, Paul ([1918] 1993) Erinnerungen an Simmel, pp. 157–62 in Kurt Gassen & Michael Landmann (eds) *Buch des Dankes an Georg Simmel. Briefe, Erinnerungen, Bibliographie. Zu seinem 100. Geburtstag am 1. März 1958*. 2. Aufl. Berlin: Duncker & Humblot.

Fine, Gary Alan & Manning, Philip (2003) Erving Goffman. In George Ritzer (ed.), *The Blackwell Companion to Major Contemporary Social Theorists*. Malden, MA: Blackwell. URL:<http://www.blackwellreference.com/public/tocnode?id=g9781405105958_chunk_g97814051059585>. Last Checked 24 Dec 2016.

Fitzi, Gregor (2002) *Soziale Erfahrung und Lebensphilosophie. Georg Simmels Beziehung zu Henri Bergson*. Konstanz: Universitätsverlag Konstanz.

Fitzi, Gregor (2016) Modernity as Solid Liquidity: Simmel's Life-Sociology, pp. 59–80 in Thomas Kemple & Olli Pyyhtinen (eds) *The Anthem Companion to Georg Simmel*. London and New York: Anthem Press.

Foucault, Michel ([1975] 1991) *Discipline and Punish*. Trans. Alan Sheridan. London: Penguin Books.

Fowler, Chris & Harris, Oliver (2015) Enduring Relations: Exploring a Paradox of New Materialism. *Journal of Material Culture*, 20(2): 127–48.

Frade, C. & Pyyhtinen, O. (2017) Weber/Simmel Antagonisms: A Philosophical & Political Stance – A Dialogue in Three Acts. *Journal of Classical Sociology, 17(2): 87–100*.

Freud, Sigmund ([1922] 2010) *Beyond the Pleasure Principle*. Trans. by C. J. M. Hubback. London and Vienna: International Psycho-Analytical Association. [Online version: Bartleby.com, 2010. www.bartleby.com/276/]

Freund, Julien (1976) Der Dritte in Simmels Soziologie, pp. 90–104 in Hannes Böhringer & Karlfried Gründer (eds) *Ästhetik und Soziologie um der Jahrhundertwende: Georg Simmel*. Frankfurt am Main: Vittorio Klostermann.
Frisby, David (1981) *Sociological Impressionism. A Reassessment of Georg Simmel's Social Theory*. London: Heinemann.
Frisby, David (1984) *Georg Simmel*. Chichester: Ellis Horwood.
Frisby, David (1985) Georg Simmel: First Theorist of Modernity. *Theory, Culture & Society*, 2(3): 49–67.
Frisby, David (1992) *Simmel and Since. Essays on Georg Simmel's Social Theory*. London and New York: Routledge.
Frisby, David (1997) Introduction to the Texts, pp. 1–28 in David Frisby & Mike Featherstone (eds) *Simmel on Culture. Selected Writings*. London: Sage.
Frisby, David (2001) *Cityscapes of Modernity. Critical Explorations*. Cambridge: Polity Press.
Frisby, David (2004a) Introduction to the Translation, pp. 1–49 in Georg Simmel, *The Philosophy of Money*. Third enlarged edition. Trans. David Frisby & Tom Bottomore. London and New York: Routledge.
Frisby, David (2004b) Transaction Introduction, pp. vii–xxxiv in Nicholas J. Spykman, *The Social Theory of Georg Simmel*. New Brunswick and London: Transaction.
Frisby, David (2006) Filosofia ja arkisten objektien luonto. David Frisbyn haastattelu. [Philosophy and the Nature of Everyday Objects: An interview with David Frisby; by Olli Pyyhtinen.] *Niin & Näin*, 51: 53–7.
Fritsch, Daniel (2009) *Georg Simmel im Kino. Die Soziologie des frühen Films und das Abenteuer der Moderne*. Bielefeld: Transcript.
Gadamer, Hans-Georg (1986/7) Erinnerungen an Heideggers Anfänge. In *Hermeneutik im Rückblick. Gesammelte Werke Band 10*. Tübingen: J.C.B. Mohr.
Gadamer, Hans-Georg ([1975] 2004) *Truth and Method*. Second, Revised Edition. Translation revised by Joel Weinsheimer & Donald G. Marshall. London & New York: Continuum.
Gassen, Kurt ([1958] 1993) Erinnerungen an Simmel, pp. 298–308 in Kurt Gassen & Michael Landmann (eds) *Buch des Dankes an Georg Simmel. Briefe, Erinnerungen, Bibliographie. Zu seinem 100. Geburtstag am 1. März 1958. Zu seinem 100. Geburtstag am 1. März 1958*. 2. Aufl. Berlin: Duncker & Humblot.
Gassen, Kurt & Landmann, Michael ([1958] 1993) *Buch des Dankes an Georg Simmel. Briefe, Erinnerungen, Bibliographie. Zu seinem 100. Geburtstag am 1. März 1958*. 2. Aufl. Berlin: Duncker & Humblot.
Gawoll, Hans-Jürgen (1993) Impulse der Lebensphilosophie. Anmerkungen zum Verhältnis von Heidegger und Simmel. *Simmel Newsletter*, 3(2): 139–51.
Giacomoni, Paola (2006) Kontinuität der Formen. Georg Simmels Interpretation einiger Begriffe der Naturforschung Goethes. *Simmel Studies*, 16(1): 5–19.
Girard, René (1979) *Violence and the Sacred*. Trans. Patrick Gregory. Baltimore and London: The John Hopkins University Press.
Goffman, Erving (1953) *Communication Conduct in an Island Community*. PhD Dissertation. University of Chicago.
Goodstein, Elizabeth (2002) Style as Substance. Georg Simmel's Phenomenology of Culture. *Cultural Critique*, 52: 209–34.

Goodstein, Elizabeth (2016) Sociology as a Sideline: Does It Matter That Georg Simmel (Thought He) Was a Philosopher?, pp. 29–58 in Thomas Kemple & Olli Pyyhtinen (eds) *The Anthem Companion to Georg Simmel*. London and New York: Anthem Press.

Goodstein, Elizabeth (2017) *Georg Simmel and the Disciplinary Imaginary*. Stanford: Stanford University Press.

Goudge, Thomas A. ([1949] 1999) Editor's Introduction, pp. 9–20 in Henri Bergson, *An Introduction to Metaphysics*. Trans. T. E. Hulme. Indianapolis: Hackett.

Gouldner, Alvin (1960) The Norm of Reciprocity. *American Sociological Review*, 25(2): 161–78.

Gronow, Jukka (1997) *The Sociology of Taste*. London and New York: Routledge.

Gross, Matthias (2000) Classical Sociology and the Restoration of Nature: The Relevance of Émile Durkheim and Georg Simmel. *Organization & Environment*, 13(3): 277–91.

Gross, Matthias (2001) Unexpected Interactions. Georg Simmel and the Observation of Nature. *Journal of Classical Sociology*, 1(3): 395–414.

Großheim, Michael (1991) *Von Georg Simmel zu Martin Heidegger. Philosophie zwischen Leben und Existenz*. Bonn: Bouvier.

Gumbrecht, Hans Ulrich (1978) Modern, Modernität, Moderne, pp. 93–131 in Otto Brunner; Werner Conze & Reinhart Koselleck (eds): *Geschichtliche Grundbegriffe. Historisches Lexikon zur politisch-sozialen Sprache in Deutschland*. Band 4. Stuttgart: Klett – Cotta.

Habermas, Jürgen (1996) Simmel als Zeitdiagnostiker. In Georg Simmel, *Philosophische Kultur. Über das Abentauer, die Geschlechter und die Krise der Moderne*. Berlin: Wagenbach.

Hacking, Ian (2002) *Historical Ontology*. Cambridge Mass: Harvard University Press.

Hare, Paul A. (1952) A Study of Interaction and Consensus in Different Sized Groups. American Sociological Review 17(3): 261–7.

Härpfer, Claudius (2014) *Georg Simmel und die Entstehung der Soziologie. Eine netzwerksoziologische Studie*. Wiesbaden: Springer.

Harrington, Austin & Kemple, Thomas (2012) Georg Simmel's 'Sociological Metaphysics': Money, Sociality, and Precarious Life. *Theory, Culture & Society (Annual Review)*, 19(4): 6–25.

Heidegger, Martin (1962) *Being and Time*. Trans. J. Macquarrie & E. Robinson. Oxford: Blackwell.

Heidegger, Martin (2010) *Grundprobleme der Phänomenologie (1919/20)*, GA 58. Frankfurt am Main: Vittorio Klosterman.

Himes, Joseph (1966) The Functions of Racial Conflict. *Social Forces*, 45(1): 1–10.

Hughes, Everett C. (1949) Social Change and Status Protest: An Essay on the Marginal Man. *Phylon*, 10(1): 58–65.

Hughes, Everett C. (1964) Robert Park. *New Society* (13 December): 18–19.

Hübner-Funk, Sibylle (1982) *Georg Simmels Konzeption von Gesellschaft. Ein Beitrag zum Verhältnis von Soziologie, Äesthetik und Politik*. Köln: Pahl-Rugstein.

Ingold, Tim (2011) *Being Alive. Essays on Movement, Knowledge and Description*. London: Routledge.

Jalava, Janne (2006) *Trust as a Decision: The Problems and Functions of Trust in Luhmannian Systems Theory*. Helsinki: University of Helsinki. PhD thesis.

Jalbert, J.E. (2003) Time, Death, and History in Simmel and Heidegger. *Human Studies*, 26(2): 259–83.
Jaworski, Gary D. (1997) *Georg Simmel and the American Prospect*. New York: State University of New York Press.
Joël, Karl ([1918] 1993) Erinnerungen an Simmel, pp. 166–9 in Kurt Gassen & Michael Landmann (eds) *Buch des Dankes an Georg Simmel. Briefe, Erinnerungen, Bibliographie. Zu seinem 100. Geburtstag am 1. März 1958*. 2. Aufl. Berlin: Duncker & Humblot.
Kandal, T. R. (1988) *The Woman Question in Classical Sociological Theory*. Miami: Florida International University Press.
Kantorowicz, Gertrud ([1923] 1959) Preface to Georg Simmel's *Fragments, Posthumous Essays, and Publications of His Last Years*. Trans. Kurt H. Wolff, pp. 3–8 in Kurt Wolff (ed.) *Georg Simmel, 1858–1918. A Collection of Essays, with Translations and a Bibliography*. Columbus: The Ohio State University Press.
Karlsruhen, Torge & Rammstedt, Otthein (2004) Editorischer Bericht, pp. 481–553 in Georg Simmel, *Postume Veröffentlichungen; Ungedrucktes; Schulpädagogik*. Georg Simmel Gesamtausgabe Band 20. Frankfurt am Main: Suhrkamp.
Kemple, Thomas (2007) Allosociality: Briges and Doors to Simmel's Social Theory of the Limit. *Theory, Culture & Society*, 24(7–8): 1–19.
Kemple, Thomas (2013a) Allegories of the End: Classical Sociologies of Economic Sustainability and Cultural Ruin. *Journal of Historical Sociology*, 26(3): 365–82.
Kemple, Thomas (2013b) Georg Simmel at UBC: The Story of a Photograph. *Sociology Newsletter*, Spring 2013. University of British California.
Kemple, Thomas (2016) Simmel and the Sources of Neoliberalism, pp. 141–60 in Thomas Kemple & Olli Pyyhtinen (eds) *The Anthem Companion to Georg Simmel*. London and New York: Anthem Press.
Kennedy, Paul (1980) *The Rise of the Anglo-German Antagonism, 1860–1914*. London: Allen & Unwin.
Kettler, David (2012) Introduction to 'Soul and Culture'. *Theory, Culture & Society*, 29(7–8): 279–85.
Koselleck, Reinhart (1988) *Vergangene Zukunft: Zur Semantik geschichtliche Zeiten*. Frankfurt am Main: Suhrkamp.
Kracauer, Siegfried (1995) *The Mass Ornament. Weimar Essays*. Trans. and ed. Thomas Y. Levin. Cambridge Mass: Harvard University Press.
Krackhardt, David (1999) The Ties That Torture: Simmelian Tie Analysis in Organizations. *Research in the Sociology of Organizations*, 16: 183–210.
Krell, David Farrell (1992) *Daimon Life: Heidegger and Life-Philosophy*. Bloomington: Indiana University Press.
Köhnke, Klaus Christian (1996) *Der junge Simmel in Theoriebeziehungen und sozialen Bewegungen*. Frankfurt am Main: Suhrkamp.
Landmann, Michael (1949) Georg Simmel: Vorbereitung eines Archivs und einer Ausgabe. In: Philosophische Vorträge und Diskussionen. Bericht über den Mainzer Philosophen-Kongreß 1948. *Zeitschrift für philosophische Forschung*, Sonderheft 1: 204–5.
Landmann, Michael ([1958] 1993) Bausteine zur Biographie, pp. 11–33 in Kurt Gassen & Michael Landmann (eds) *Buch des Dankes an Georg Simmel. Briefe,*

Erinnerungen, Bibliographie. Zu seinem 100. Geburtstag am 1. März 1958. 2. Aufl. Berlin: Duncker & Humblot.
Landmann, Michael (1968) Einleitung des Herausgebers, pp. 7–29 in Georg Simmel, *Das Individuelle Gesetz. Philosophische Exkurse*. Ed. Michael Landmann. Frankfurt am Main: Suhrkamp.
Landmann, Michael (1976) Georg Simmel: Konturen seines Denkens, pp. 3–17 in Hannes Böhringer & Karlfried Gründer (eds) *Ästhetik und Soziologie um die Jahrhundertwende: Georg Simmel*. Frankfurt am Main: Vittorio Klostermann.
Landmann, Michael & Susman, Margarete (1957). Einleitung, pp. v–xxiii in Georg Simmel: *Brücke und Tür. Essays des Philosophen zur Geschichte, Religion, Kunst und Gesellschaft*. Ed. Landmann, in collaboration with Susman. Stuttgart: K. F. Koehler.
Lash, Scott (1999) *Another Modernity, a Different Rationality*. Oxford: Blackwell.
Lash, Scott (2005) Lebenssoziologie. Georg Simmel in the Information Age. *Theory, Culture & Society*, 22(3): 1–23.
Lash, Scott (2006) Life (Vitalism). *Theory, Culture & Society*, 23(2–3): 323–9.
Latour, Bruno (2005) *Reassembling the Social. An Introduction to Actor-Network-Theory*. Oxford and New York: Oxford University Press.
Latour, Bruno & Lépinay, Vincent Antonine (2009) *The Science of Passionate Interests: An Introduction to Gabriel Tarde's Economic Anthropology*. Chicago: Prickly Paradigm Press.
Lechner, Frank J. (1991) Simmel on Social Space. *Theory, Culture & Society*, 8(3): 195–201.
Leck, Ralph M. (2000) *Georg Simmel and Avant-Garde Sociology. The Birth of Modernity, 1880–1920*. New York: Humanity Books.
Lee, Monica & Silver, David (2012) Simmel's Law of the Individual and the Ethics of the Relational Self. *Theory, Culture & Society*, 29(7–8): 124–45.
Léger, François (1989) *La pensée de Georg Simmel. Contribution à l'histoire des idées en Allemagne au début du xxe siècle*. Paris: Éditions KIME.
Levine, Donald N. (1959) The structure of Simmel's social thought, pp. 9–32 in Kurt H. Wolff (ed.) *Georg Simmel. 1858–1918*. Columbus: Ohio State University Press.
Levine, Donald N. (1971) Introduction, pp. ix–lxv in Georg Simmel, *On Individuality and Social Forms. Selected Writings*. Chicago and London: The University of Chicago Press.
Levine, Donald N. (1981) Sociology's Quest for the Classics: The Case of Simmel, pp. 60–80 in Buford Rhea (ed.) *The Future of the Sociological Classics*. London: George Allen and Unwin.
Levine, Donald N. (1985) *The Flight from Ambiguity: Essays in Social and Cultural Theory*. Chicago: University of Chicago Press.
Levine, Donald N. (2012) *Soziologie* and *Lebensanschauung*: Two Approaches to Synthesizing 'Kant' and 'Goethe' in Simmel's Work. *Theory Culture & Society*, 29(7–8): 26–52.
Levine, Donald N., Carter, Ellwood B. & Gorman, Eleanor Miller (1976a) Simmel's Influence on American Sociology I. *American Journal of Sociology*, 81(4): 813–45.
Levine, Donald N., Carter, Ellwood B. & Gorman, Eleanor Miller (1976b) Simmel's Influence on American Sociology II. *American Journal of Sociology*, 81(5): 1112–32.

Lichtblau, Klaus (1991) Causality or Interaction? Simmel, Weber, and Interpretive Sociology. *Theory, Culture & Society*, 8(3): 33–62.
Lichtblau, Klaus (1995) Sociology and the Diagnosis of the Times or: The Reflexivity of Modernity. *Theory, Culture & Society*, 12(1): 25–52.
Lichtblau, Klaus (1997) *Georg Simmel*. Frankfurt/New York: Campus Verlag.
Lindemann, Gesa (2006) Die Emergenzfunktion und die konstitutive Funktion des Dritten. Perspektiven einer kritisch-systematischen Theorieentwicklung. *Zeitschrift für Soziologie*, 35(2): 82–101.
Lipman, Matthew (1959) Some Aspects of Simmel's Conception of the Individual, pp. 119–38 in Kurt Wolff (ed.) *Georg Simmel, 1858 –1918. A Collection of Essays, with Translations and a Bibliography*. Columbus: The Ohio State University Press.
Litt, Theodor (1926) *Individuum und Gemeinschaft. Grundlegung der Kulturphilosophie*. Leipzig: B. G. Teubner.
Lofland, Lynn H. (1985) *A World of Strangers: Order and Action in Public Urban Space*. New York: Waveland Press.
Ludwig, Emil ([1914, 1918, and 1931] 1993) Erinnerungen an Simmel, pp. 152–7 in Kurt Gassen & Michael Landmann (eds) *Buch des Dankes an Georg Simmel. Briefe, Erinnerungen, Bibliographie. Zu seinem 100. Geburtstag am 1. März 1958*. 2. Aufl. Berlin: Duncker & Humblot.
Luhmann, Niklas (1979) *Trust and Power*. Chichester: John Wiley.
Luhmann, Niklas (1987) Tautologie and Paradoxie in den Selbstbeschreibungen der modernen Gesellschaft. *Zeitschrift für Soziologie*, 16: 161–74.
Lukács, Georg (1914) Soziologie des modernen Dramas. *Archiv für Sozialwissenschaft und Sozialpolitik*, 38: 303–45, 662–706.
Lukács, Georg (1972) *Schriften zur Literatursoziologie*. Neuwied: Luchterhand.
Lukács, Georg (1986) *Pensée vecue, mémoires parlés*. Paris: L'arche.
Lukács, Georg ([1918] 1991) Georg Simmel. Trans. Margaret Cerullo. *Theory, Culture & Society*, 8(3): 145–50.
Lukács, Georg ([1918] 1993) Georg Simmel, pp. 171–6 in Kurt Gassen & Michael Landmann (eds) *Buch des Dankes an Georg Simmel. Briefe, Erinnerungen, Bibliographie. Zu seinem 100. Geburtstag am 1. März 1958*. 2. Aufl. Berlin: Duncker & Humblot.
Lukács, Georg ([1910] 2010) *Soul and Form*. Ed. John T. Sanders & Katie Terezakis. Columbia University Press.
Lüschen, Gerd & Stone, Gregory P. (1977) Introduction, pp. 1–45 in Gerd Lüschen & Gregory P. Stone (eds) *Herman Schmalenbach: On Society and Experience*. Chicago: The University of Chicago Press.
Lyotard, Jean-Francois (1988) *Peregrinations. Law, Form, Event*. New York: Columbia University Press.
Löw, Martina (2001) *Raumsoziologie*. Frankfurt am Main: Suhrkamp.
Maioli, Esteban (2010) La recepción de la obra de Georg Simmel en la Argentina. *VI Jornadas de Sociología de la UNLP*. Universidad Nacional de La Plata. Facultad de Humanidades y Ciencias de la Educación. Departamento de Sociología, La Plata.
Mamelet, Alfred (1965) Sociological Relativism, pp. 64–73 in Lewis A. Coser (ed.) *Georg Simmel*. Englewood Cliffs: Prentice-Hall.
Marston, Sallie A., Jones, John Paul III & Woodward, Keith (2005) Human Geography Without Scale. *Transactions of the Institute of British Geographers*, 30(4): 416–32.

Matthias, Leo ([1928] 1993) Erinnerungen an Simmel, pp. 192–4 in Kurt Gassen & Michael Landmann (eds) *Buch des Dankes an Georg Simmel. Briefe, Erinnerungen, Bibliographie. Zu seinem 100. Geburtstag am 1. März 1958*. 2. Aufl. Berlin: Duncker & Humblot.
Maus, Heinz (1959) Simmel in German Sociology, pp. 180–200 in Kurt Wolff (ed.) *Georg Simmel, 1858–1918. A Collection of Essays, with Translations and a Bibliography*. Columbus: The Ohio State University Press.
McCracken, Grant (1988) *Culture and Consumption. New Approaches to the Symbolic Character of Consumer Goods and Activities*. Bloomington: Indiana University Press.
Merton, Robert K. (1949) *Social Theory and Social Structure*. New York: Free Press.
Miller, Daniel (1987) *Material Culture and Mass Consumption*. Oxford, UK: Blackwell.
Mills, C. Wright (2000 [1959]) *The Sociological Imagination*. Fortieth Anniversary Edition. Oxford: Oxford University Press.
Mills, Theodore (1958) Some Hypotheses on Small Groups from Simmel. *American Journal of Sociology*, 63(6): 642–50.
Muller, Jerry Z. (1987) *The Other God that Failed: Hans Freyer and the Deradicalization of German Conservatism*. Princeton, NJ: Princeton University Press.
Möllering, Guido (2001) The Nature of Trust: From Georg Simmel to Theory of Expectation, Interpretation and Suspension. *Sociology*, 35(2): 403–20.
Naegele, Kaspar D. (1958) Attachment and Alienation: Complementary Aspects of the Work of Durkheim and Simmel. *The American Journal of Sociology*, 63(6): 580–9.
Nedelmann, Birgitta (1984) Georg Simmel als Klassiker soziologischer Prozeßanalysen, pp. 91–115 in Heinz-Jürgen Dahme & Otthein Rammstedt (eds) *Georg Simmel und die Moderne. Neue Interpretationen und Materialien*. Frankfurt am Main: Suhrkamp.
Nietzsche, Friedrich (2003) *The Genealogy of Morals*. Trans. H. B. Samuel. Mineola and New York: Dover.
Nisbet, Robert A. (1959) Comment. *American Sociological Review*, 24(4): 479–81.
Noro, Arto (1991) *Muoto, moderniteetti ja "kolmas". Tutkielma Georg Simmelin sosiologiasta*. [Form, Modernity, and the 'Third'. A Study of the Sociology of Georg Simmel.] Helsinki: Tutkijaliitto.
Noro, Arto (2005) Esipuhe suomennosvalikoimaan. [Foreword.], pp. 7–24 in Georg Simmel, *Suurkaupunki ja moderni elämä. Kirjoituksia vuosilta 1895–1917*. Trans. Tiina Huuhtanen, ed. Arto Noro. Helsinki: Gaudeamus.
Oakes, Guy (1977) Introduction: Simmel's Problematic, pp. 1–37 in Georg Simmel, *The Problems of the Philosophy of History. An Epistemological Essay*. Trans. and ed. Guy Oakes. New York: The Free Press.
Oakes, Guy (1984) The Problem of Women in Simmel's Theory of Culture, pp. 3–62 in Georg Simmel, *On Women, Sexuality, and Love*. Ed. Guy Oakes. New Haven, CT & London: Yale University Press.
Outhwaite, William (2006) *The Future of Society*. Oxford: Blackwell.
Papilloud, Christian (2002) Critical Relations. Anthropology of Exchange in Georg Simmel and Marcel Mauss. *Simmel Studies*, 12(1): 85–107.
Park, Robert Ezra (1915) The City: Suggestions for the Investigation of Human Behavior in the City Environment. *The American Journal of Sociology*, 20(5): 577–612.

Park, Robert Ezra & Burgess, Ernest W. ([1921] 1969) *Introduction to the Science of Sociology*. Chicago: Chicago University Press.
Parsons, Talcott (1934) Some Reflections on 'The Nature and Significance of Economics'. *Quarterly Journal of Economics*, 48(3): 511–45.
Parsons, Talcott (1935) The Place of Ultimate Values in Sociological Theory. *International Journal of Ethics*, 45(3): 282–316.
Parsons, Talcott ([1937] 1968) *The Structure of Social Action*. New York: Free Press.
Parsons, Talcott ([1936] 2001) Georg Simmel and Ferdinand Tönnies: Social Relationships and the Elements of Action, pp. 71–92 in Gabriel Pollini & Giuseppe Sciortino (eds) *Parsons' The Structure of Social Action and Contemporary Debates*. Milano: Franco Angeli.
Parsons, Talcott, Shils, Edward, Naegele, Kaspar, D. & Pitts, Jesse R. (eds) (1961) *Theories of Society: Foundations of Modern Sociological Theory*. New York: The Free Press of Glencoe.
Partyga, Dominika (2016) Simmel's Reading of Nietzsche: The Promise of 'Philosophical Sociology'. *Journal of Classical Sociology*, 16(4): 414–37.
Perec, Georges ([1974] 1999) *Species of Spaces and Other Pieces*. Ed. and trans. John Sturrock. London: Penguin Books.
Pietilä, Kauko (2011) *Reason of Sociology: George Simmel and Beyond*. London: Sage.
Polanyi, Karl (1944) *The Great Transformation*. New York: Rinehart.
Portioli, Claudia (2012) Les chemins de la pensée de G. Simmel en Italie. *Sociologie & Sociétés*, 44(2): 263–87.
Powell, Christopher & Dépelteau, François (eds) (2013) *Conceptualizing Relational Sociology: Ontological and Theoretical Issues*. New York: Palgrave Macmillan.
Prigogine, Ilya & Stengers, Isabelle (1984) *Order out of Chaos: Man's New Dialogue with Nature*. London: Heinemann.
Pyyhtinen, Olli (2009) Being-with: Georg Simmel's Sociology of Association. *Theory, Culture & Society*, 26(5): 108–28.
Pyyhtinen, Olli (2010) *Simmel and 'the Social'*. Basingstoke and New York: Palgrave Macmillan.
Pyyhtinen, Olli (2012) Life, Death and Individuation: Simmel on the Problem of Life Itself. *Theory, Culture & Society*, 29(7–8): 78–100.
Pyyhtinen, Olli (2014) *The Gift and its Paradoxes*. Surrey and Burlington: Ashgate.
Pyyhtinen, Olli (2015) *More-than-Human Sociology: A New Sociological Imagination*. Basingstoke and New York: Palgrave Macmillan.
Pyyhtinen, Olli (2016) The Real as Relation: Simmel as a Pioneer of Relational Sociology, pp. 101–20 in Thomas Kemple & Olli Pyyhtinen (eds) *The Anthem Companion to Georg Simmel*. London and New York: Anthem Press.
Pyyhtinen, Olli & Joronen, Mikko (forthcoming) Die Dinge aufleben lassen. Simmel, Heidegger und Deleuze über den Sinn des Lebens. In Gallina Tasheva & Johannes Weiß (eds) *Die Existenzialanalytik Martin Heideggers in ihren sozialtheoretischen und soziologischen Bezügen*. Mohr Siebeck Verlag.
Rammstedt, Otthein (1986) *Deutsche Soziologie 1933–1945. Die Normalität einer Anpassung*. Frankfurt am Main: Suhrkamp.
Rammstedt, Otthein (1994) Georg Simmel. *Soziologie: Mitteilungsblatt der Deutschne Gesellschaft für Soziologie*. Sonderheft, 3/1994: 103–13.

Rammstedt, Otthein (2005) Foreword, pp. 9–11 in Natàlia Cantó-Milà (2005) *A Sociological Theory of Value: Georg Simmel's Sociological Relationism*. Bielefeld: Transcript.
Rammstedt, Otthein (2012) On the Genesis of a Collected Edition of Simmel's Works, 1918–2012. Trans. Austin Harrington. *Theory, Culture & Society (Annual Review)*, 24 (7–8): 302–16.
Rickert, Sophie ([1948] 1993) Erinnerungen an Simmel, pp. 211–12 in Kurt Gassen & Michael Landmann (eds) *Buch des Dankes an Georg Simmel. Briefe, Erinnerungen, Bibliographie. Zu seinem 100. Geburtstag am 1. März 1958*. 2. Aufl. Berlin: Duncker & Humblot.
Ritzer, George (2011) *Sociological Theory*. Eighth Edition. New York: McGraw-Hill.
Rose, Peter I. (1977) *Strangers in Their Midst: Small-Town Jews and Their Neighbors*. Merrick, N.Y.: Richwood Publishing.
Rossi, Peter H. (1958) Emile Durkheim-Georg Simmel, 1858–1958: An Editorial Foreword. *The American Journal of Sociology*, 63(6): 579.
Salomon, Albert ([1957] 1993) Erinnerungen an Simmel, pp. 277–8 in Kurt Gassen & Michael Landmann (eds) *Buch des Dankes an Georg Simmel. Briefe, Erinnerungen, Bibliographie. Zu seinem 100. Geburtstag am 1. März 1958*. 2. Aufl. Berlin: Duncker & Humblot.
Salomon, Albert ([1963] 1997) Georg Simmel Reconsidered. Edited, with an Introduction and Notes by Gary D. Jaworski, pp. 91–108 in Gary D. Jaworski, *Georg Simmel and the American Prospect*. New York: State University of New York Press.
Salz, Arthur (1959) A Note From a Student of Simmel's, pp. 233–6 in Kurt Wolff (ed.) *Georg Simmel, 1858–1918*. Columbus: Ohio State University Press.
Sassatelli, Roberta (2000) From Value to Consumption. A Social-theoretical Perspective on Simmel's Philosophie des Geldes. *Acta Sociologica*, 43(3): 207–18.
Scaff, Lawrence (1987) Weber, Simmel und die Kultursoziologie. *Kölner Zeitschrift für Soziologie und Sozialpsychologie*, 39(2): 255–77.
Scaff, Lawrence (1991) *Fleeing the Iron Cage: Culture, Politics, and Modernity in the Thought of Max Weber*. Berkeley, Los Angeles & London: University of California Press.
Scaff, Lawrence (2005) The Mind of The Modernist: Simmel on Time. *Time & Society*, 14(1): 5–23.
Scaff, Lawrence (2015) Personal communication (email from 17 Dec 2015).
Schermer, Henry & Jary, David (2013) *Form and Dialectic in Georg Simmel's Sociology. A New Interpretation*. Basingstoke and New York: Palgrave Macmillan.
Schmalenbach, Herman (1919) Simmel. *Sozialistische Monatshefte*, 52: 283–8.
Schnabel, Peter-Ernst (1974) *Die Soziologische Gesamtkonzeption Georg Simmels. Ein wissenschaftshistorische und wissenschaftstheoretische Untersuchung*. Stuttgart: Gustav Fisscher.
Schrader-Klebert, Karin (1968) Der Begriff der Gesellschaft als regulative Idee. Soziale Welt. *Zeitschrift für sozialwissenschaftliche Forschung und Praxis*, 19(2): 97–118.
Schroer, Markus (2006) *Räume, Orte, Grenzen. Auf dem Weg zu einer Soziologie des Raumes*. Frankurt am Main: Suhrkamp.
Schwartz, Barry (1967) The Social Psychology of the Gift. *American Journal of Sociology*, 73(1): 1–11.
Schwerdtfeger, Johannes (1995) Bergson und Simmel. *Simmel Newsletter*, 5(2): 89–96.

Scott, Alan & Staubmann, Helmut (2005) Editors' introduction, pp. xi–xix in Georg Simmel, *Rembrandt*. Trans. Alan Scott and Helmut Staubmann. New York and London: Routledge.

Serres, Michel (2007) *The Parasite*. Trans. Lawrence R. Schehr. Minneapolis: University of Minnesota Press.

Shimmei, Masamicha (1959) Georg Simmel's Influence on Japanese Thought, pp. 201–15 in Kurt Wolff (ed.) *Georg Simmel, 1858 –1918. A Collection of Essays, with Translations and a Bibliography*. Columbus: The Ohio State University Press.

Small, Albion W. (1909) Review of *Soziologie*, by Georg Simmel *The American Journal of Sociology*, 14(4): 544–5.

Small, Albion W. (1925) Review of Nicholas Spykman, *The Social Theory of Georg Simmel. The American Journal of Sociology*, 31(1): 84–7.

Smith, Gregory (1989) *A Simmelian Reading of Goffman*. Unpublished doctoral dissertation. University of Salford. URL: <http://usir.salford.ac.uk/14705/1/D092734.pdf> Last Checked 23 Dec 2016.

Sombart, Werner (1903) *Die deutsche Volkswirtschaft im neunzehnten Jahrhundert*, Berlin: Georg Bondi.

Sorokin, Pitirim (1928) *Contemporary Sociological Theories*. New York and London: Harper & Brothers.

Spykman, Nicholas J. ([1925] 2004) *The Social Theory of Georg Simmel*. New Brunswick and London: Transaction.

Staubmann, Helmut (1998) Overcoming Flawed Dichotomies: The Impact of Georg Simmel on American Sociology. *International Journal of Politics, Culture and Society*, 11(3): 501–15.

Stonequiest, Everett V. (1937) *The Marginal Man*. New York: Scribner's.

Susman, Margarete ([1957] 1993) Erinnerungen an Simmel, pp. 278–91 in Kurt Gassen & Michael Landmann (eds) *Buch des Dankes an Georg Simmel. Briefe, Erinnerungen, Bibliographie. Zu seinem 100. Geburtstag am 1. März 1958*. 2. Aufl. Berlin: Duncker & Humblot.

Swedberg, Richard (2014) *The Art of Social Theory*. Princeton and Oxford: Princeton University Press.

Tenbruck, Friedrich (1958) Georg Simmel (1858–1918). *Kölner Zeitschrift für Soziologie und Sozialpsychologie*, 10: 587–614.

Tenbruck, Friedrich (1959) Formal Sociology, pp. 61–99 in Kurt H. Wolff (ed.) *Georg Simmel, 1858–1918. A Collection of Essays, with Translations and a Bibliography*. Columbus: The Ohio State University Press.

Tennen, Hanoch (1976) Simmel und Karl Jaspers. Ein Vergleich, pp. 135–74 in Hannes Böhringer & Karlfried Gründer (eds) (1976) *Ästhetik und Soziologie um die Jahrhundertwende: Georg Simmel*. Frankfurt am Main: Vittorio Klostermann.

Thacker, Eugene (2010) *After Life*. Chicago: University of Chicago Press.

Theunissen, Michael (1984) *The Other. Studies in the Social Ontology of Husserl, Heidegger, Sartre, and Buber*. Trans. Christopher Macann. Cambridge, Mass: MIT Press.

Thiess, Frank ([1918] 1993) Erinnerungen an Simmel, pp. 176–9 in Kurt Gassen & Michael Landmann (eds) *Buch des Dankes an Georg Simmel. Briefe, Erinnerungen, Bibliographie. Zu seinem 100. Geburtstag am 1. März 1958*. 2. Aufl. Berlin: Duncker & Humblot.

Timasheff, Nicholas S. (1955) *Sociological Theory: Its nature and growth.* Garden City, New York: Doubleday & Co.
Tönnies, Ferdinand (1965) Simmel as Sociologist, pp. 50–2 in Lewis A. Coser (ed.) *Georg Simmel.* Englewood Cliffs: Prentice-Hall.
Vandenberghe, Frédéric (2009) *A Philosophical History of German Sociology.* London and New York: Routledge.
van Vucht Tjissen, Lieteke (1991) Women and Objective Culture: Georg Simmel and Marianne Weber. *Theory, Culture & Society*, 8(3): 203–18.
Veblen, Thorstein ([1899] 1992) *The Theory of the Leisure Class.* New Brunswick and London: Transaction Publishers.
Vierkandt, Alfred (1916) Die Beziehung als Grudnkategorie des sozialen Denkens. (Bruchstücke aus dem Manuskript einer "Gesellschaftslehre".) (Schluss). *Archiv für Rechts- und Wirtschaftsphilosophie*, 9(2): 214–25.
von Naso, Eckart ([1954] 1993) Erinnerungen an Simmel, pp. 222–3 in Kurt Gassen & Michael Landmann (eds) *Buch des Dankes an Georg Simmel. Briefe, Erinnerungen, Bibliographie. Zu seinem 100. Geburtstag am 1. März 1958.* 2. Aufl. Berlin: Duncker & Humblot.
von Wiese, Leopold ([1924/9] 1933) *System der allgemeinem Soziologie als Lehre von den sozialen Prozessen und den sozialen Gebilden der Menschen (Beziehungslehre).* München–Leipzig: Duncker & Humblot.
von Wiese, Leopold (1951) The Place of Social Science in Germany Today. *The American Journal of Sociology*, 57(1): 1–6.
von Wiese, Leopold (1965) Simmel's Formal Method, pp. 53–7 in Lewis A. Coser (ed.) *Georg Simmel.* Englewood Cliffs: Prentice-Hall.
Waizbort, Leopold (2008) Simmel in Brazil. Trans. Anthony Doyle. (Originally published in Portuguese in *Dados – Revista de Ciências Sociais*, 50(1): 11–48. 2007.) URL: <http://socialsciences.scielo.org/pdf/s_dados/v4nse/scs_a05.pdf>. Last Checked 24 Dec 2016.
Weber, Max (1972) Georg Simmel as a Sociologist and Theorist of Modernity. Trans. Donald N. Levine. *Social Research*, (39)1: 155–63.
Weber, Max (1985) *Gesammelte Aufsätze zur Wissenschaftslehre.* Tübingen: Mohr.
Weingartner, Rudolph H. (1960) *Experience and Culture. The Philosophy of Georg Simmel.* Middletown Connecticut: Wesleyan University Press.
Weinstein, Deena & Weinstein, Michael A. (1991) Georg Simmel: Sociological Flâneur Bricoleur. *Theory, Culture & Society*, 8(3): 151–68.
Welty, Gordon (1996) Simmel on 'The Lie'. *European Journal for Semiotic Studies*, 7(2): 273–98.
Wessely, Anna (1990) Simmel's Influence on Lukács' Conception of the Sociology of Art, pp. 357–73 in Michael Kaern, Bernard Phillips & Robert S. Cohen (eds), *Georg Simmel and Contemporary Sociology.* Dordrecht: Kluwert.
Whitehead, Alfred North ([1929] 1978) *Process and Reality.* Corrected edition. New York: Free Press.
Wirth, Louis (1925) A Bibliography of the Urban Community, pp. 161–228 in Robert E. Park, Ernest W. Burgess & Roderick D. Mckenzie. *The City.* Chicago: University of Chicago Press.
Wirth, Louis (1938) Urbanism as a Way of Life. *American Journal of Sociology*, 44(1): 1–24.

Witz, Anne (2001) Georg Simmel and the Masculinity of Modernity. *Journal of Classical Sociology*, 1(3): 353–70.
Wolff, Kurt H. (1950) Introduction, pp. xvii–lxiv in Kurt H. Wolff (ed.) *The Sociology of Georg Simmel*. Translated, edited and with an introduction by Kurt H. Wolff. New York: Free Press.
Zelizer, Viviana (1994) *The Social Meaning of Money. Pin Money, Paychecks, Poor Relief, & Other Currencies*. New York: Basic Books.
Ziemann, Andreas (2000) *Die Brücke zur Gesellschaft. Erkenntniskritische und topographische Implikationen der Soziologie Georg Simmels*. Konstanz: Universitätsverlag Konstanz.
Žižek, Slavoj (2004) Notes on a Debate "From Within the People". *Criticism*, 46(4): 661–6.

Index

Abel, Theodor   161, 165, 172
Adorno, Theodor   4, 139, 156
Agamben, Giorgio   103
analogies   26, 29n, 132
Appadurai, Arjun   77
Arendt, Hannah   139, 158n
art   120, 136
association   18, 30–49, 55, 67, 71, 80, 84, 88, 95–98, 151, 181
    forms of   19, 83–101, 151

Baehr, Peter   156
Baudelaire, Charles   51–52, 53, 58, 63, 117
Bauman, Zygmunt   36
Bean, Susan S.   169
becoming   6, 20, 36, 38–39, 45, 111–113
    and being   36, 102, 114–116
    fashion as   54–57
Becker, Howard   169
being-alone   89
being-with   31, 89, 113
Benjamin, Walter   63–64, 139, 156
Bentham, Jeremy   88
Bergson, Henri   1, 20, 21, 36, 83, 106–111, 123n, 145–146
Berlin, Isaiah   98
Bevers, Antonius M.   16, 27, 29n, 104, 176
blasé attitude   65–67
Blau, Peter M.   168
Bleicher, Josef   102
Bloch, Ernst   130–131
Blumer, Herbert   170–171
Bouglè, Cèlestin   1, 30, 143–144, 159n
boundaries   26, 66, 86, 94, 116–117

Buber, Martin   128, 138
Burgess, Ernest W.   152–153, 167

Caplow, Theodore   169
Cantó-Milà, Natàlia   92
Campbell, Colin   59
calculative reasoning   77
Carter, Ellwood B.   147
Christian, Petra   22, 40, 175
competition   19, 27–28, 152
Comte, Auguste   33, 34
conflict   28, 31, 73, 88, 90, 100n, 151, 152, 153, 161, 167–168, 173
contradiction/s   12–13, 171
Coser, Lewis A.   159n, 161, 166, 167–168, 176–177
coquetry   97–98
culture   103–104, 117–122, 177
    crisis of   138
    tragedy of   104, 119–122, 136

Dahme, Heinz Jürgen   36, 156, 174, 176–177
Dasein   139–142
Deleuze, Gilles   xi, 100n, 185–186
desire   72–73, 79
Dilthey, Wilhelm   17, 22, 103, 112, 140
distance and proximity   41, 73, 83, 87, 92–95, 100n, 173
    see also desire
    and refugees   94–95
Dodd, Nigel   82n
Duncan, Hugh Danziel   4
Durkheim, Èmile   1, 3, 5, 33, 48n, 50, 89, 127–128, 143–146, 151, 152, 157n, 162, 165, 167, 177
dyad vs. triad   14, 88–91, 100n, 169

205

economic sociology   70, 81n
economy   19, 21, 92, 119, 121
    see also society and economy
Elias, Norbert   6, 25
Emirbayer, Mustafa   32
exchange   15, 16, 19, 69, 70–75, 82n, 168

fashion   51, 53–60, 66–67, 68n, 85, 99n, 119, 130, 170–171
Fechter, Paul   128, 129
fixity   86–87
Fitzi, Gregor   36, 144, 146, 183, 187n
friendship   87, 91–93, 99
Frisby, David   20, 51, 81n, 153, 176, 182
form/s   21, 30–36, 83, 99, 132, 173
    dissolution of   36
    vs. formalism   83, 99, 139
    sociology of   18, 27, 31, 34, 55, 83–99, 122, 132–133, 134
form-content distinction   11, 15–21, 34–35, 96–98, 99
    in epistemology   16–17
    in metaphysics   20–21
    in sociology   18–20
    and Wechselwirkung   26–28
    see also sociability
Foucault, Michel   88
Frade, Carlos   158n
Freud, Sigmund   64, 69
Freyer, Hans   135, 136–137, 155
fundamental dualisms and general polarities   12

Gadamer, Hans Georg   140
Gassen, Kurt   129, 161, 174
Girard, Renè   73
Goethe, Johann Wolfgang von   14, 20, 102, 106, 108
Goffman, Erving   161, 166–167, 172, 186
Goodstein, Elizabeth   68n, 183–184

Gouldner, Alvin   168
Goudge, Thomas A.   110
Groman, Eleanor Miller   147
Gronow, Jukka   171
Guattari, Félix   185–186
Gumbrecht, Hans Ulrich   52

Habermas, Jürgen   177–178
Hare, Paul A.   169
Hegel, Georg Wilhelm Friedrich   13, 22, 53, 175, 177
Heraclitus   36, 114
Heidegger, Martin   138–143
Hughes, Everett C.   95, 155, 168, 172, 179n
Husserl, Edmund   1, 68n, 69, 174
Hübner-Funk, Sybille   176, 177

inclusion/exclusion   13, 93–94, 100n
individual   12–14, 18–19, 22, 32–39, 41–43
    as assembled being   45
Ingold, Tim   28
I/you-relation   40–43, 89, 91, 92, 138
    see also dyad vs. triad
    see also preconditions of society

Jary, David   12
Jaspers, Karl   149, 158n
Jaworski, Gary D.   159n, 163, 171
Jöel, Karl   128, 129

Kant, Immanuel   14, 16–17, 22, 38, 40, 68n, 81n, 85, 102, 107, 108, 110, 112, 114, 119, 120–121, 123n, 128, 134, 146, 147, 175, 177
Kantorowitz, Gertrud   110, 115, 157, 160n, 167
Kemple, Thomas   48n, 101n, 185
knowledge   15, 16–17, 22–24, 26–28, 84, 104, 105, 110, 119–120
    interpersonal   41, 92
    topological or geographical   28

Index

Koselleck, Reinhart 52
Kracauer, Siegfried 25, 35

Landmann, Michael 11, 13, 157, 161, 174–175, 177, 179
Lash, Scott 187n
Latour, Bruno 181
Lechner, Farank 85
Leck, Ralph M. 8n
Levine, Donald N. 92, 131, 147–148, 151–152, 154, 155, 162–163, 165, 167, 171, 172–173, 174, 177, 179n, 182
Lichtblau, Klaus viii, 158n, 177
life 102–103, 106–117, 133, 137, 159n, 171, 186
　as becoming 20–21, 111–114
　and death 113, 139, 141–143
　vs. form 16, 20–22, 27, 28n, 44, 46, 84–85, 111–112, 113–117, 119–121, 122
　more-life 46, 109–110, 113–116, 117
　more-than-life 46, 113–116, 117
　vs. sociability 96, 98
life-philosophy 16, 20–21, 26–27, 29n, 84, , 103, 106–117, 119, 122, 123n, 140–143, 147, 153, 159n, 171, 173, 176, 183, 187n
　see also life-philosophy of Georg Simmel
Lindemann, Gesa 100n
Lipman, Matthew 83
Litt, Theodor 134
Lofland, Lynn H. 94
love 87, 91–93
Ludwig, Emil 128, 158
Luhmann, Niklas 59, 177, 179n
Lukács, Georg 2, 128, 130, 132, 135–136, 137, 156, 158n
Lyotard, Jean-Francis 57

Mamelet, Alfred 146–147
Mannheim, Karl 137–138, 155, 156
Marshall, Albert 162

Marx, Karl 3, 5, 21, 50, 71–72, 81n, 152, 158n, 186
matter 38
McCracken, Grant 68n
meal 98
Merton, Robert 161, 167–168, 178
methodological individualism 43–44, 133
metropolis 5, 51–53, 55, 60–67, 70, 87, 150, 152–153
　as coincidence of opposites 61
　vs. rural life 55, 62–63, 65–66, 68n
micro-macro-reductionism 43–47
Mills, C. Wright 35
Mills, Theodore 169
modern experience 5, 50–51, 52–53, 63–64, 66–67, 85
　and fashion 58–60
modernity
　aesthetic 51, 52–53, 58, 63
　phenomenology of 66
　restlessness of 52–54, 79
　three meanings of 51, 52–53
modernization 50
molar vs. molecular 38, 48n
money 3, 25–26, 47, 60, 69–82
　as frightful leveller 65
　as mediator 25–26, 74, 79–80
　and modern life 69–70, 76–81
　money economy 65, 70, 75, 77
　as an object 75–76
　and trust 75–76
morphogenesis 99

Naegele, Kaspar D. 171–172
Nietzsche, Friedrich 14, 20, 53, 60, 102, 106–110, 112, 116, 123n, 134, 158n, 177
Nisbet, Robert 165

Oakes, Guy 15, 184
Outhwaite, William 44

Parmenides 36, 114, 123n
Pareto, Vilfredo 162
Park, Robert E. 2, 27, 149–153, 166
Parsons, Talcott 161, 162–165, 167, 171, 172, 177, 178, 179n
Partyga, Dominika 123n
Perec, Georges 68n
Polanyi, Karl 70
poor 100–101n
process 5, 6, 18, 20, 21, 24, 25, 35–36, 37–39, 44, 45, 104, 111, 181, 186

Rammstedt, Otthein 29n, 81n, 155, 157, 158n, 176, 177, 179
reciprocity 35, 37, 45, 168, 173
relations 4–5, 32, 91–92
  real as 25–26, 27, 71, 185
  relation of 47
  see also Wechselwirkungen
relationalism/relational mode of thought 4–6, 22–26, 27–28, 29n, 32, 45–47, 51, 68n, 71, 80, 83–84, 146, 147, 153, 161, 168, 178, 182–183, 186
  epistemological 23–24
  metaphysical 25–27
  sociological 24–25
religion 15, 120
Rickert, Heinrich 1, 22, 157n, 158, 174
Rickert, Sophie 134
Ritzer, George 46
Rossi, Peter H. 165

Salomon, Albert 104, 129, 158, 166, 178
Scaff, Lawrence 99n, 158n, 172
Schermer, Henry 12
Schnabel, Peter-Ernest 175
Schopenhauer, Arthur 14, 102, 106–109
science 104, 119–120
Simmel, Georg
  as adventurer in ideas 11
  and Durkheim, Èmile 143–146
  life-philosophy of 20–21, 27, 29n, 84, 103, 106–117, 119

  philosophy of 102–124, 173, 182–183
  as sociological flâneur 182
  and Tarde, Gabriel de 144
  and Weber, Max 131–134, 158n
Simmel, Hans 157
Small, Albion W. 1, 148–149, 152, 154, 155, 159n, 166
Schmalenbach, Herman 138, 157
Shimmei, Masamicha 154–155, 179n
sociability 26, 83, 95–98, 122
society
  container model of 33, 37
  and economy 70
  preconditions of 39–43
  as a process 36, 37–39
  vs. nature 40
  as relations 4, 24, 37–39, 123
sociology
  and biology 37
  canon of 3, 161, 165, 180, 185
  foundation of 24, 30–47
  relational 24–25, 181
  reifying tendencies of 6, 32, 77–78
  of space 85–88
Sombart, Werner 30, 62, 65
Spencer, Herbert 33, 149
Spykman, Nikolas 153–154, 155
stranger 13–14, 80, 92, 93–95, 137, 151, 152–153
  Simmel as 1, 2, 100
substantialism 4, 32, 39, 113, 123n, 164, 170, 185
Sumner, William G. 151, 152
Susman, Margarete 2, 175

Tarde, Gabriel 1, 25, 144
Tenbruck, Friedrich 19, 20, 99, 167, 183
Thacker, Eugene 103
Theunissen, Michael 40
the third 11, 13–15, 22, 56, 88–91, 100n, 114
  money as 80
trust 75, 76, 92, 100n, 177
Tönnies, Ferdinand 30, 65

value/valuation   70–73
Veblen, Thorstein   57–58
Vierkandt, Alfred   134–135
von Wiese, Leopold   27, 28n, 134, 135, 156

Weber, Alfred   155
Weber, Marianne   134, 174
Weber, Max   1, 3, 5, 7, 26, 28n, 30, 50, 131 – 134, 152, 158n, 162, 167, 174, 177, 186
Wechselwirkung   22–28, 29n, 31, 32, 34, 37–39, 45, 46, 71, 99, 124n, 132, 133, 135, 150–151, 158n, 175, 176, 178,
   dadic and triadic   88–91

and life   112–113
and space   85–88
as a third   22
see also relationalism
Weingartner, Rudolph   167, 173
Wessely, Anna   13
Whitehead, Alfred North   6, 8n
Windelband, Wilhelm   17
Wirth, Luis   68n, 150
Wolff, Kurt H.   100n, 165–166, 167, 179, 184
Worms, Renè   1, 30, 47n, 143, 159n

Zelizer, Viviana   78
Ziemann, Andreas   22

Printed by Printforce, the Netherlands